The LEAST

YOU SHOULD KNOW ABOUT

English

TERESA FERSTER GLAZIER

WRITING SKILLS

FORM **B**
SEVENTH EDITION

PAIGE WILSON

PASADENA CITY COLLEGE

HARCOURT COLLEGE PUBLISHERS

Fort Worth   Philadelphia   San Diego   New York   Orlando   Austin   San Antonio
Toronto   Montreal   London   Sydney   Tokyo

PUBLISHER	Earl McPeek
ACQUISITIONS EDITOR	Steve Dalphin
MARKET STRATEGIST	John Meyers
DEVELOPMENTAL EDITOR	Michell Phifer
PROJECT EDITOR	CJ Jasieniecki
ART DIRECTOR	Vicki Whistler
PRODUCTION MANAGER	Cindy Young

ISBN: 0-15-506987-x
Library of Congress Catalog Card Number: 00-101370

Address for Domestic Orders
Harcourt College Publishers, 6277 Sea Harbor Drive, Orlando, FL 32887-6777
800-782-4479

Address for International Orders
International Customer Service
Harcourt, Inc., 6277 Sea Harbor Drive, Orlando, FL 32887-6777
407-345-3800
(fax) 407-345-4060
(e-mail) hbintl@harcourtbrace.com

Address for Editorial Correspondence
Harcourt College Publishers, 301 Commerce Street, Suite 3700, Fort Worth, TX 76102

Web Site Address
http://www.harcourtcollege.com

Printed in the United States of America

0 1 2 3 4 5 6 7 8 9   016   9 8 7 6 5 4 3

Harcourt College Publishers

This book is for students who need to review basic English skills and who may profit from a simplified "least you should know" approach. Parts 1 to 3 cover the essentials of spelling, sentence structure, and punctuation. Part 4 on writing teaches students the basic structures of the paragraph and the essay, along with the writing skills necessary to produce them.

Throughout the book, we try to avoid the use of linguistic terminology whenever possible. A conjunction is a connecting word; gerunds and present participles are *ing* words; an infinitive is the *to* ___ form of a verb. Students work with words they know instead of learning a vocabulary they may never use again.

There are abundant exercises, including practice with writing sentences and proofreading paragraphs—enough so that students learn to use the rules automatically and thus *carry over their new skills into their writing*. Exercises consist of sets of ten thematically related, informative sentences on such subjects as one of the rarest butterflies in the world (which happens to live in South Central Los Angeles), vending-machine dating in Japan, the invention of the chocolate chip cookie, the phenomenon of tennis shoes thrown over power lines, and so on. Such exercises reinforce the need for coherence and details in student writing. With answers provided at the back of the book, students can correct their own work and progress at their own pace.

For the seventh edition, we have completely revised Part 4 on writing, which covers the writing process and which stresses the development of the student's written "voice." Writing assignments follow each discussion, and there are samples by both student and professional writers. Part 4 ends with a section designed to help students with writing assignments based on readings. It includes articles to read, react to, and summarize. Students improve their reading by learning to spot main ideas and their writing by learning to write meaningful reactions and concise summaries.

The Least You Should Know about English functions equally well in the classroom and at home as a self-tutoring text. The simple explanations, ample exercises, and answers at the back of the book provide students with everything they need to progress on their own. Students who have previously been overwhelmed by the complexities of English should, through mastering simple rules and through writing and rewriting simple papers, gain enough competence to succeed in further composition courses.

Acknowledgments

For their thoughtful commentary on the book, we would like to thank the following reviewers: Irene Badaracco, Fordham University; Cheryl Delk, Western Michigan University; Nancy Dessommes, Georgia Southern University; Donna Ross Hooley, Georgia Southern University; Sandra Jensen, Lane Community College; Anastasia Lankford, Eastfield College; Ben Larson, York College; Sue McKee, California State University at Sacramento; Karen McGuire, Pasadena City College; Kevin Nebergall, Krikwood Community College; Peggy Porter, Houston Community College; and Anne Simmons, Olean Business Institute.

In addition, we would like to thank our publishing team for their expertise and hard work: Steve Dalphin, Acquisitions Editor; Michell Phifer, Developmental Editor; CJ Jasieniecki, Project Editor; Cindy Young, Production Manager; and Vicki Whistler, Art Director.

Finally, we are indebted to Herb and Moss Rabbin, Kenneth Glazier, and the rest of our families and friends for their support and encouragement.

Teresa Ferster Glazier

Paige Wilson

Form B differs from Form A in that all of the exercises, writing samples, and assignments are new. The explanations and examples remain the same.

A **Test Packet** with additional exercises and ready-to-photocopy tests accompanies this text and is available to instructors.

CONTENTS

Writing Skills   206

What Is the Least You Should Know?

Most English textbooks try to teach you more than you need to know. This one will teach you the least you need to know—and still help you learn to write acceptably. You won't have to bother with grammatical terms like gerunds and modal auxiliary verbs and demonstrative pronouns and all those others you've been hearing about for years. You can get along without knowing these terms if you'll learn thoroughly a few basic concepts. You *do* have to know how to spell common words; you *do* have to recognize subjects and verbs to avoid writing fragments; you *do* have to know a few rules of sentence structure and punctuation—but rules will be kept to a minimum.

The English you'll learn in this book is sometimes called Standard Written English, and it may differ slightly or greatly from the spoken English you use. Standard Written English is the accepted form of writing in business and the professions. So no matter how you speak, you will communicate better in writing when you use Standard Written English. You might *say* something like "That's a whole nother problem," and everyone will understand, but you would probably want to *write,* "That's a completely different problem." Knowing the difference between spoken English and Standard Written English is essential in college, in business, and in life.

Unless you learn the least you should know, you'll have difficulty communicating in writing. Take this sentence for example:

I hope my application will be excepted by the scholarship committee.

We assume the writer will not actually be happy to be overlooked by the committee but merely failed to use the right word. If the sentence had read

I hope my application will be *accepted* by the scholarship committee.

then the writer would convey the intended meaning. Or take this sentence.

The manager fired Lee and Dave and I received a hundred dollar raise.

The sentence needs a comma.

The manager fired Lee and Dave, and I received a hundred dollar raise.

But perhaps the writer meant

The manager fired Lee, and Dave and I received a hundred dollar raise.

Punctuation makes all the difference, especially if you are Dave. What you'll learn from this text is simply to make your writing so clear that no one will misunderstand it.

As you make your way through the book, it's important to master every rule as you come to it because many rules depend on previous ones. For example, unless you learn to pick out subjects and verbs, you'll have trouble with fragments, with subject–verb agreement, and with punctuation. The rules are brief and clear, and it won't be difficult to master all of them—*if you want to*. But you do have to want to!

HERE'S THE WAY TO MASTER THE LEAST YOU SHOULD KNOW

1. Study the explanation of each rule carefully.

2. Do the first exercise. Correct your answers using the answer section at the back of the book. If you miss even one answer, study the explanation again to find out why.

3. Do the second exercise and correct it. If you miss a single answer, go back once more and study the explanation. You must have missed something. Be tough on yourself. Don't just think, "Maybe I'll get it right next time." Go back and master the rules, and *then* try the next exercise. It's important to correct each group of ten sentences before going on so that you'll discover your mistakes while you still have sentences to practice on.

4. You may be tempted to quit after you do one or two exercises perfectly. Don't! Make yourself finish another exercise. It's not enough to *understand* a rule. You have to *practice* it.

If you're positive, however, after doing several exercises, that you've mastered the rule, take the next exercise as a test. If you miss even one answer, you should do all the rest of the questions. But if you again make no mistakes, move on to the proofreading and sentence composing exercises so that your understanding of the rule carries over into your writing.

Mastering the essentials of spelling, sentence structure, and punctuation will take time. Generally, college students spend a couple of hours outside of class for each hour in class. You may need more. Undoubtedly, the more time you spend, the more your writing will improve.

P A R T   1

Spelling

Anyone can learn to spell better. You can eliminate most of your spelling errors if you want to. It's just a matter of deciding you're going to do it. If you really intend to learn to spell, study each of the seven parts of this section until you make no more mistakes in the exercises.

Your Own List of Misspelled Words

Words Often Confused (Sets 1 and 2)

Contractions

Possessives

Words That Can Be Broken into Parts

Rule for Doubling the Final Letter

Using a Dictionary

Study these seven parts, and you'll be a better speller.

Your Own List of Misspelled Words

On the inside cover of your English notebook or in some other obvious place, write correctly all the misspelled words in the papers handed back to you. Review them until you're sure of them.

Words Often Confused (Set 1)

Learning the differences between these often-confused words will help you overcome many of your spelling problems. Study the words carefully, with their examples, before trying the exercises.

a, an   Use *an* before a word that begins with a vowel *sound (a, e, i,* and *o,* plus *u* when it sounds like *uh)* or silent *h.*

Note that it's not the letter but the *sound* of the letter that matters.

> an apple, an essay, an inch, an onion
>
> an umpire, an ugly design (the *u*'s sound like *uh*)
>
> an hour, an honest person (silent *h*)

Use *a* before a word that begins with a consonant sound (all the sounds except the vowels, plus *u* or *eu* when they sound like *you*).

> a chart, a pie, a history book (the *h* is not silent in *history*)
>
> a union, a uniform, a unit (the *u*'s sound like *you*)
>
> a European vacation, a euphemism *(eu* sounds like *you)*

accept, except   *Accept* means "to receive willingly."

> I *accept* your apology.

Except means "excluding" or "but."

> Everyone arrived on time *except* him.

advise, advice   *Advise* is a verb (pronounce the *s* like a *z*).

> I *advise* you to take your time finding the right job.

Advice is a noun (it rhymes with *rice*).

> My counselor gave me good *advice*.

affect, effect   *Affect* is a verb and means "to alter or influence."

> All quizzes will *affect* the final grade.
>
> The happy ending *affected* the mood of the audience.

Effect is most commonly used as a noun and means "a result." If *a, an*, or *the* is in front of the word, then you'll know it isn't a verb and will use *effect*.

> The strong coffee had a powerful *effect* on me.
>
> We studied the *effects* of sleep deprivation in my psychology class.

all ready, already   If you can leave out the *all* and the sentence still makes sense, then *all ready* is the form to use. (In that form, *all* is a separate word and could be left out.)

We're *all ready* for the trip. (*We're ready for the trip* makes sense.)

The banquet is *all ready*. (*The banquet is ready* makes sense.)

But if you can't leave out the *all* and still have the sentence make sense, then use *already* (the form in which the *al* has to stay in the word).

They've *already* eaten. (*They've ready eaten* doesn't make sense.)

We have seen that movie *already*.

are, our   *Are* is a verb.

We *are* going to Colorado Springs.

Our shows we possess something.

We painted *our* fence to match the house.

brake, break   *Brake* used as a verb means "to slow or stop motion." It's also the name of the device that slows or stops motion.

I had to *brake* quickly to avoid an accident.

Luckily I just had my *brakes* fixed.

Break used as a verb means "to shatter" or "to split." It's also the name of an interruption, as in "a coffee break."

She never thought she would *break* a world record.

Enjoy your spring *break*.

choose, chose   The difference here is one of time. Use *choose* for present and future; use *chose* for past.

I will *choose* a new major this semester.

We *chose* the wrong time of year to get married.

clothes, cloths   *Clothes* are something you wear; *cloths* are pieces of material you might clean or polish something with.

I love the *clothes* that characters wear in movies.

The car wash workers use special *cloths* to dry the cars.

coarse, course   *Coarse* describes a rough texture.

I used *coarse* sandpaper to smooth the surface of the board.

Course is used for all other meanings.

> Of *course* we saw the golf *course* when we went to Pebble Beach.

complement, compliment   The one spelled with an *e* means to complete something or bring it to perfection.

> Use a color wheel to find a *complement* for purple.

> Juliet's personality *complements* Romeo's; she is practical, and he is a dreamer.

The one spelled with an *i* has to do with praise. Remember "*I* like compliments," and you'll remember to use the *i* spelling when you mean praise.

> My evaluation included a really nice *compliment* from my coworkers.

> We *complimented* them on their new home.

conscious, conscience   *Conscious* means "aware."

> They weren't *conscious* of any problems before the accident.

Conscience means that inner voice of right and wrong. The extra *n* in *conscience* should remind you of *No,* which is what your conscience often says to you.

> My *conscience* told me to turn in the expensive watch I found.

dessert, desert   *Dessert* is the sweet one, the one you like two helpings of. So give it two helpings of *s.*

> We had a whole chocolate cheesecake for *dessert.*

The other one, *desert,* is used for all other meanings and has two pronunciations.

> I promise that I won't *desert* you.

> The snake slithered slowly across the *desert.*

do, due   *Do* is a verb, an action. You *do* something.

> I always *do* my best work at night.

But a payment or an assignment is *due;* it is scheduled for a certain time.

> Our first essay is *due* tomorrow.

Due can also be used before *to* in a phrase that means *because of.*

> The outdoor concert was canceled *due to* rain.

feel, fill   *Feel* describes *feelings.*

> Whenever I stay up late, I *feel* sleepy in class.

Fill describes what you do to a cup or a gas tank.

> Did they *fill* the pitcher to the top?

fourth, forth   The word *fourth* has *four* in it. (But note that *forty* does not. Remember the word *forty-fourth.*)

> This is our *fourth* quiz in two weeks.

> My grandparents celebrated their *forty-fourth* anniversary.

If you don't mean a number, use *forth.*

> We wrote back and *forth* many times during my trip.

have, of   *Have* is a verb. Sometimes, in a contraction, it sounds like *of.* When you say *could've,* the *have* may sound like *of,* but it is not written that way. Always write *could have, would have, should have, might have.*

> We should *have* planned our vacation sooner.

> Then we could *have* used our coupon for a free one-way ticket.

Use *of* only in a prepositional phrase (see p. 55).

> She sent me a box *of* chocolates for my birthday.

hear, here   The last three letters of *hear* spell "ear." You *hear* with your ear.

> When I listen to a sea shell, I *hear* ocean sounds.

The other spelling *here* tells "where." Note that the three words indicating a place or pointing out something all have *here* in them: *here, there, where.*

> I'll be *here* for three more weeks.

it's, its   *It's* is a contraction and means "it is" or "it has."

> *It's* hot. (*It is* hot.)

> *It's* been hot all week. (*It has* been hot . . . .)

Its is a possessive. (Possessives such as *its, yours, hers, ours, theirs, whose* are already possessive and never need an apostrophe. See p. 31)

The jury had made *its* decision.

The dog pulled at *its* leash.

knew, new   *Knew* has to do with knowledge (both start with *k*).

New means "not old."

They *knew* that she wanted a *new* bike.

know, no   *Know* has to do with knowledge (both start with *k*).

By Friday, I must *know* all the state capitals.

No means "not any" or the opposite of "yes."

My boss has *no* patience. *No,* I need to work late.

E X E R C I S E S

Underline the correct word. Don't guess! If you aren't sure, turn back to the explanatory pages. When you've finished ten sentences, compare your answers with those at the back of the book. Correct each group of ten sentences before continuing so you'll catch your mistakes while you still have sentences to practice on.

Exercise 1

1. The (affects, effects) of caffeine on our society would be hard to measure.

2. Of (coarse, course), we were (all ready, already) comfortable with caffeine before trendy coffee houses were introduced to America in the early 1980s.

3. That's when Howard Schultz, founder of Starbucks, made (a, an) observation while traveling in Italy.

4. He was especially impressed with (it's, its) espresso bars.

5. (Conscience, Conscious) of their success, he (knew, new) that (a, an) expanded version of the Italian espresso bar would work in America too.

6. With (are, our) love of (deserts, desserts) and socializing, we were (all ready, already) for a new kind of store—not to sell (clothes, cloths) but to sell coffee.

7. Many people did not (feel, fill) immediately attracted by the Starbucks concept, however.

8. First they had to (accept, except) coffee as a (complement, compliment) to their lives instead of just something to drink on a coffee (brake, break).

9. By the early 1990s, half a decade after Schultz (choose, chose) to bring the coffee house concept to America, there were just over one hundred and fifty Starbucks stores.

10. But those numbers nearly doubled in 1993, mainly (do, due) to world-wide, round-the-clock access to the Internet; and by the end of the 1990s, Starbucks was (a, an) billion-dollar industry.

Source: Inc., 20th Century Anniversary Issue 1999

Exercise 2

1. I used to (hear, here) the expression "hobo" when I was growing up, but I didn't (know, no) what it meant.

2. Now after reading (a, an) obituary of Irving Stevens, the "King of the Hobos," I understand (it's, its) meaning better.

3. The word "hobo" was a shortened form of "hoe boy"; it described a man who would (do, due) temporary farm work and travel from place to place in open railway cars.

4. It was a life that people (choose, chose) to live rather than were forced to live, and it brought (it's, its) own kind of rewards.

5. Stevens, whose hobo nickname was Fishbones, became (conscience, conscious) of people's perceptions of hobos as worthless "bums."

6. Such negative stereotypes did not (affect, effect) Stevens' self-image or his love of the hobo lifestyle, and he prospered in spite of them.

7. Stevens' insights and stories, as well as some of his (advise, advice) for other hobos, (feel, fill) two books called *Dear Fishbones* and *Hoboing in the 1930s.*

8. He even invented (a, an) insect repellent sold under the name of Irving's Fly Dope, and he was especially proud of (it's, its) success.

9. Despite the original name "hoe *boy*," some women (choose, chose) to be hobos and were readily (accepted, excepted) by their male counterparts; Boxcar Bertha was one famous example.

10. Irving Stevens' own daughter, Connie Hall, became "Queen of the Hobos" at the end of her father's reign, and to her that was a real (complement, compliment).

Source: The Economist, 15 May 1999

Exercise 3

1. Dinosaur footprints bring (fourth, forth) images of huge creatures and (feel, fill) us with wonder.

2. The fact that the footprints are still (hear, here) but the creatures aren't (affects, effects) us deeply.

3. These reactions (are, our) especially true when we see not one footprint but many in (a, an) unbroken row; scientists call them dinosaur "trackways."

4. Before 1995, the longest trackway that we (knew, new) of measured just under five hundred feet long; (it's, its) located in Portugal.

5. That was (all ready, already) an incredible discovery, but then scientists found five new trackways between six hundred and one thousand feet long in Uzbekistan and Turkmenistan.

6. The tracks were made by megalosaurs, meat eaters a lot like Tyrannosaurus Rex, (accept, except) that these dinosaurs lived earlier—more than one hundred and fifty million years ago.

7. The tracks' sizes and shapes (complement, compliment) what we (all ready, already) (know, no) about the creatures of the late Jurassic period.

8. But the megalosaurs that made the tracks in Uzbekistan seem to (have, of) walked with their feet far apart.

9. Perhaps these creatures used to (feel, fill) up on dinosaur (desserts, deserts).

10. Their tracks reveal them to (have, of) been almost forty feet long and a little wider than usual.

Source: Discover, Dec. 1995

Exercise 4

1. I've lived on my own for two years, and I'm (all ready, already) tired of trying to decide what to (do, due) for dinner every night.

2. When I lived at home, I used to come home from school, change my (clothes, cloths), and (choose, chose) from all of the things my mom, dad, or siblings were eating for dinner.

3. I could take a plate of Dad's famous macaroni and cheese back to my room and then go downstairs later for a slice of Mom's lemon pie with (it's, its) fluffy meringue on top.

4. Now I have to come up with a main (coarse, course) and a (dessert, desert) all by myself.

5. (Do, Due) to my lack of cooking experience, dinners of my own are either burned or bought.

6. I'm beginning to (feel, fill) a little self-(conscience, conscious) about my limitations in the kitchen.

7. I could call my parents for (advise, advice), but I don't want them to worry about me.

8. Without a doubt, I should (have, of) paid more attention when both my parents were cooking, not just have (complemented, complimented) them on the results.

9. I guess I could take a cooking (coarse, course) or get a roommate to (do, due) the cooking for reduced rent.

10. I like everything about living away from home (accept, except) making my own dinner.

Exercise 5

1. There is (a, an) old, commonly held belief that if you (choose, chose) to wash your car today, it will rain tomorrow.

2. Of (coarse, course) that's just a saying; (it's, its) not true.

3. However, if you take my (advise, advice) and wash your car at home, it will save you considerable expense should this happen to you.

4. To avoid the undesirable (affect, effect) of clouding or streaking of the finish, never wash your car in direct sunlight.

5. But don't park your car under a tree to take advantage of (it's, its) shade, or you may be sorry later (do, due) to the possibility of sap falling from the tree.

6. Also, be sure that the (clothes, cloths) you use to wipe the surface are clean and have (know, no) (coarse, course) stitching or texture.

7. You don't want to (brake, break) your antenna, so it should be removed if possible.

8. Once your car is (all ready, already) to be washed, use circular motions and (feel, fill) the surface every now and then to be sure (it's, its) been cleaned.

9. Take the time to dry the whole surface of the car with a chamois if you want to get a lot of (complements, compliments) from your friends.

10. If you've done a thorough job, the (clothes, cloths) you are wearing will be wet, but your car will be dry and as shiny as it was the day you bought it.

PROOFREADING EXERCISE

Find and correct the ten errors contained in the following student paragraph. All of the errors involve Words Often Confused (Set 1).

I like all of the classes I chose this semester accept my tennis class. Its not what you might think. The teacher is nice, my classmates have a good attitude, and I like wearing tennis cloths. Its just that I don't no how to serve the ball. Everyone has given me advise, but I can't seem to coordinate the toss and the stroke. Or I get the toss and the stroke right, but then the ball lands in the middle of the net. At first, it wasn't too embarrassing. But now that everyone knows my weakness, I am very self-conscience whenever its my turn to serve. I new that I should of taken bowling or archery instead.

SENTENCE WRITING

The surest way to learn these Words Often Confused is to use them immediately in your own writing. Choose the five pairs or groups of words that you most often confuse from Set 1. Then use each of them correctly in a new sentence. No answers are provided at the back of the book, but you can see if you are using the words correctly by comparing your sentences to the examples in the explanations.

Words Often Confused (Set 2)

Study this second set of words carefully, with their examples, before attempting the exercises. Knowing all of the word groups in these two sets will take care of many of your spelling problems.

lead, led   *Lead* is the metal that rhymes with *head*.

Old paint is dangerous because it often contains *lead*.

The past form of the verb "to lead" is *led*.

What factors *led* to your decision?

I *led* our school's debating team to victory last year.

If you don't mean past time, use *lead*, which rhymes with *bead*.

I will *lead* the debating team again this year.

loose, lose   *Loose* means "not tight." Note how *l o o s e* that word is. It has plenty of room for two *o*'s.

My dog's tooth is *loose*.

Lose is the opposite of win.

If we *lose* this game, we will be out for the season.

passed, past   The past form of the verb "to pass" is *passed*.

She easily *passed* her math class.

The runner *passed* the baton to her teammate.

We *passed* your house twice before we saw the address.

Use *past* when it's not a verb.

We drove *past* your house. (the same as "We drove *by* your house")

I always use my *past* experiences to help me solve problems.

In the *past,* he had to borrow his brother's car.

personal, personnel   Pronounce these two correctly, and you won't confuse them—*pérsonal, personnél*.

She shared her *personal* views as a parent.

Personnel means "a group of employees."

I had an appointment in the *personnel* office.

piece, peace   Remember "piece of pie." The one meaning "a *piece* of something" always begins with *pie*.

One child asked for an extra *piece* of candy.

The other one, *peace,* is the opposite of war.

The two gangs discussed the possibility of a *peace* treaty.

principal, principle

Principal means "main." Both words have *a* in them: princip*a*l, m*a*in.

The *principal* concern is safety. (main concern)

He lost both *principal* and interest. (main amount of money)

Also, think of a school's "princi*pal*" as your "*pal*."

An elementary school *principal* must be kind. (main administrator)

A *principle* is a "rule." Both words end in *le:* princip*le,* ru*le*

I am proud of my high *principles*. (rules of conduct)

We value the *principle* of truth in advertising. (rule)

quiet, quite

Pronounce these two correctly, and you won't confuse them. *Quiet* means "free from noise" and rhymes with *diet.*

Tennis players need *quiet* in order to concentrate.

Quite means "very" and rhymes with *bite.*

It was *quite* hot in the auditorium.

right, write

Right means "correct" or "proper."

You will find your keys if you look in the *right* place.

It also means in the exact location, position, or moment.

Your keys are *right* where you left them.

Let's go *right* now.

Write means to compose sentences, poems, essays, and so forth.

I asked my teacher to *write* a letter of recommendation for me.

than, then

Than compares two things.

I am taller *than* my sister.

Then tells when (*then* and *when* rhyme, and both have *e* in them).

I always write a rough draft of a paper first; *then* I revise it.

their, there, they're

Their is a possessive, meaning belonging to them.

Their cars have always been red.

There points out something. (Remember that the three words indicating a place or pointing out something all have *here* in them: *here, there, where*.)

I know that I haven't been *there* before.

There was a rainbow in the sky.

They're is a contraction and means "they are."

They're living in Canada. (*They are* living in Canada now.)

threw, through

Threw is the past form of "to throw."

We *threw* snowballs at each other.

I *threw* away my chance at a scholarship.

If you don't mean "to throw something," use *through*.

We could see our beautiful view *through* the new curtains.

They worked *through* their differences.

two, too, to

Two is a number.

We have written *two* papers so far in my English class.

Too means "extra" or "also," and so it has an extra *o*.

The movie was *too* long and *too* violent. (extra)

They are enrolled in that biology class *too*. (also)

Use *to* for all other meanings.

They like *to* ski. They're going *to* the mountains.

weather, whether

Weather refers to conditions of the atmosphere.

Snowy *weather* is too cold for me.

Whether means "if."

I don't know *whether* it is snowing there or not.

Whether I travel with you or not depends on the weather.

were, wear, where

These words are pronounced differently but are often confused in writing.

Were is the past form of the verb "to be."

We *were* interns at the time.

Wear means to have on, as in wearing clothes.

I always *wear* a scarf in winter.

Where refers to a place. (Remember that the three words indicating a place or pointing out something all have *here* in them: *here, there, where.*)

Where is the mailbox? There it is.

Where are the closing papers? Here they are.

who's, whose   *Who's* is a contraction and means "who is" or "who has."

Who's responsible for signing the checks? (*Who is* responsible?)

Who's been reading my journal? (*Who has* been . . . ?)

Whose is a possessive. (Possessives such as *whose, its, yours, hers, ours, theirs* are already possessive and never take an apostrophe. See p. 31.)

Whose keys are these?

woman, women   The difference here is one of number: wo*man* refers to one female; wo*men* refers to two or more females.

I know a *woman* who won eight thousand dollars on a single horse race.

I bowl with a group of *women* from my work.

you're, your   *You're* is a contraction and means "you are."

You're as smart as I am. (*You are* as smart as I am.)

Your is a possessive meaning belonging to you.

I borrowed *your* lab book.

E X E R C I S E S

Underline the correct word. When you've finished ten sentences, compare your answers with those at the back of the book. Do only ten sentences at a time so you can teach yourself while you still have sentences to practice on.

Exercise 1

1. I don't know (weather, whether) I should (right, write) my own resume or pay a service do it for me.

2. I have a friend (who's, whose) just been hired at a law firm; he told me, "(You're, Your) crazy if you don't let an expert put together (you're, your) resume."

3. Maybe he's (right, write); he's been (threw, through) the process already and was (quiet, quite) satisfied with the result.

4. He has never (lead, led) me astray before, and I'm not (two, too, to) sure I know how to (right, write) all of my (personal, personnel) information in a clear format.

5. For instance, I can't figure out how much of my (passed, past) experience I should include.

6. (Personal, Personnel) offices do have strict requirements about the length and styles of documents.

7. (Their, There, They're) often harder to get (passed, past) (than, then) the people on the hiring committees.

8. In fact, the one (woman, women) who helped me last time I tried to get a job told me that the (principal, principle) problem with my file was the poor quality of my resume.

9. I think I'll ask my friend (were, wear, where) he got his resume done and how much it cost.

10. I would rather (loose, lose) a little money (than, then) (loose, lose) another job opportunity.

Exercise 2

1. When most of us picture a (piece, peace) of ice, we think of little see-(threw, through) cubes of frozen water.

2. And we consider (their, there, they're) (principal, principle) job (two, too, to) be cooling our lemonade when the (weather, whether) gets hot.

3. Scientists, however, know less (than, then) they would like to about the behavior of water when it freezes.

4. A few of them, including physicist William Harrison, have made the study of ice (their, there, they're) (personal, personnel) mission in life.

5. Harrison, (who's, whose) especially intrigued by the curious movements and emissions of glaciers, is not alone; George Ashton studies ice (two, too, to), but he focuses on places (were, wear, where) ice forms on top of rivers and lakes.

6. One of the things ice experts are (quiet, quite) sure of already is that ice covers just under ten percent of the earth's surface.

7. When frozen, water acts more strangely (than, then) other substances; it gets bigger rather (than, then) smaller, first of all.

8. And it melts instead of getting more solid when pressure is applied to it; a (piece, peace) of wire can be pulled (threw, through) a chunk of ice, and the ice will just freeze again behind it.

9. Minute pieces of ice in the atmosphere have also been discovered to play a part in the thinning of the earth's ozone layer (threw, through) (their, there, they're) interaction with chloroflourocarbons.

10. If the ice now covering a tenth of the globe were to melt, the oceans would rise between (two, too, to) and three hundred feet, and we would (loose, lose) nearly all of the big cities in the world.

Source: Discover, June 1999

Exercise 3

1. After my exercise class, my feet feel as heavy as (lead, led), and I can still hear my instructor saying, "(You're, Your) not lifting (you're, your) feet high enough!"

2. My (personal, personnel) goal is to (loose, lose) ten pounds.

3. Lately, the indicator on the scale has gone (passed, past) my ideal weight, and I'm not (two, too, to) happy about it.

4. I am (quiet, quite) sure that I don't want to (were, wear, where) only (loose, lose) clothes for the rest of my life.

5. Luckily, I'm taller (than, then) the other members of my family, so (their, there, they're) not aware of my recent weight gain yet.

6. But once the warm (weather, whether) arrives, my family will head for the lake.

7. (Than, Then) I won't be able (two, too, to) hide in baggy clothes.

8. My brother and (two, too, to) of my sisters love to water-ski (their, there, they're) at the lake.

9. They don't care (weather, whether) anybody joins them; (their, there, they're) a party all by themselves.

10. I just don't want to be the one (who's, whose) still wearing a T-shirt after everyone else is in the water just because of a ten-pound spare tire around my waist.

Exercise 4

1. Lately, it seems people have forgotten the (principal, principle) "Mind (you're, your) own business, and let other people mind theirs."

2. Private moments are becoming more public (than, then) ever, especially when it comes (two, too, to) marriage proposals.

3. In the (passed, past), people asked each other the big question in the secure setting of a home or perhaps in a (quiet, quite) corner of a restaurant.

4. Now a stadium full of baseball fans or the readership of a whole newspaper must be (their, there, they're) to witness the event.

5. One man decided to (right, write) a crossword puzzle that would spell out the question "Will you marry me?" for his beloved to discover.

6. The (woman, women) he wanted to marry did the puzzle in the paper every morning.

7. On the morning of the proposal, she went (threw, through) the clues, answered all of them correctly, and when she saw the proposal and her name spelled out in the puzzle, she looked up at her boyfriend and said, "Yes!"

8. Some men and (woman, women) don't think it's (right, write) to be put on the spot in public, however.

9. In one instance, the intended (threw, through) the ring overboard after being asked in front of the entire population of a cruise ship.

10. (Weather, Whether) it's other people's portable phone calls or marriage proposals, we (loose, lose)—or maybe we give away—a little more privacy every day.

Exercise 5

1. The Girls' Middle School in Mountain View, California, is attempting to (right, write) the wrongs of the (passed, past).

2. GMS is an all-girl campus (were, wear, where) the (principal, principle) aim is to teach girls science, math, and technology.

3. The American Association of University (Woman, Women) studied the treatment of children in schools and published its results in 1992.

4. The study showed that girls (loose, lose) interest in the tough subjects due (two, too, to) lack of attention by teachers and decreased access to computers.

5. And standard test scores (threw, through) the years (quiet, quite) clearly show the results: girls' math scores have been consistently lower (than, then) boys' scores.

6. Kathleen Bennett, the (woman, women) who founded GMS in 1998, wants to harness girls' willingness to learn and (their, there, they're) ability to excel at math, science, and all subjects.

7. Like Bennett, (who's, whose) background in technology is extensive, other teachers at GMS provide role models for their students.

8. The school offers more (than, then) just science and math classes; (their, there, they're) are also classes in languages and the arts.

9. (Weather, Whether) a GMS student is studying a circuit board or a (piece, peace) of music, she does so without boy/girl distractions.

10. Many parents gain (piece, peace) of mind by enrolling (their, there, they're) children in single-sex schools.

Source: Newsweek, 21 June 1999

PROOFREADING EXERCISE

See if you can correct the ten errors in this student paragraph. All errors involve Words Often Confused (Set 2).

Now that the whether is nice, my husband and I have decided to repaint the outside of our house. We are going to paint it ourselves. But it isn't going to be an easy job since many of the shingles have come lose over the years. In the passed before we moved in, the house had been repainted without the scraping and sanding necessary, so big chunks of paint have just started falling off onto the grass. We worry that their is led in the old paint, but we can't decide weather to call in a professional. One of my husband's friends, a women who's house was just remodeled, told him, "Your going to regret doing it yourselves. After what I've been threw, I would strongly recommend hiring a professional. That's the only way to guarantee your piece of mind."

SENTENCE WRITING

Write several sentences using any words you missed in doing the exercises for Words Often Confused (Set 2).

Sentence writing is a good idea not only because it will help you remember these words often confused, but also because it will be a storehouse for ideas you can later use in writing papers. Here are some topics you might consider writing your sentences about:

Your study habits

Your favorite musician or group

One of your best qualities

Something you would like to change

Your favorite sport to watch on TV

Contractions

When two words are condensed into one, the result is called a contraction:

is not ········▶ isn't   you have ········▶ you've

The letter or letters that are left out are replaced with an apostrophe. For example, if the two words *do not* are condensed into one, an apostrophe is put where the *o* is left out.

do not   don't

Note how the apostrophe goes in the exact place where the letter or letters are left out in these contractions:

I am	I'm
I have	I've
I shall, I will	I'll
I would	I'd
you are	you're
you have	you've
you will	you'll
she is, she has	she's
he is, he has	he's
it is, it has	it's

we are	we're
we have	we've
we will, we shall	we'll
they are	they're
they have	they've
are not	aren't
cannot	can't
do not	don't
does not	doesn't
have not	haven't
let us	let's
who is, who has	who's
where is	where's
were not	weren't
would not	wouldn't
could not	couldn't
should not	shouldn't
would have	would've
could have	could've
should have	should've
that is	that's
there is	there's
what is	what's

One contraction does not follow this rule: *will not* becomes *won't.*

In all other contractions that you're likely to use, the apostrophe goes exactly where the letter or letters are left out. Note especially *it's, they're, who's,* and *you're.* Use them when you mean two words. (See pp. 31–32 for the possessive forms—*its, their, whose,* and *your*—which don't have an apostrophe.)

E X E R C I S E S

Put an apostrophe in each contraction. Then compare your answers with those at the back of the book. Be sure to correct each group of ten sentences before going on so you'll catch your mistakes while you still have sentences to practice on.

Exercise 1

1. We've all seen images of and heard stories about Cleopatra VII, the incredibly beautiful and powerful queen of Egypt.

2. The facts of Cleopatra's life don't need to be exaggerated to be intriguing and fantastic.

3. There isn't any disagreement that her appearance was stunning and her manner mesmerizing.

4. However, the picture on a coin she's said to have commissioned portrays her as more of a ruler than a lover; this coin is the closest thing we've got to a photograph of Cleopatra, and it's on display at the British Museum in London.

5. Cleopatra certainly wasn't ordinary: she knew as many as eight languages, understood science and philosophy, and wrote scholarly works.

6. Theres also the famous story of Cleopatra rolling herself up in a rug or some blankets to be delivered to Julius Caesar; he's said to have been very impressed.

7. For political reasons, she'd wanted to meet with Caesar in private, but she couldn't do so without attracting the attention of possible enemies.

8. This bold move and a longer, more complicated alliance with Marc Antony don't touch the surface of Cleopatra's accomplishments.

9. And scholars can't explain all of the evidence following Cleopatra's famous suicide.

10. Although we've been led to believe she used an asp, there weren't any marks on her dead body, and the snake was never found.

Source: Smithsonian, Feb. 1997

Exercise 2

1. My friends and I needed some extra money for a trip wed planned, so we decided to have a group yard sale.

2. I didnt think that Id find very many items to sell in my own house.

3. But I couldnt believe how much stuff I discovered that I hadnt ever used.

4. There wasnt any reason to hang onto an old exercise bicycle, for instance.

5. And I knew I didnt want to keep the cat-shaped clock that hung in my room when I was a kid.

6. My parents werent willing to part with the clock, though; I guess theyre more sentimental than I am right now.

7. It isnt easy to get rid of some things, and my friends didnt have any better luck with their parents than Id had.

8. Still, since there were so many of us, we ended up with a yard full of merchandise.

9. We spent the weekend selling a cup here and a bike there until wed made over two hundred dollars.

10. Now were convinced that without our yard-sale profits, we couldnt have had such a fun-filled trip.

Exercise 3

1. Leonardo da Vinci's mural *The Last Supper* hasnt been treated well over the years.

2. If hed known, in the 1490s when he created the mural, that it would suffer so, da Vinci mightve reconsidered doing it at all.

3. In the past, its been painted over and even covered with glue in unsuccessful efforts to preserve it.

4. Often there wasnt any attempt to protect the mural; at one time, the room containing the masterpiece was even used as a stable for horses.

5. Napoleon's soldiers didnt treat it any better; in fact, theyre known to have vandalized it on purpose.

6. Although the room hasnt held horses or soldiers recently, its been filled with the exhaust from nearby cars and moisture from the breath of too many visitors.

7. In the late 1970s, Italy decided that it wouldnt allow the mural to suffer any further abuse.

8. The Italian government enlisted a team of experts to clean and repair da Vinci's famous painting, and theyd been working for more than twenty years on the project before it was finished in 1999.

9. Whats on the wall now that theyve finished hasnt been universally well received.

10. Its hard to tell how much of da Vinci's work remains after layers and chunks of grime and coverings have been removed.

Source: Newsweek, 7 June 1999

Exercise 4

1. Every semester, theres a blood drive at my school, and usually I tell myself Im too busy to participate.

2. But this time, Ive decided to give blood with a couple of my friends.

3. Weve all wanted to donate before, but individually we havent had the nerve.

4. Well visit the "blood-mobile" together and support each other if any of us cant do it.

5. My friend Carla has donated before, so shes the one weve asked about how it feels.

6. She described the whole process and assured us that its easy and painless.

7. First, a volunteer asks us some questions and takes a small blood sample from one of our earlobes to see if we are or arent able to give blood.

8. Once were cleared to donate, well be asked to lie down and have one of our arms prepared for the actual donation.

9. Thats the part Ill be dreading, but Carla says its just the first stick that stings a little.

10. After that, she says that theres no sensation at all except the satisfaction of helping with such a worthy cause.

Exercise 5

1. "Whos Gene Moore?" people might ask.

2. Ive just read an article about his life, and hes definitely someone most people whove ever been to New York City would know.

3. They wouldnt recognize his face or his name, but they probably wouldve seen his work.

4. For forty years before his death in 1998, Mr. Moore dressed the gorgeous and sometimes outrageous windows of Tiffany's on Fifth Avenue.

5. Moore's first dreams were to play piano or to paint professionally, but he wasnt satisfied with the results of either of these endeavors.

6. His artistic spirit and creative talents werent wasted, however.

7. After succeeding in the display departments of several smaller stores, Moore's future was sealed when he was hired by Tiffany's.

8. Over the years, its been impossible not to notice Moore's innovative displays.

9. Theyve included jewels presented on vegetables and broken necklaces being used as nesting material for birds.

10. In his early work, Moores even credited with starting the practice of using strands of tiny white lights for holiday displays, instead of the overused colored ones.

Source: The Economist, 12 Dec. 1998

PROOFREADING EXERCISE

Can you correct the ten errors in this student paragraph? They could be from any of the areas studied so far.

I cant even think of a roller coaster anymore without being afraid. I used to look forward to the warm whether and frequent trips to our local amusement parks. I loved everything about the rides—the speed, the dips, the turns, the loops. Then I was in a minor car accident wear I injured my knee after crashing into the rear end of another car. It was'nt to bad, and only my knee was hurt. I thought that a sore knee would be the only negative affect. I was wrong. For some reason, since the accident, I've become really frightened of going fast. I found out the hard way, by going threw the most terrifying minutes of my life on a coaster that Id been on several times in the passed. I guess its time for me to find new ways of having fun.

SENTENCE WRITING

Doing exercises helps you learn a rule, but even more helpful is using the rule in writing. Write ten sentences using contractions. You might write about your reaction to the week's big news story, or you can choose your own subject.

Possessives

The trick in writing possessives is to ask yourself the question, "Who (or what) does it belong to?" (Modern usage has made *who* acceptable when it comes first in a sentence, but some people still say, "*Whom* does it belong to?" or even "*To whom* does it belong?") If the answer to your question doesn't end in *s*, then add an apostrophe and *s*. If the answer to your question ends in *s*, add an apostrophe. Then you must see if you need another sound to make the possessive clear. If you need another *s* sound, add the apostrophe and another *s* (as in the last of the following examples).

one girl (uniform)	Who does it belong to?	girl	Add *'s*	girl's uniform
two girls (uniforms)	Who do they belong to?	girls	Add *'*	girls' uniforms
a man (coat)	Who does it belong to?	man	Add *'s*	man's coat
mens (coats)	Who do they belong to?	men	Add *'s*	men's hats
children (game)	Who does it belong to?	children	Add *'s*	children's game
a month (pay)	What does it belong to?	month	Add *'s*	month's pay
Brahms (Lullaby)	Who does it belong to?	Brahms	Add *'*	Brahms' lullaby
my boss (office)	Who does it belong to?	boss	Add *'s*	boss's office

This trick will always work, but you must ask the question every time. Remember that the key word is *belong*. Who (or what) does it belong to? If you ask the question another way, you may get an answer that won't help you. Also, if you just look at a word without asking the question, you may think the name of the owner ends in *s* when it really doesn't.

TO MAKE A POSSESSIVE

1. Ask "Who (or what) does it belong to?"
2. If the answer doesn't end in *s*, add an apostrophe and *s*.
3. If the answer ends in *s*, add just an apostrophe *or* an apostrophe and *s* if you need the extra sound to show a possessive (as in *boss's office*).

E X E R C I S E S

Follow the directions carefully for each of the following exercises. Because possessives can be tricky, explanations follow some exercises to help students understand them better.

Exercise 1

Cover the right column and see if you can write the following possessives correctly. Ask the question "Who (or what) does it belong to?" each time. Don't look at the answer before you try!

1. the women (soccer team)   _____   the women's soccer team

2. an umpire (decisions)   _____   an umpire's decisions

3. Phyllis (career)   _____   Phyllis' or Phyllis's career

4. Anthony (new dog)   _____   Anthony's new dog

5. the Porters (mailbox)   _____   the Porters' mailbox

6. Ms. Ross (picture)   _____   Ms. Ross's picture

7. parents (responsibilities)   _____   parents' responsibilities

8. a butterfly (wings)   _____   a butterfly's wings

9. two butterflies (wings)   _____   two butterflies' wings

10. a lawsuit (success)   _____   a lawsuit's success

(Sometimes you may see a couple of choices when the word ends in *s. Phyllis' career* may be written *Phyllis's career*. That is also correct, depending on how you want your reader to say it. Be consistent when given such choices.)

CAUTION- Don't assume that any word that ends in *s* is a possessive. The *s* may indicate more than one of something, a plural noun. Make sure the word actually possesses something before you add an apostrophe.

A few commonly used words are already possessive and don't need an apostrophe added to them. Memorize this list:

our, ours   its

your, yours   their, theirs

his, her, hers   whose

Note particularly *its, their, whose,* and *your.* They are already possessive and don't take an apostrophe. (These words sound just like *it's, they're, who's,* and *you're,* which are *contractions* that use an apostrophe in place of their missing letters.)

Exercise 2

Cover the right column below and see if you can write the correct form. The answer might be a *contraction* or a *possessive.* If you miss any, go back and review the explanations.

1. (There) someone here to see you.	There's
2. (They) lease runs out next month.	Their
3. Are these keys (you) or hers?	yours
4. Let me know when (it) time to begin.	it's
5. (Who) taking you to the mall?	Who's
6. The car is so old that (it) paint is fading.	its
7. (We) looking for a new apartment.	We're
8. (Who) textbook is this?	Whose
9. (She) the one who called the radio station.	She's
10. Are you sure that (you) right?	you're

Exercise 3

Here's another chance to check your progress with possessives. Cover the right column again as you did in Exercises 1 and 2, and add apostrophes to the possessives. Each answer is followed by an explanation.

1. My cousins spent the weekend at my parents mountain cabin.	parents' (You didn't add an apostrophe to *cousins,* did you? The cousins don't possess anything.)
2. The border guard collected all of the tourists passports.	tourists' (Who did the passports belong to?)
3. I attended my sisters graduation.	sister's (if it is one sister), sisters' (two or more sisters)
4. Two of my friends borrowed the camp directors boat.	director's (The friends don't possess anything.)
5. Patricks salad was larger than hers.	Patrick's (*Hers* is already possessive and doesn't take an apostrophe.)

6. After a moments rest, the dog wagged its tail again.

moment's (*Its* is already possessive and doesn't take an apostrophe.)

7. Overnight, someone covered the Smiths house with tissue.

Smiths' (The house belongs to the Smiths.)

8. Childrens shoe sizes differ from adults sizes.

children's, adults' (Did you use the "Who do they belong to" test?)

9. The sign read, "Buses only."

No apostrophe, no possessive.

10. A toothpastes flavor affects its sales.

toothpaste's (*Its* is already possessive and doesn't take an apostrophe.)

Exercises 4 and 5

Now you're ready to put the apostrophe in each possessive that follows. But be careful. *First,* make sure the word really possesses something; not every word ending in *s* is a possessive. *Second,* remember that certain words are already possessive and don't take an apostrophe. *Third,* remember that even though a word ends in *s,* you can't tell where the apostrophe goes until you ask the question, "Who (or what) does it belong to?" Check your answers at the back of the book after the first set.

Exercise 4

1. One of Pablo Picassos famous paintings was recently vandalized at a museum in Amsterdam.

2. Before the incident, the painting, *Woman Nude in Front of the Garden,* was worth approximately six million dollars, but to the art world it was priceless.

3. A man who had been treated for psychological problems destroyed the masterpieces monetary and artistic value in a single moment.

4. When a museum guards back was turned, the deranged man used a kitchen knife to carve a huge hole in the paintings center.

5. He effectively removed the womans image and the canvas behind her.

6. Art historians know that Picasso put three days effort into creating the painting in 1956.

7. But its life was cut short at forty-three; and unfortunately, the museums security team did not catch the attacker in the act.

8. Later, the vandal made the authorities job easier when he told his story to one of Amsterdams newspapers; the mans criminal record included an airline hijacking attempt in the late 1970s.

9. The future of Picassos *Woman Nude in Front of the Garden* is uncertain.

10. According to museum experts, the painting can be restored—but never to its unharmed state.

Source: U.S. News & World Report, 31 May 1999

Exercise 5

1. Nearly everyone knows of *The Simpsons* success as an animated television program.

2. At the height of the shows popularity in 1998, several products participated in the promotion of a contest called "The Simpsons House Giveaway."

3. Each of the contestants was hoping to win the following prize: a full-scale, exact duplicate of Homer, Marge, Bart, Lisa, and Maggies beloved home.

4. The prize houses color scheme would even match the cartoon series hues of bright yellow, pink, orange, blue, and green—inside and out.

5. The contests winner was a woman from Kentucky, 63-year-old Barbara Howard.

6. Howards entry form came from a box of iced tea mix, but she never expected to hold the big yellow key to The Simpsons Houses front door.

7. For one thing, the 2,200-square-foot, four-bedroom prize propertys location was far from Kentucky.

8. It was built in Henderson, Nevada, not far from Las Vegas bright lights and casinos.

9. The sponsoring house builder named the area Springfield after the Simpsons own cartoon town, but there are no other similarities.

10. Howard and her family won't find Ned Flanders house, Principal Skinners elementary school, Apus Kwik-E-Mart, or Chief Wiggums police station anywhere nearby.

PROOFREADING EXERCISE

Find the five errors in this student paragraph. All of the errors involve possessives.

You might not know of Marion Donovans claim to fame. She invented some-thing most parents use thousands of times. When her babys' crib became wet each night, Donovan used a shower curtain to create the worlds first plastic diaper cover. After patenting her device and calling it the "Boater," Donavans' business sense guided her to sell the idea, which she received one million dollars for in 1951. The Boater design led to the birth of the disposable diaper, and its' sales cur-rently bring in nearly five billion dollars a year.

Source: People, 7 Dec. 1998

SENTENCE WRITING

Write ten sentences using the possessive forms of the names of members of your family or the names of your friends. You could write about a recent event where your family or friends got together. Just tell the story of what happened that day.

REVIEW OF CONTRACTIONS AND POSSESSIVES

Here are two review exercises. First, add the necessary apostrophes to the following sentences. Try to get all the correct answers. Don't excuse an error by saying, "Oh, that was just a careless mistake." A mistake is a mistake. Be tough on yourself.

1. Theres a popular tradition most of us celebrate on Valentines Day.

2. We give each other little candy hearts with sayings on them, such as "Im Yours," "Youre Cute," and "Be Mine."

3. Americas largest maker of these candies is Necco; thats short for New England Confectionery Company.

4. Necco calls its version of the candies "Sweethearts Brand Conversation Hearts," and Neccos sayings have only two basic requirements: theyve got to be short and "sweet."

5. The candy hearts recipe is very sweet indeed—its ninety percent sugar.

6. The companys history goes back to the mid-1800s, and at first the sayings were printed on paper and placed inside a shell-shaped candy, more like a fortune cookies design than the tiny printed hearts we buy now.

7. In 1902, the candys shape was changed to a heart, and the sayings were printed directly on the candy.

8. Necco now makes eight billion of its candy hearts each year to satisfy the countrys desire to continue the hundred-year-old tradition.

9. Stores may begin stocking boxes of conversation hearts as early as New Years Day, but statistics show that over seventy-five percent of each years boxes are purchased in the three days before Valentines Day.

10. And if a couple of boxes are left over after February 14th, theyll stay fresh for up to five years.

Source: The Washington Post, 11 Feb. 1998

Second, add the necessary apostrophes to the following short student essay.

Bowling for Values

Growing up as a child, I didnt have a set of values to live by. Neither my mother nor my father gave me any specific rules, guidelines, or beliefs to lead me through the complicated journey of childhood. My parents approach was to set me free, to allow me to experience lifes difficulties and develop my own set of values.

They were like parents taking their young child bowling for the first time. They hung their values on the pins at the end of the lane. Then they put up the gutter guards and hoped that Id hit at least a few of the values theyd lived by themselves.

If I had a son today, Id be more involved in developing a set of standards for him to follow. Id adopt my mom and dads philosophy of letting him discover on his own what hes interested in and how he feels about life. But Id let him bowl in other lanes or even in other bowling alleys. And, from the start, hed know my thoughts on religion, politics, drugs, sex, and all the ethical questions that go along with such subjects.

Now that Im older, I wish my parents wouldve shared their values with me. Being free wasnt as comfortable as it mightve been if Id had some basic values to use a foundation when I had tough choices to make. My childrens lives will be better, I hope. At least theyll have a base to build on or to remodel—whichever they choose.

Words That Can Be Broken into Parts

Breaking words into their parts will often help you spell them correctly. Each of the following words is made up of two shorter words. Note that the word then contains all the letters of the two shorter words.

chalk board	. . .	chalkboard	room mate	. . .	roommate
over due	. . .	overdue	home work	. . .	homework
super market	. . .	supermarket	under line	. . .	underline

Becoming aware of prefixes such as *dis, inter, mis,* and *un* is also helpful. When you add a prefix to a word, note that no letters are dropped, either from the prefix or from the word.

dis appear	disappear	mis represent	misrepresent
dis appoint	disappoint	mis spell	misspell
dis approve	disapprove	mis understood	misunderstood

dis satisfy	dissatisfy	un aware	unaware
inter act	interact	un involved	uninvolved
inter active	interactive	un necessary	unnecessary
inter related	interrelated	un sure	unsure

Have someone dictate the previous list for you to write and then mark any words you miss. Memorize the correct spellings by noting how each word is made up of a prefix and a word.

Rule for Doubling a Final Letter

Most spelling rules have so many exceptions that they aren't much help. But here's one worth learning because it has almost no exceptions.

Double a final letter [consonants only] when adding an ending that begins with a vowel (such as *ing, ed, er*) if all three of the following are true:

1. The word ends in a single consonant,

2. which is preceded by a single vowel (the vowels are *a, e, i, o, u*),

3. and the accent is on the last syllable (or the word only has one syllable).

We'll try the rule on a few words to which we'll add *ing, ed,* or *er.*

begin   **1.** It ends in a single consonant—*n,*
       2. preceded by a single vowel—*i,*
       3. and the accent is on the last syllable—be gin´.
       Therefore we double the final consonant and write *beginning, beginner.*

stop   **1.** It ends in a single consonant—*p,*
       2. preceded by a single vowel—*o,*
       3. and the accent is on the last syllable (there is only one).
       Therefore we double the final consonant and write *stopping, stopped, stopper.*

filter   **1.** It ends in a single consonant—*r,*
       2. preceded by a single vowel—*e,*
       3. But the accent isn't on the last syllable. It's on the first—*fil´ter.*
       Therefore we don't double the final consonant. We write *filtering, filtered.*

keep   **1.** It ends in a single consonant—*p,*
        2. but it isn't preceded by a single vowel. There are two *e*'s.
        Therefore we don't double the final consonant. We write *keeping, keeper.*

NOTE- Be aware that *qu* is treated as a consonant because *q* is almost never written without *u*. Think of it as *kw.* In words like *equip* and *quit,* the *qu* acts as a consonant. Therefore *equip* and *quit* both end in a single consonant preceded by a single vowel, and the final consonant is doubled in *equipped* and *quitting.*

E X E R C I S E S

Add *ing* to these words. Correct each group of ten before continuing so you'll catch any errors while you still have words to practice on.

Exercise 1

1. eat		**6.** confer
2. cut		**7.** clap
3. slip		**8.** trim
4. talk		**9.** quiz
5. weed		**10.** mop

Exercise 2

1. snap		**6.** cancel
2. tear		**7.** prefer
3. heal		**8.** dream
4. flop		**9.** drip
5. suggest		**10.** transmit

Exercise 3

1. pat		**6.** brush
2. span		**7.** gather
3. feed		**8.** knot
4. alarm		**9.** offer
5. occur		**10.** hog

Exercise 4

1. dig	**6.** unhook
2. review	**7.** run
3. deal	**8.** push
4. clog	**9.** aim
5. click	**10.** deliver

Exercise 5

1. mourn	**6.** wish
2. dress	**7.** cook
3. pass	**8.** construct
4. button	**9.** polish
5. sit	**10.** lead

PROGRESS TEST

This test covers everything you've studied so far. One sentence in each pair is correct. The other is incorrect. Read both sentences carefully before you decide. Then write the letter of the incorrect sentence in the blank. Try to isolate and correct the error if you can.

1. _A_ **A.** This years' roses are the most beautiful I've ever seen.

   B. The men's team will travel more than the women's team this season.

2. _A_ **A.** I don't know how to play chess, but I want to learn.

   B. We could of gone to the movies last weekend.

3. _A_ **A.** We submited our names to the scholarship committee for consideration.

   B. Classes were canceled because of the heavy snowfall.

4. _A_ **A.** I always loose my car keys, especially when I'm running late.

   B. The dog next door loves to put its paws up on the fence and watch us swim.

5. _B_ **A.** The flavors of beans and rice complement each other perfectly.

   B. I would like to complement you on your choice of major.

6. _A_ **A.** Do you know were Yosemite is?

   B. We've seen that video several times, and I'm tired of it.

7. _A_ **A.** Our suitcases were all ready on the plane when we heard the announcement.

   B. We were all ready to go on our trip to the Bahamas.

8. _A_ **A.** Blooming plants and trees have no affect on my husband.

   B. But they do affect me, especially in the summer.

9. _B_ **A.** Firefighters worried that someone was inside the empty building.

   B. Their principle goal was to save lives.

10. _B_ **A.** We bought an umbrella that would last for many years.

   B. It was made of an unique material developed by NASA.

Using a Dictionary

Some dictionaries are more helpful than others. A tiny pocket-sized dictionary or one that fits on a single sheet in your notebook might help you find the spelling of very common words, but for all other uses, you will need a complete, recently published dictionary. Spend some time at a bookstore looking through the dictionaries to find one that you feel comfortable reading. Look up a word that you have had trouble with in the past, and see if you understand the definition. Try looking the same word up in another dictionary and compare. If all else fails, stick with the big names, and you probably can't go wrong.

Work through the following thirteen exercises using a good dictionary. Then you will understand what a valuable resource it is.

1. Pronunciation

Look up the word *generic* and copy the pronunciation here.

_____

_____

_____

_____

Now under each letter with a pronunciation mark over it, write the key word having the same mark. You'll find the key words at the bottom of one of the two dictionary pages open before you. Note especially that the upside-down e (ə) always has the sound of *uh* like the *a* in *ago* or *about*. Remember that sound because it's found in many words.

Next, pronounce the key words you have written, and then slowly pronounce *generic,* giving each syllable the same sound as its key word.

Finally, note which syllable has the heavy accent mark. (In most dictionaries the accent mark points to the stressed syllable, but in one dictionary it is in front of the stressed syllable.) The stressed syllable is *ner.* Now say the word, letting the full force of your voice fall on that syllable.

When more than one pronunciation is given, the first is more common. If the complete pronunciation of a word isn't given, look at the word above it to find the pronunciation.

Look up the pronunciation of these words, using the key words at the bottom of the dictionary page to help you pronounce each syllable. Then note which syllable has the heavy accent mark, and say the word aloud.

depot   sibilant   ambivalent   chorister

2. Definitions

The dictionary may give more than one meaning for a word.

Read all the meanings for each italicized word and then write a definition appropriate to the sentence.

1. The woman left her *stole* in the taxi. *taking something that isn't yours,*

2. At the museum, I always find the *period* furniture most interesting. _____

_____

3. They were taught how to *thread* the needle of a sewing machine. _____

_____

4. Artistic *license* allows for the expansion of creativity. _____

_____

3. Spelling

By making yourself look up each word you aren't sure how to spell, you'll soon become a better speller. When two spellings are given in the dictionary, the first one (or the one with the definition) is preferred.

Use a dictionary to find the preferred spelling for each of these words.

travelled, traveled   canceling, cancelling

millennium, millenium   judgment, judgement

4. Compound Words

If you want to find out whether two words are written separately, written with a hyphen between them, or written as one word, consult your dictionary. For example:

half brother   is written as two words

sister-in-law   is hyphenated

stepchild   is written as one word

Write each of the following correctly:

week end_____   care free   _____

off season_____   half truth   _____

5. Capitalization

If a word is capitalized in the dictionary, that means it should always be capitalized. If it is not capitalized in the dictionary, then it may or may not be capitalized, depending on how it is used (see p. 190). For example, *Asian* is always capitalized, but *high school* is capitalized or not, according to how it is used.

Last year, I graduated from high school.

Last year, I graduated from Jefferson High School.

Write the following words as they're given in the dictionary (with or without a capital) to show whether they must always be capitalized or not. Take a guess before looking them up.

republican   _____   spanish   _____

dyslexia   _____   earth   _____

6. Usage

Just because a word is in the dictionary doesn't mean that it's in standard use. The following labels indicate whether a word is used today and, if so, where and by whom.

obsolete	no longer used
archaic	not now used in ordinary language but still found in some biblical, literary, and legal expressions
colloquial, informal	used in informal conversation but not in formal writing
dialectal, regional	used in some localities but not everywhere
slang	popular but nonstandard expression
nonstandard, substandard	not used in Standard Written English

Look up each italicized word and write the label indicating its usage. Dictionaries differ. One may list a word as slang whereas another will call it colloquial. Still another may give no designation, thus indicating that that particular dictionary considers the word in standard use.

1. That party was really *cheesy.* _____

2. She *ain't* going with us, is she? _____

3. I borrowed a *thou* from my brother—he's *loaded!* _____

4. The class hamster was a *goner* as soon as the teacher brought him through the door. _____

5. Are they *privy* to your thoughts?_____

7. Derivations

The derivations or stories behind words will often help you remember the current meanings. For example, if you read that someone is *narcissistic* and you consult your dictionary, you'll find that *narcissism* is a condition named after Narcissus, who was a handsome young man in Greek mythology. One day Narcissus fell in love with his own reflection in a pool, but when he tried to get closer to it, he fell in the water and drowned. A flower that grew nearby is now named for Narcissus. And *narcissistic* has come to mean "in love with oneself."

Look up the derivation of each of these words. You'll find it in square brackets either just before or just after the definition.

Cheddar _____

Milquetoast _____

Caesarian section _____

amphora_____

8. Synonyms

At the end of a definition, a group of synonyms is sometimes given. For example, at the end of the definition of *injure,* you'll find several synonyms, such as *damage* or *harm.* And if you look up *damage* or *harm,* you'll be referred to the same synonyms listed under *injure.*

List the synonyms given for the following words.

vapid_____

educate_____

cover_____

9. Abbreviations

Find the meaning of the following abbreviations.

MIA   _____   mg   _____

SRO   _____   cc   _____

10. Names of People

The names of famous people will be found either in the main part of your dictionary or in a separate biographical names section at the back.

Identify the following famous people.

Pablo Casals _____

Sappho _____

Buckminster Fuller _____

Octavio Paz _____

11. Names of Places

The names of places will be found either in the main part of your dictionary or in a separate geographical names section at the back.

Identify the following places.

Caudine Forks _____

Okefenokee _____

Port Said _____

Sandwich _____

12. Foreign Words and Phrases

Find the language and the meaning of the italicized expressions.

1. Jason committed a real *faux pas* when he forgot his host's name. _____

2. For a modern example of *deus ex machina,* just watch the end of that new movie. _____

3. We used *tromp l'œil* to paint a doorway on the garden wall. _____

4. The two fighters went at it *mano a mano.* _____

13. Miscellaneous Information

See if you can find these miscellaneous bits of information in a dictionary.

1. Would you put a *valence* or a *valance* at the top of your window? _____

2. Where would you expect to see an example of *stichomythia?* _____

3. What seasoning is used in *goulash?* _____

4. How long did the *Trojan War* last? _____

5. How often does *biweekly* mean? _____

Sentence Structure

Sentence structure refers to the way sentences are built using words, phrases, and clauses. Words are single units, and words link up in sentences to form clauses and phrases. Clauses are word groups *with* subjects and verbs, and phrases are word groups *without* subjects and verbs. Clauses are the most important because they make statements—they tell who did what (or what something is) in a sentence. Look at the following sentence for example:

We bought oranges at the farmer's market on Main Street.

It contains ten words, each playing its own part in the meaning of the sentence. But which of the words together tell who did what? *We bought oranges* is correct. That word group is a clause. Notice that *at the farmer's market* and *on Main Street* also link up as word groups but don't have somebody (subject) doing something (verb). Instead, they are phrases to clarify *where* we bought the oranges.

Importantly, you could leave out one or both of the phrases and still have a sentence—*We bought oranges*. However, you cannot leave the clause out. Then you would just have *At the farmer's market on Main Street*. Remember, every sentence needs at least one clause that can stand by itself.

Learning about the structure of sentences helps you control your own. Once you know more about sentence structure, then you can understand writing errors and learn how to correct them.

Among the most common errors in writing are fragments, run-ons, and awkward phrasing.

Here are some fragments:

Wandering around the mall all afternoon.

Because I tried to do too many things at once.

By interviewing the applicants in groups.

They don't make complete statements—not one has a clause that can stand by itself. Who was *wandering*? What happened *because you tried to do too many things at once?* What was the result of *interviewing the applicants in groups?* These incomplete sentence structures fail to communicate a complete thought.

In contrast, here are some run-ons:

Computer prices are dropping they're still beyond my budget.

The forecast calls for rain I'll wait to wash my car.

A truck parked in front of my driveway I couldn't get to school.

Unlike fragments, run-ons make complete statements, but the trouble is they make *two* complete statements; the first *runs on* to the second without correct punctuation. The reader has to go back to see where there should have been a break.

So fragments don't include enough information, and run-ons include too much. Another problem occurs when the information in a sentence just doesn't make sense.

Here are a few sentences with awkward phrasing:

The problem from my grades started to end.

It was a time at the picnic.

She won me at chess.

Try to find the word groups that show who did what, that is, the clauses. Once you find them, then try to put the clauses and phrases together to form a precise meaning. It's difficult, isn't it? You'll see that many of the words themselves are misused or unclear, such as *from, it,* and *won.* These sentences don't communicate clearly because the clauses, phrases, and even words don't work together. They suffer from awkward phrasing.

Fragments, run-ons, awkward phrasing, and other sentence structure errors confuse the reader. Not until you get rid of them will your writing be clearer and easier to read. Unfortunately there is no quick, effortless way to learn to avoid errors in sentence structure. First, you need to understand how clear sentences are built. Then you will be able to avoid common errors in your own writing.

This section will describe areas of sentence structure one at a time and then explain how to correct errors associated with the different areas. For instance, we start by helping you find subjects and verbs and understand dependent clauses; then we show you how to avoid fragments. You can go through the whole section yourself to master all of the areas. Or your teacher may assign only parts based on errors the class is making.

Finding Subjects and Verbs

The most important words in sentences are those that make up its independent clause, the subject and the verb. When you write a sentence, you write about *something* or *someone.* That's the subject. Then you write what the subject *does* or *is.* That's the verb.

> Lightning strikes.

The word *Lightning* is the something you are writing about. It's the subject, and we'll underline it once. *Strikes* tells what the subject does. It shows the action in the sentence. It's the verb, and we'll underline it twice. But most sentences do not include only two words—the subject and the verb. However, these two words still make up the core of the sentence even if other words and phrases are included with them.

> Lightning strikes back and forth from the clouds to the ground very quickly.

> Often lightning strikes people on golf courses or in boats.

When many words appear in sentences, the subject and verb can be hard to find. Because the verb often shows action, it's easier to spot than the subject. Therefore, always look for it first. For example, in the sentence

> The neighborhood cat folded its paws under its chest.

which word shows the action? Folded. It's the verb: Underline it twice. Now ask yourself who or what folded? Cat. It's the subject. Underline it once.

Study the following sentences until you understand how to pick out subjects and verbs.

> Tomorrow our school celebrates its fiftieth anniversary. (Which word shows the action? Celebrates. It's the verb. Underline it twice. Who or what celebrates? School. It's the subject. Underline it once.)

> The team members ate several boxes of chocolates. (Which word shows the action? Ate. Who or what ate? Members ate.)

> Internet users crowd the popular services. (Which word shows the action? Crowd. Who or what crowd? Users crowd.)

Often the verb doesn't show action but merely tells what the subject *is* or *was.* Learn to spot such verbs—*is, am, are, was, were, seems, feels, appears, becomes, looks,* and so forth. (For more information on these verbs, see the discussion of sentence patterns on p. 127).

> Marshall is a neon artist. (First spot the verb is. Then ask who or what is? Marshall is.)

The bread appears moldy. (First spot the verb appears. Then ask who or what appears? Bread appears.)

Sometimes the subject comes after the verb.

In the audience were two reviewers from the *Times.* (Who or what were in the audience? Reviewers were.)

There was a fortune-teller at the carnival. (Who or what was there? Fortune-teller was there.)

There were name tags for all the participants. (Who or what were there? Name tags were there.)

Here are the worksheets. (Who or what are here? Worksheets are here.)

NOTE- Remember that *there* and *here* (as in the last three sentences) are not subjects. They simply point to something.

In commands, often the subject is not expressed. It is *you* (understood).

Sit down. (You sit down.)

Place flap A into slot B. (You place flap A into slot B.)

Meet me at 7:00. (You meet me at 7:00.)

There may be more than one subject in a sentence.

Toys and memorabilia from the 1950s are high-priced collectibles.

Celebrity dolls, board games, and even cereal boxes from that decade line the shelves of antique stores.

There may also be more than one verb.

Water boils at a consistent temperature and freezes at another.

The ice tray fell out of my hand, skidded across the floor, and landed under the table.

As you pick out subjects in the following exercises, you may wonder whether you should say the subject is, for example, *memories* or *pleasant childhood memories*. It makes no difference so long as you get the main subject, *memories,* right. In the answers at the back of the book, usually—but not always—the single word is used. Don't waste your time worrying whether to include an extra word or two with the subject. Just make sure you get the main subjects right.

EXERCISES

Underline the subjects once and the verbs twice. When you've finished ten sentences, compare your answers carefully with those at the back of the book.

Exercise 1

1. Pleasant childhood memories are often quite vivid.

2. We remember special places, people, and things from our youth.

3. The image of our first house stays in our minds, for instance.

4. There are the neighborhood children to recall.

5. Such memories include favorite furniture and decorative objects.

6. Think back to your childhood now.

7. Most likely, it brings back a flood of memories.

8. Perhaps colors and smells seemed brighter and sweeter then.

9. Such sensations strike most of us at some point in our lives.

10. At these times, we cherish the past and look forward to the future.

Exercise 2

1. Your brain has two halves—a right side (hemisphere) and a left side (hemisphere).

2. But one side of your brain is stronger in different ways.

3. Scientists refer to this fact as "hemispheric lateralization" and test it this way.

4. Open your eyes and hold up your thumb with your arm far out.

5. Next, point your thumb at something on the other side of the room.

6. Keep both eyes open but cover the thing with the image of your thumb.

7. One at a time, shut one eye and then the other.

8. Your thumb moves to the right or left or stays the same.

9. For most people, the thumb jumps to the right with a closed right eye.

10. Very few people experience the opposite effect and are left-eyed.

Source: Discover, June 1999

Exercise 3

1. Amateur talent shows celebrate the performer or "ham" in all of us.

2. Schools and charities organize these events and raise funds for their organizations.

3. There are singers, dancers, comics, and acrobats in nearly every community.

4. They are not always good singers, dancers, comics, and acrobats, however.

5. In fact, crowds often love the worst performers in talent shows.

6. A sense of humor in the audience and the performers helps enormously.

7. Otherwise, participants feel embarrassment instead of encouragement.

8. Laughing with someone is not the same as laughing at someone.

9. Amateur performers need courage and support.

10. Every celebrity started somewhere, perhaps even in a talent show.

Exercise 4

1. The word *toast* has a couple of different meanings.

2. We toast pieces of bread and eat them with butter and jam.

3. People also make toasts to the bride and groom at weddings.

4. There are Old French and Latin word roots for *toast.*

5. Both *toster* (Old French) and *torrere* (Latin) refer to cooking and drying.

6. *Toast* as the word for cooked bread slices arrived in the 1400s.

7. The story of *toast*'s other meaning makes sense from there.

8. In the 1600s, there was a tradition in taverns.

9. Revelers placed spicy croutons in their drinks for added flavor.

10. Then they drank to the health of various ladies and invented the other meaning of *toast.*

Source: Dictionary of Word Origins (Arcade Publishing, 1990)

Exercise 5

1. Actors in the 1997 movie *Titanic* worked under difficult conditions.

2. The script required several hundred extras besides the actors in the leading roles.

3. For nearly four months, the filmmakers shot only nighttime scenes in water.

4. At the end of each night's filming, there were hundreds of cold actors in wet costumes.

5. Earlier in production, the actors complained about another scene.

6. Jack teaches Rose the art of spitting off the ship's deck.

7. That scene took five days to film and was very unpopular at the time.

8. Later, by chance, it connected with Rose's final moment of rebellion.

9. In the original script of the lifeboat scene, Rose's character stabs her fiancé with a hairpin.

10. But Kate Winslet thought of spitting in his face instead and tied the two moments together.

Source: Newsweek, 28 June 1999

PARAGRAPH EXERCISE

Underline the subjects once and the verbs twice in the following student paragraph.

My aunt and uncle have an incredible cookie jar collection. At the moment, they own about eight hundred jars and get new ones every day. Some of their cookie jars date back to the late nineteenth century. But others commemorate more current cartoon or movie characters. Celebrity cookie jars bring my aunt special happiness and add to the glamour of the collection. There are Elvis, Marilyn Monroe, and James Dean jars and even ones depicting The Grateful Dead's bus or The Beatles' psychedelic car. I really appreciate my aunt and uncle's collection and hope for one of my own someday.

SENTENCE WRITING

Write ten sentences about any subject—your favorite color, for instance. Keeping your subject matter simple in these sentence writing exercises will make it easier to find your sentence structures later. After you have written your sentences, go back and underline your subjects once and your verbs twice.

Locating Prepositional Phrases

Prepositional phrases are among the easiest structures in English to learn. Remember that a phrase is just a group of words (at least two) without a subject and a verb. And don't let a term like *prepositional* scare you. If you look in the middle of that long word, you'll find a familiar one—*position*. In English, we tell the *positions* of people and things in sentences using prepositional phrases. Look at the following sentence with its prepositional phrases in parentheses:

Our field trip (to the desert) begins (at 6:00) (in the morning) (on Friday).

One phrase tells where the field trip is going *(to the desert),* and three phrases tell when the trip begins *(at 6:00, in the morning,* and *on Friday).* As you can see, prepositional phrases show the position of someone or something in space or in time.

Here is a list of prepositions that can show positions in space:

under	across	outside	against
around	by	inside	at
through	beyond	over	below
above	among	on	in
below	near	behind	past
between	with	from	to

Here are prepositions that can show positions in time:

before	throughout	past	within
after	by	until	in
since	at	during	for

These lists include only individual words, *not phrases.* Remember, a preposition must be followed by an object—someone or something—to create a prepositional phrase. Notice that in the added prepositional phrases that follow, the position of the plane in relation to the object, *the clouds,* changes completely.

The passenger plane flew *above the clouds.*
below the clouds.
within the clouds.
between the clouds.
past the clouds.
around the clouds.

Now notice the different positions in time:

The plane landed *at 3:30.*
by 3:30.
past 3:30.
before the thunderstorm.
during the thunderstorm.
after the thunderstorm.

NOTE- A few words—such as *of, as,* and *like*—are prepositions that do not fit neatly into either the space or time category, yet they are very common prepositions (box *of candy,* note *of apology,* type *of bicycle*—act *as a substitute,* use *as an example,* as happy *as my little brother*—vitamins *like A, C, and E,* shaped *like a watermelon,* moved *like a snake).*

By locating prepositional phrases, you will be able to find subjects and verbs more easily. For example, you might have difficulty finding the subject and verb in a long sentence like this:

> After the rainy season, one of the windows in the attic leaked at the corners of its molding.

But if you put parentheses around all the prepositional phrases like this

> (After the rainy season), <u>one</u> (of the windows) (in the attic) <u><u>leaked</u></u> (at the corners) (of its molding).

then you have only two words left—the subject and the verb. Even in short sentences like the following, you might pick the wrong word as the subject if you don't put parentheses around the prepositional phrases first.

> <u>Many</u> (of the characters) <u><u>survived</u></u> (in that movie).

> The <u>waves</u> (around the ship) <u><u>looked</u></u> real.

NOTE- Don't mistake *to* plus a verb for a prepositional phrase. For example, *to quit* is not a prepositional phrase because *quit* is not the name of something. It's a form of verb.

E X E R C I S E S

Locate and put parentheses around the prepositional phrases in the following sentences. Be sure to start with the preposition itself *(in, on, to, at, of . . .)* and include the word or words that go with it *(in the morning, on our sidewalk, to Hawaii . . .).* Then underline the subjects once and the verbs twice. Remember that subjects and verbs are never inside prepositional phrases. Review the answers given at the back for each group of ten sentences before continuing.

Exercise 1

1. My family and I live in a house at the top of a hilly neighborhood in Los Angeles.

2. On weekday mornings, nearly everyone drives down the steep winding roads to their jobs or to school.

3. In the evenings, they all come back up the hill to be with their families.

4. For the rest of the day, we see only an occasional delivery van or compact school bus.

5. But on Saturdays and Sundays, there is a different set of drivers on the road.

6. Then tourists in minivans and prospective home buyers in convertibles cram the narrow streets.

7. On these weekend days, most of the neighborhood residents stay at home.

8. Frequently, drivers unfamiliar with the twists and turns of the roads up here cause accidents.

9. The expression "Sunday driver" really means something to those of us on the hill.

10. And we could add "Saturday driver" to the list as well.

Exercise 2

1. In England, Bob Martin is a man with a very strange claim to fame.

2. The seventy-year-old Martin lives in Eastleigh, a town approximately one hundred miles south of London.

3. For ten years, he traveled by train to London hundreds of times for one specific purpose.

4. During these trips, Martin attended six hundred and twenty-five performances of *Cats,* the long-running musical by Andrew Lloyd Webber.

5. Martin's interest in the show started the first time he listened to the original cast album.

6. This devoted *Cats* fan always sat in the orchestra section, but not always in the same seat.

7. Many of the actors and crew members in the productions befriended Bob Martin over the years.

8. In the eyes of his extended family, Martin is just a happy eccentric.

9. Without a wife or children to think about, Martin indulged his interest in *Cats.*

10. As a result, he traveled more than one hundred thousand miles over the rails and spent more than twenty thousand dollars on tickets to see the same play over and over again.

Source: People, 2 Aug. 1999

Exercise 3

1. Through NASA's space-exploration projects, we learn more about everything from our fellow planets to our sun and moon.

2. *Galileo* already discovered a layer of ice on Europa, Jupiter's moon, and in 2003 will look for signs of life beneath the ice's surface.

3. With the help of the *Hubble Space Telescope,* NASA retrieved pictures of the planet Uranus—its system of rings and its weather patterns.

4. NASA launched *Cassini* in 1997 to study Saturn, with an expected arrival time of 2004.

5. In an effort to put an American on Mars by 2020, NASA will use information from *Mars Surveyor 2001.*

6. NASA's *Pluto-Kuiper Express* will study Pluto, the most distant planet in our solar system.

7. With the *Contour Mission* in 2002, NASA hopes to learn about the origin of comets.

8. The *Terra* satellite will look at changes in Earth's weather as part of NASA's Earth Observing System.

9. The *Genesis* probe will fly around the sun and gather new information about its unique properties.

10. Finally, the mission for the *Lunar Prospector* is to discover habitable places on the moon.

Source: George, June 1999

Exercise 4

1. An engraved likeness of Pocahontas, the famous Powhatan Indian princess, is the oldest portrait on display at the National Portrait Gallery.

2. In 1607, Pocahontas—still in her early teens—single-handedly helped the British colonists in Virginia to survive.

3. Later, in 1616, Pocahontas traveled to England after her marriage to John Rolfe and the birth of their son.

4. She visited the court of King James I and impressed the British with her knowledge of English and her conversion to Christianity.

5. For her new first name, she chose Rebecca.

6. During her seven-month stay in England, she became extremely ill.

7. At some point before or during her illness, Simon Van de Passe engraved her portrait on copper.

8. The portrait shows Pocahontas in a ruffled collar and ornate Anglicized clothes but with very strong Indian features.

9. Successful sales of prints from the portrait illustrate her fame abroad.

10. Pocahontas died on that trip to England at the age of twenty-two.

Source: *Smithsonian*, Jan. 1999

Exercise 5

1. Gorgons have been extinct for two hundred and fifty million years.

2. These creatures lived and died millions of years before dinosaurs.

3. They perished along with almost all life on the planet in a huge cataclysmic event.

4. In fact, dinosaurs met a similar fate of their own.

5. Gorgons were beasts with both lion-like and lizard-like qualities.

6. Recently, scientists discovered a full-size fossilized skeleton of a gorgon in South Africa.

7. At seven feet long, the fossil tells a lot about these animals.

8. They had eyes in the sides of their nearly three-foot-long heads.

9. And they hunted successfully with the help of their four-inch-long teeth.

10. The gorgons' extreme physical features reveal the harshness of their prehistoric surroundings.

Source: *Discover*, Apr. 1999

PARAGRAPH EXERCISE

Put parentheses around the prepositional phrases in this paragraph from *You Can't Show Kids in Underwear and Other Little-Known Facts about Television*, by Barbara Seuling.

On November 17, 1968, during the last seconds of a football game between the New York Jets and the Oakland Raiders, in which the Jets were leading by a score of 32 to 29, NBC cut the game to show the children's story *Heidi*. The switchboard was so overwhelmed with calls from angry viewers that the circuit broke down. Meanwhile, the Jets were defeated 43 to 32. NBC was forced to show the last fifty seconds of the game on the following morning's *Today* show broadcast.

SENTENCE WRITING

Write ten sentences on the topic of your favorite snack—or choose any topic you like. When you go back over your sentences, put parentheses around your prepositional phrases and underline your subjects once and your verbs twice.

Understanding Dependent Clauses

All clauses contain a subject and a verb; however, there are two kinds of clauses: independent and dependent. An independent clause has a subject and a verb and can stand alone as a sentence. A dependent clause has a subject and a verb but can't stand alone because it begins with a dependent word (or words) such as

after	since	where
although	so that	whereas

as	than	wherever
as if	that	whether
because	though	which
before	unless	whichever
even if	until	while
even though	what	who
ever since	whatever	whom
how	when	whose
if	whenever	why

Whenever a clause begins with one of these dependent words, it is a dependent clause (unless it's a question, which would be followed by a question mark). If we take an independent clause such as

We ate dinner together.

and put one of the dependent words in front of it, it becomes a dependent clause and can no longer stand alone:

After we ate dinner together . . .

Although we ate dinner together . . .

As we ate dinner together . . .

Before we ate dinner together . . .

Since we ate dinner together . . .

That we ate dinner together . . .

When we ate dinner together . . .

While we ate dinner together . . .

With the added dependent words, these do not make complete statements. They leave the reader expecting something more. Therefore, these clauses can no longer stand alone. Each would depend on another clause—an independent clause—to make a sentence. We'll place a broken line beneath the dependent clauses.

After we ate dinner together, we went to the evening seminar.

We went to the evening seminar *after* we ate dinner together.

The speaker didn't know *that* we ate dinner together.

While we ate dinner together, the restaurant became crowded.

Note that in the preceeding examples, *when a dependent clause comes at the beginning of a sentence, it is followed by a comma*. Often the comma prevents misreading, as in the following sentence:

When he returned, the video was almost over.

Without a comma after *returned,* the reader would read *When he returned the video* before realizing that this was not what the author meant. The comma prevents misreading. Sometimes if the dependent clause is short and there is no danger of misreading, the comma can be left off, but it's safer simply to follow the rule that a dependent clause at the beginning of a sentence is followed by a comma.

You'll learn more about the punctuation of dependent clauses on pages 171 and 177, but right now just remember the previous rule.

Note that sometimes the dependent word is the subject of the dependent clause:

Theirs is the house that was remodeled last month.

The children understood what was happening.

Sometimes the dependent clause is in the middle of the independent clause:

The house that was remodeled last month is theirs.

The events that followed were confusing.

And sometimes the dependent clause is the subject of the entire sentence:

What you do also affects me.

Whichever they choose will be best for them.

How it looks doesn't mean anything.

Also note that sometimes the *that* of a dependent clause is omitted.

I know *that* you can tell the difference between red and green.

I know you can tell the difference between red and green.

Did everyone get the classes *that* they wanted?

Did everyone get the classes they wanted?

The word *that* doesn't always introduce a dependent clause. It may be a pronoun and serve as the subject of the sentence.

That was a big mistake.

That is my book.

That can also be a descriptive word.

That movie makes me cry every time.

I will take him to *that* restaurant tomorrow.

E X E R C I S E S

Underline the subjects once and the verbs twice in both the independent and the dependent clauses. Then put a broken line under the dependent clauses. Some sentences may have no dependent clauses, and others may have more than one.

Exercise 1

1. Jo Ann Altsman is a woman who is lucky to be alive.

2. When she had a second heart attack, no other person was there to help her.

3. Because she was in such pain, she couldn't move or easily call for help.

4. She did have two pets that she looked to as she lay on the floor of her home in what she considered her final moments.

5. She wondered if her dog might help, but he only barked at her.

6. Then Altsman's 150-pound potbellied pig LuLu took action when it became obvious that no one else could help her master.

7. The pig somehow made it through the little door that allows smaller pets to go in and out.

8. As she went through the opening, LuLu suffered big scratches on her tummy, but she persisted.

9. While she whined loudly for help, LuLu walked to the nearest highway and waited for a car.

10. The man who stopped followed LuLu to Altsman's house, and he called for an ambulance.

Source: People, 2 Nov. 1998

Exercise 2

1. On June 8, 1924, two British men, George Mallory and Andrew Irvine, disappeared as they were climbing to the top of Mount Everest.

2. When a reporter earlier asked Mallory why he climbed Everest, his response became legendary.

3. "Because it is there," Mallory replied.

4. No living person knows whether the two men reached the summit of Everest before they died.

5. Nine years after Mallory and Irvine disappeared, English climbers found Irvine's ice ax.

6. But nothing else of Mallory's or Irvine's was found until a Chinese climber spotted their bodies in 1975.

7. He kept the news of his sighting secret for several years but finally decided to tell a fellow climber on the day before he died himself in an avalanche on Everest.

8. In May 1999, a team of mountaineers searched the area where the Chinese man had seen something, and they found George Mallory's frozen body still intact after seventy-five years.

9. After they took DNA samples for identification, the mountaineers buried the famous climber on the mountainside where he fell.

10. Mallory and Irvine were the first climbers to try to get to the top of Everest, and the question remains whether they were on their way up or on their way down when they met their fate.

Source: Newsweek, 17 May 1999

Exercise 3

1. If you ever plan a trip to Bangkok, be sure to visit the Royal Dragon restaurant.

2. Somchai T. Amornrat designed the Royal Dragon so that it would break the world's record for the largest restaurant in the world.

3. Since the previous record-holding restaurant was also in Bangkok, Amornrat did some research and made his restaurant even bigger.

4. The Royal Dragon covers twelve acres and is so sprawling that servers must wear roller skates to get around.

5. As many as ten thousand people a day eat at the Royal Dragon or Mangkorn Luang, as it is called in Thai.

6. After customers enter the huge park-like complex, they dine at tables that encircle a large reflecting pool.

7. And once every evening, a waitress entertains the diners as she flies from the top of a Pagoda that is seven stories high to a stage in the middle of the pool.

8. Before the flying waitress takes off, speakers play the theme song from *Mission: Impossible.*

9. If guests want to make their own music, they can visit one of the Royal Dragon's fifty karaoke bars.

10. The one thousand people who cook and serve the food and who do the dishes afterward never worry about being late to work since most of them live in the restaurant complex.

Source: Avenues, Nov./Dec. 1998

Exercise 4

1. I just read an article that described the history of all the presidents' dogs.

2. Our first president, George Washington, cared so much about dogs that he bred them; Washington even interrupted a battle to return a dog that belonged to a British general.

3. Abraham Lincoln, whose dog was actually named Fido, left his loyal pet in Illinois after the Lincolns moved to the White House.

4. Teddy Roosevelt had lots of dogs but met and adopted Skip, the one that he loved best, as the little terrier held a bear at bay in the Grand Canyon.

5. FDR's pooch was always with him; he was a black Scottie named Fala, and they say that Roosevelt was so devoted to this pet that he made a U.S. Navy ship return to the Aleutians to pick Fala up after the diplomatic party accidentally left the dog behind.

6. Warren G. Harding's Laddie Boy was the most pampered of the presidential dogs since the Hardings gave him birthday parties and ordered a specially made chair for Laddie Boy to sit in during presidential meetings.

7. Soviet leader Nikita Khrushchev brought with him Pushinka, a dog that he gave to John F. Kennedy's daughter Caroline.

8. At a filling station in Texas, Lyndon Johnson's daughter Luci found a little white dog, Yuki, whom President Johnson loved to have howling contests with in the Oval Office.

9. Of course, Nixon had his famous Checkers, and George Bush had a spaniel named Millie, who wrote her own best-selling book with the help of Barbara Bush.

10. And just when it seemed that all presidents prefer dogs, Bill Clinton arrived with Socks, a distinctively marked black-and-white cat.

Source: Smithsonian, June 1997

Exercise 5

1. When Susan Lucci won a Daytime Emmy award in 1999, everyone was happy and surprised.

2. For Lucci, the award ended a losing steak that lasted nineteen years.

3. Since she has played the part of Erika Cane on *All My Children* for nearly thirty years, Lucci naturally wanted to win.

4. And whenever she didn't win, Lucci's family and friends gave her extra support.

5. Her children decorated the house while she attended the award ceremonies so that she felt appreciated even if she lost again.

6. As her string of losses got longer, Lucci revealed a good sense of humor when she did commercials that alluded to her infamous losing streak.

7. For a long time, nothing that Lucci did seemed to help her chances, however, and many thought that she might never win.

8. Some believe that she won the Emmy in 1999 because the scenes that Lucci submitted to the award board showed her as Erika the mom, dealing with a daughter who suffered from anorexia.

9. Since Lucci has a daughter herself, the scenes had the power of true emotions behind them.

10. Lucci's own daughter Liza is now a soap opera actress too, and everyone hopes that, as far as awards go, she will have better luck than her mother did.

Source: People, 6 June 1999

PARAGRAPH EXERCISE

Underline the subjects once, the verbs twice, and put a broken line under the dependent clauses in these paragraphs from *The Sense of Wonder,* by Rachel Carson.

If the moon is full and the night skies are alive with the calls of bird migrants, then the way is open for [an] adventure with your child, if he [or she] is old enough to use a telescope or a good pair of binoculars. The sport of watching migrating birds pass across the face of the moon has become popular and even scientifically important in recent years, and it is as good a way as I know to give an older child a sense of the mystery of migration.

Seat yourself comfortably and focus your glass on the moon. You must learn patience, for unless you are on a well-traveled highway of migration you may have to wait many minutes before you are rewarded. In the waiting periods you can study the topography of the moon, for even a glass of moderate power reveals enough detail to fascinate a space-conscious child. But sooner or later you should begin to see the birds, lonely travelers in space glimpsed as they pass from darkness into darkness.

SENTENCE WRITING

Write ten sentences about your morning routine (getting up, getting ready for school or work, eating breakfast, etc.). Try to write sentences that contain both independent and dependent clauses. Then underline your subjects once, your verbs twice, and put a broken line under your dependent clauses.

Correcting Fragments

Sometimes a group of words looks like a sentence—with a capital letter at the beginning and a period at the end—but it is missing a subject or a verb or both. Such incomplete sentence structures are called fragments. Here are a few examples:

Just ran around hugging everyone in sight. (no subject)

Paul and his sister with the twins. (no verb)

Nothing to do but wait. (no subject and no verb)

To change these fragments into sentences, we must make sure each has a subject and an adequate verb:

The sweepstakes winner just ran around hugging everyone in sight. (We added a subject.)

Paul and his sister with the twins reconciled. (We added a verb.)

We had nothing to do but wait. (We added a subject and a verb.)

Sometimes we can simply attach such a fragment to the sentence before or after it.

I want to find a fulfilling job. A career like teaching, for example.

I want to find a fulfilling job, a career like teaching, for example.

Or we can change a word or two in the fragment and make it into a sentence.

A teaching career is one example.

PHRASES

Phrases by definition are word groups without subjects and verbs, so whenever a phrase is punctuated as a sentence, it is a fragment. Look at this example of a sentence followed by a phrase fragment beginning with *hoping* (see p. 116 for more about verbal phrases).

I waited outside the director's office. Hoping to have a chance for an audition.

We can correct this fragment by attaching it to the previous sentence.

I waited outside the director's office, hoping to have a chance for an audition.

Or we can change it to include a subject and a real verb.

I waited outside the director's office. I hoped to have a chance for an audition.

Here's another example of a sentence followed by a phrase fragment:

The actor's profile was striking. Sketched on an envelope by a famous artist.

Here the two have been combined into one complete sentence:

The actor's striking profile was sketched on an envelope by a famous artist.

Or a better revision might be

A famous artist sketched the actor's striking profile on an envelope.

Sometimes, prepositional phrases are also incorrectly punctuated as sentences. Here a prepositional phrase follows a sentence, but the word group is a fragment—it has no subject and verb of its own. Therefore, it needs to be corrected.

I have lived a simple life so far. With my family on our farm in central California.

Here is one possible correction:

I have lived a simple life so far with my family on our farm in central California.

Or it could be corrected this way:

My family and I have lived a simple life on our farm in central California.

DEPENDENT CLAUSES

Dependent clauses punctuated as sentences are still another kind of fragment. A sentence needs a subject, a verb, *and* a complete thought. As discussed in the previous section, a dependent clause has a subject and a verb, but it begins with a word that makes its meaning incomplete, such as *after, while, because, since, although, when, if, where, who, which,* and *that.* (see p. 61 for a list). To correct such fragments, you need to take off the word that makes the clause dependent *or* add an independent clause.

FRAGMENT
   While some of us practiced our speeches.

CORRECTED
> Some of us practiced our speeches.

or

> *While* some of us practiced our speeches, we heard the bell.

FRAGMENT
> *Which* signaled the start of class.

CORRECTED
> The bell signaled the start of class.

or

> We heard the bell, *which* signaled the start of class.

Are fragments ever permissible? Fragments are sometimes used in advertising and in other kinds of writing. But such fragments are used by professional writers who know what they're doing. These fragments are used intentionally, not in error. Until you're an experienced writer, stick with complete sentences. Especially in college writing, fragments should not be used.

E X E R C I S E S

Some—but not all—of the following word groups are sentences. The others suffer from incomplete sentence structure. Put a period after each of the sentences. Make any fragments into sentences by assuring that each has a subject and an adequate verb.

Exercise 1

1. Sarah Winchester was a rich, eccentric woman

2. Her husband being William Winchester

3. William inherited the Winchester rifle fortune

4. The weapon responsible for the deaths of more people and animals than any gun before it

5. After William's death, the Winchester millions passing down to Sarah

6. But bad luck and other deaths in her family made her superstitious

7. A psychic calling it revenge by all those spirits killed by Winchester rifles

8. To avoid more trouble, the psychic told Sarah to buy a house out west and use her money to constantly rebuild it

9. The spirits guiding the renovation along the way to give them a nice place to visit and keep them happy

10. That way avoiding the curse of the Winchester ghosts

Source: America's Strangest Museums (Carol Publishing, 1996)

Exercise 2

1. The Winchester Mystery House, located in San Jose, California, built by Sarah Winchester

2. Growing from its original form—a small field house with fewer than ten rooms—to a sprawling mansion with more than one hundred rooms

3. Thousands of windows and doors, some without openings on the other side

4. One Sarah-sized door just five feet high right next to one of normal size

5. Nearly fifty bedrooms and as many staircases, several leading to a dead end at the ceiling

6. Thirteen was Sarah's lucky number

7. So she set twelve other table settings at dinner for her ghost guests

8. Even signing her will (with thirteen sections) thirteen times

9. Sarah died in 1922 and left the Winchester Mystery House behind as a museum

10. Many people visiting Sarah's strange house and exploring its odd interiors every year.

Source: America's Strangest Museums (Carol Publishing, 1996)

Exercise 3

Correct each phrase fragment by changing or adding words or by attaching the phrase to the complete sentence nearby.

1. Finding a parking space on the first day of classes seems impossible. Driving endlessly around campus and looking for an empty spot.

2. With hope that the situation will improve. I always spend the sixty dollars for a parking permit.

3. My old car's engine doesn't like the long periods of idling. Stalling a lot and not starting up again easily.

4. In order to get a space close to my first class. I always follow anyone walking through the parking lot closest to the science building.

5. I am usually disappointed by this method, however. Most people just walking through the parking lot to get to farther lots or to the bus stop.

6. I was really lucky on the first day of classes two semesters ago. Driving right into a spot vacated by a student from an earlier class.

7. Maybe I should get up before dawn myself. A fool-proof way to secure a perfect parking place.

8. Every morning, I see these early birds in their cars with their seats back. Sleeping there for hours before class but in a great spot.

9. I don't think I can solve the problem this way. Finding it hard to get out of bed in the dark.

10. Due to the rise in college populations. Campus parking problems will most likely only get worse.

Exercise 4

Correct each dependent clause fragment by eliminating its dependent word or by attaching the dependent clause to the independent clause before or after it.

1. We were writing in our journals. When suddenly the fire alarm rang.

2. Everyone in the class looked at each other first and then at the teacher. Who told us to gather up our things and follow him outside.

3. The series of short bells continued. As we left the room and noisily walked out into the parking lot beside the main building.

4. The sunlight was very warm and bright compared to the classroom's flo-rescent lights. Which make everything look more clinical than natural.

5. As we stood in a large group with students and teachers from other classes. We wondered about the reason for the alarm.

6. I have never been roused by a fire alarm. That was anything but a planned drill.

7. Without the danger of injury, a party atmosphere quickly develops. Since we all get a break from our responsibilities.

8. I've noticed that the teachers seem the most at ease. Because they don't have to be in control during these situations.

9. After we students and the teachers chatted for ten minutes or so. The final bell rang to signal the end of the drill.

10. When we sat down at our desks again. The teacher asked us to continue writing in our journals until the end of the hour.

Exercise 5

All of the following word groups are clauses. If the clause has a subject and a verb and *does not* begin with a dependent word (such as *when, while, after, because, since, although, where, if, who, which,* or *that*), put a period after it. If the clause has a subject and a verb and *does* begin with a dependent word (making it a dependent clause fragment), add an independent clause either before or after it to make it a sentence. Remember that if the dependent clause comes first, a comma should follow it. These ten clauses are not about the same topic.

1. That you know so much about the politics of South American countries

2. While the jury deliberated

3. But that story sounds unbelievable

4. Be sure to send me a postcard

5. Harry Houdini promised to visit his wife after his death

6. Taking artistic photographs requires skill and patience

7. The restaurant where we first met

8. Until he noticed the price tag hanging from the side of the couch

9. A woman who traveled extensively during her childhood

10. If the rain stops

PROOFREADING EXERCISE

Correct the five fragments in the following paragraph.

When a ten-year-old girl named Stephanie Taylor heard about the shooting death of a police dog in New Jersey. She decided to do something to protect the dogs. Who work for the police in Oceanside, California. Where Stephanie lives with her family. Raising enough money to buy bulletproof vests for all of Oceanside PD's K-9 (canine) officers. Stephanie is glad now. Knowing that the dogs who serve and protect her neighborhood will be protected themselves.

Source: People, 16 Aug. 1999

SENTENCE WRITING

Write ten fragments and then revise them so that they are complete sentences. Or exchange papers with another student and turn your classmate's ten fragments into sentences.

Correcting Run-On Sentences

Any word group having a subject and a verb is a clause. As we have seen, the clause may be independent (able to stand alone) or dependent (unable to stand alone). If two independent clauses are written together without proper punctuation between them, the result is called a run-on sentence. Here are some examples.

Classical music is soothing I listen to it in the evenings.

I love the sound of piano therefore, Chopin is one of my favorites.

Run-on sentences can be corrected in one of four ways:

1. Make the two independent clauses into two sentences.

Classical music is soothing. I listen to it in the evenings.

I love the sound of piano. Therefore, Chopin is one of my favorites.

2. Connect the two independent clauses with a semicolon.

Classical music is soothing; I listen to it in the evenings.

I love the sound of piano; therefore, Chopin is one of my favorites.

When a connecting word such as

also	however	otherwise
consequently	likewise	then
finally	moreover	therefore
furthermore	nevertheless	thus

is used to join two independent clauses, the semicolon comes before the connecting word, and a comma usually comes after it.

Mobile phones are convenient; however, they are very expensive.

Earthquakes scare me; therefore, I don't live in Los Angeles.

We traveled to London; then we took the "Chunnel" to Paris.

The college recently built a large new library; thus students have more quiet study areas.

NOTE- The use of the comma after the connecting word depends on how long the connecting word is. If it is only a short word, like *then* or *thus,* no comma is needed.

---

3. Connect the two independent clauses with a comma and one of the following seven words (the first letters of which create the word *fanboys*): *for, and, nor, but, or, yet, so.*

Classical music is soothing, *so* I listen to it in the evenings.

Chopin is one of my favorites, *for* I love the sound of piano.

Each of the *fanboys* has its own meaning (for example, *so* means "as a result," and *for* means "because").

Swans are beautiful birds, *and* they mate for life.

Students may register for classes by phone, *or* they may do so in person.

I applied for financial aid, *but* or *yet* I was still working at the time.

Beth doesn't know how to use a computer, *nor* does she plan to learn.

But before you put a comma before a *fanboys,* be sure there are two independent clauses. The first sentence that follows has two independent clauses. The second sentence is merely one independent clause with two verbs, so no comma should be used.

The snow began falling at dusk, and it continued to fall through the night.

The snow began falling at dusk and continued to fall through the night.

4. Make one of the clauses dependent by adding a dependent word (such as *since, when, as, after, while,* or *because*—see p. 61 for a full list).

Since classical music is soothing, I listen to it in the evenings.

Chopin is one of my favorites *because* I love the sound of piano.

WAYS TO CORRECT RUN-ON SENTENCES

They learned a new routine. They needed to practice it. (two sentences)

They learned a new routine; they needed to practice it. (semicolon)

They learned a new routine; therefore, they needed to practice it.
(semicolon + transition)

They learned a new routine, so they needed to practice it.
(comma + *fanboys*)

Because they learned a new routine, they needed to practice it.
(dependent clause first)

They needed to practice because they learned a new routine.
(dependent clause last)

Learn these ways to join two clauses, and you'll avoid run-on sentences.

Exercises 1 and 2

CORRECTING RUN-ONS WITH PUNCTUATION

Most—but not all—of the following sentences are run-ons. If the sentence has two independent clauses, separate them with correct punctuation. For the first two exercises, *don't create any dependent clauses*; use only a period, a semicolon, or a comma to separate the two independent clauses. Your answers may differ from those at the back of the book depending on how you choose to separate them. Remember that a comma may be used only before the words *for, and, nor, but, or, yet, so.*

Exercise 1

1. Frank Epperson invented something delicious and refreshing and it comes on a stick.

2. In 1905, Epperson was an eleven-year-old boy he lived in San Francisco.

3. On the porch outside his house, he was mixing a fruity drink with a stick and forgot to put it away before going to bed.

4. The drink sat outside all night with the stick still in it.

5. There was a record-breaking cold snap that evening and the drink froze.

6. In the morning, Frank Epperson ate his frozen juice creation it made a big impression.

7. Epperson grew up and kept making his frozen "Epsicles" they came in seven varieties.

8. Eighteen years after that cold night, Epperson patented his invention but with a different name.

9. Epperson's kids loved their dad's treat and they always called them "pop's sicles."

10. So Popsicles were born and people have loved them ever since.

Source: Biography Magazine, July 1999

Exercise 2

1. Last week I decided to adopt a pet from an animal shelter so I visited the SPCA near my house.

2. There were lots of great potential pets there at first I couldn't choose between the dogs or the cats.

3. I imagined the changes in my life with the addition of each type of pet.

4. My house doesn't have a fenced yard so a dog would need to be walked in the mornings and evenings.

5. I like small dogs anyway and could easily envision myself taking a tiny terrier for a stroll.

6. But I am at work for most of the day it might bark and disturb the neighbors.

7. A cat, on the other hand, can stay inside and doesn't make any noise.

8. Cats are also independent therefore, a cat wouldn't miss me during the day.

9. By coincidence, the shelter had just received a litter of gray and white kittens I was lucky enough to have first choice and picked the best one.

10. I named her Dizzy for she loved to chase the white tip of her tail around.

Exercises 3 and 4
CORRECTING RUN-ONS WITH DEPENDENT CLAUSES

Most—but not all—of the following sentences are run-ons. Correct any run-on sentences by making one of the clauses dependent. You may change the words. Use a dependent word (such as *since, when, as, after, while, because* or the others listed on p. 61) to begin the dependent clause. In some sentences you will want to put the dependent clause first; in others you may want to put it last (or in the middle of the sentence). Since various words can be used to start a dependent clause, your answers may differ from those suggested at the back of the book.

Exercise 3

1. I've been learning about sleep in my psychology class I now know a lot more about it.

2. Sleep has five stages we usually go through all these stages many times during the night.

3. The first stage of sleep begins our muscles relax and mental activity slows down.

4. During stage one, we are still slightly awake.

5. Stage two takes us deeper than stage one we are no longer aware of our surroundings.

6. We spend about half our sleeping time in the second stage.

7. Next is stage three in it we become more and more relaxed and are very hard to awaken.

8. Stage four is the deepest in this stage we don't even hear loud noises.

9. The fifth stage of sleep is called REM (rapid-eye-movement) sleep our eyes move back and forth quickly behind our eyelids.

10. REM sleep is only about as deep as stage two we do all our dreaming during the REM stage.

Exercise 4

1. The first time a Titan Arum, the largest flower in the world, bloomed in the United States was at New York's Botanical Gardens in 1937.

2. The New York police had to break up the crowds they got out of control after seeing and *smelling* the amazing plant.

3. The Titan Arum is known for its size and its odor it is native to Sumatra.

4. The blooming plant smells like dirty feet or dead animals some people call it the "corpse flower."

5. In July 1999, a Titan Arum began the blooming process at the Huntington Gardens in San Marino, California.

6. No Titan had ever bloomed in California thousands of people visited the Huntington to experience the spectacle.

7. Visitors came in such large numbers the Huntington extended its hours and even stayed open on Monday it's normally closed on Mondays.

8. Within a couple of days, the Huntington gift shop ran out of Titan Arum souvenirs the souvenirs depicted the tall plant in full bloom.

9. The blossom finished growing it measured six feet tall and nearly four feet across.

10. The Huntington Gardens usually close at 4:30 the Huntington's Titan Arum bloomed at 5:00 on August 1, 1999, to the "delight" of everyone.

Source: Christian Science Monitor, 3 Aug. 1999

Exercise 5

Correct the following run-on sentences using any of the methods studied in this section: adding a period, a semicolon, a semicolon + a transition word, a comma + a *fanboys,* or using a dependent word to create a dependent clause.

1. In 1999, the BBC released its documentary series called *The Life of Birds* Sir David Attenborough was the host.

2. The series took nearly three years to complete the crew filmed in more than forty countries they shot about two hundred miles of film.

3. The BBC spent fifteen million dollars making *The Life of Birds* the cost included Attenborough's traveling the equivalent of ten times around the world.

4. The BBC takes such shows very seriously this one about birds comes after the BBC's amazing documentary called *The Private Life of Plants.*

5. For the plant series, BBC filmmakers even invented new ways to film plants and record the sounds they make a lot of the filming had to take place under artificial conditions however, for the bird series, the BBC wanted a more realistic feeling.

6. All of the filming was done in the birds' own habitats it showed their natural behavior some of this behavior had never been seen or filmed before.

7. To capture these rare moments, filmmakers had to live with birds in the wild it was not a very safe environment at times.

8. A tree full of BBC filmmakers was struck by lightning in an Amazon rainforest they were covered with insects in Jamaica and Attenborough had to speak to the camera in total darkness in a cave in Venezuela.

9. Makers of the series were especially proud of their bird of paradise footage they shot it in New Guinea.

10. It turned out to be one of their biggest disappointments the priceless film was erased by an especially powerful X-ray machine at the airport.

Source: Christian Science Monitor, 3 Aug. 1999

REVIEW OF FRAGMENTS AND RUN-ON SENTENCES

If you remember that all clauses include a subject and a verb, but only independent clauses can be punctuated as sentences (since only they can stand alone), then you will avoid fragments in your writing. And if you memorize these six rules for the punctuation of clauses, you will be able to avoid most punctuation errors.

PUNCTUATING CLAUSES	
I am a student. I am still learning.	(two sentences)
I am a student; I am still learning.	(two independent clauses)
I am a student; therefore, I am still learning.	(two independent clauses connected by a word such as *also, consequently, finally, furthermore, however, likewise, moreover, nevertheless, otherwise, then, therefore, thus*)
I am a student, so I am still learning.	(two independent clauses connected by *for, and, nor, but, or, yet, so*)
Because I am a student, I am still learning.	(dependent clause at beginning of sentence)
I am still learning because I am a student.	(dependent clause at end of sentence) The dependent words are *after, although, as, as if, because, before, even if, even though, ever since, how, if, in order that, since, so that, than, that, though, unless, until, what, whatever, when, whenever, where, whereas, wherever, whether, which, whichever, while, who, whom, whose, why.*

It is essential that you learn the italicized words in the previous table—which ones come between independent clauses and which ones introduce dependent clauses.

PROOFREADING EXERCISE

Rewrite the following paragraph, making the necessary changes so there will be no fragments or run-on sentences.

Most people would not recognize the name Joseph Ignace Guillotin but they probably have heard of the machine named after him. The guillotine. The device used when many a king or queen said, "Off with his—or her—head!" The guillotine consists of a slanted blade the blade falls down a window-frame-shaped tower and can be reset after it does its job. Guillotin was a doctor in France during the French Revolution. He was not the inventor of the machine he did suggest that it be used to behead people quickly and easily. Guillotin's name was first associated with the device in 1793 now doctors everywhere also use the word *guillotine*. To describe cutting procedures that they perform during tonsillectomies and other surgeries.

Source: Dictionary of Word Origins (Arcade Publishing, 1990)

SENTENCE WRITING

Write a sample sentence of your own to demonstrate each of the six ways a writer can use to punctuate two clauses. You may model your sentences on the examples used in the preceding review chart.

Identifying Verb Phrases

Sometimes a verb is one word, but often the whole verb includes more than one word. These are called verb phrases. Look at several of the many forms of the verb *speak,* for example. Most of them are verb phrases, made up of the main verb *(speak)* and one or more helping verbs.

speak	is speaking	had been speaking
speaks	am speaking	will have been speaking
spoke	are speaking	is spoken
will speak	was speaking	was spoken
has spoken	were speaking	will be spoken
have spoken	will be speaking	can speak
had spoken	has been speaking	must speak
will have spoken	have been speaking	should have spoken

Note that words like the following are never verbs even though they may be near a verb or in the middle of a verb phrase:

already	finally	now	probably
also	just	often	really
always	never	only	sometimes
ever	not	possibly	usually

Jason has *never* spoken to his instructor before. She *always* talks with other students.

Two verb forms—*speaking* and *to speak*—look like verbs, but neither can ever be the verb of a sentence. No *ing* word by itself can ever be the verb of a sentence; it must be helped by another verb in a verb phrase. (See the discussion of verbal phrases on p. 116.)

Jeanine speaking French. (not a sentence because there is no complete verb phrase)

Jeanine is speaking French. (a sentence with a verb phrase)

And no verb with *to* in front of it can ever be the verb of a sentence.

Ted to speak in front of groups. (not a sentence because there is no real verb)

Ted <u>hates</u> to speak in front of groups. (a sentence with *hates* as the verb)

These two forms, *speaking* and *to speak* may be used as subjects, or they may have other uses in the sentence.

<u>Speaking</u> on stage <u>is</u> scary. <u>To speak</u> on stage <u>is</u> scary. <u>Ted</u> <u>had</u> a *speaking* part in that play.

But neither of them alone can ever be the verb of a sentence.

E X E R C I S E S

Underline the subjects once and the verbs or verb phrases twice. It's a good idea to put parentheses around prepositional phrases first. (See p. 54 if you need help in locating prepositional phrases.) The sentences may contain independent *and* dependent clauses, so there could be several verbs and verb phrases.

Exercise 1

1. I have always wondered how an Etch-A-Sketch works.

2. This flat TV-shaped toy has been popular since it first came out in the 1960s.

3. Now I have discovered a Web site that answers questions like the following: "How does an Etch-A-Sketch work?"

4. An Etch-A-Sketch is filled with a combination of metal powder and tiny plastic particles.

5. This mixture clings to the inside of the Etch-A-Sketch screen.

6. When the pointer that is connected to the two knobs moves, the tip of it "draws" lines in the powder on the back of the screen.

7. The powder at the bottom of the Etch-A-Sketch does not fill in these lines because it is too far away.

8. But if the Etch-A-Sketch is turned upside down, the powder clings to the whole underside surface of the screen and "erases" the image again.

9. Although the basic Etch-A-Sketch has not changed since I was a kid, it now comes in several different sizes.

10. Best of all, these great drawing devices have never needed batteries, and I hope that they never will.

Exercise 2

1. Most people would not think of bar codes and cockroaches together.

2. We would expect bar codes on products in supermarkets and shopping malls.

3. And we might not be surprised if a cockroach showed up by a trash can behind the supermarket or shopping mall.

4. But we would definitely look twice if we saw a cockroach with a bar code on its back.

5. That is just what exterminator Bruce Tennenbaum wanted everyone to do in 1999, however.

6. He attached bar codes to one hundred of these insects and released them in Tucson, Arizona, as a public-awareness campaign.

7. When people found a bar-coded bug, they could return it for a hundred-dollar prize.

8. In an effort to increase public participation, one of the roaches was tagged with a unique bar code that would earn its finder fifty thousand dollars.

9. Many of the citizens of Tucson searched for these "prizes," and some of the tagged roaches were found.

10. But Tennenbaum should have put a tracking device on the fifty-thousand-dollar bug because it was never seen again.

Source: Today's Homeowner, May 1999

Exercise 3

1. When we think of ancient structures, Stonehenge in England and the Great Pyramids of Egypt come to mind.

2. Fairly recently, Fred Wendorf discovered an arrangement of stones possibly a thousand years older than Stonehenge.

3. Wendorf uncovered the stone structures of Nabta Playa while he was researching nomadic people in Egypt.

4. Wendorf dug down to the level where eight huge stone tablets formed a circle.

5. He and other anthropologists believe that nomads must have created the site for astronomical purposes.

6. The slabs and their arrangement date back seven thousand years.

7. They were placed in groups of two and were aligned with different points of the compass.

8. Near the circle of stones was a tomb that had not been found before.

9. It had been used not for a dead king but for the nomads' cattle.

10. These nomadic people may have been the first citizens of the Nile Valley so many thousands of years ago.

Source: Discover, July 1998

Exercise 4

1. During the last semester of high school, my English teacher assigned a special paper.

2. He said that he was becoming depressed by all the bad news out there, so each of us was assigned to find a piece of good news and write a short research paper about it.

3. I must admit that I had no idea how hard that assignment would be.

4. Finally, I found an article while I was reading my favorite magazine.

5. The title of the article was a pun; it was called "Grin Reaper."

6. I knew instantly that it must be just the kind of news my teacher was searching for.

7. The article explained that one woman, Pam Johnson, had started a club that she named The Secret Society of Happy People.

8. She had even chosen August 8 as "Admit You're Happy Day" and had already convinced more than fifteen state governors to recognize the holiday.

9. The club and the holiday were created to support people who are happy so that the unhappy, negative people around will not bring the happy people down.

10. As I was writing my essay, I visited the Happy People Web site and, for extra credit, signed my teacher up for their newsletter.

Source: *People*, 30 Aug. 1999

Exercise 5

1. Last night I took my daughter to a performance by her favorite group.

2. The tickets were not too expensive, and I remembered how much fun I had had at concerts in my younger days.

3. I had not been to an open-air event for several years, however, and I was expecting the same kind of experience.

4. I should have considered the changes that have occurred since then.

5. The first difference was that, when we arrived, people were waiting in a long line in the hot sunshine to get into the stadium even though everyone had assigned seats.

6. I asked a staff member why they weren't spending time in their cars or in the cool shade.

7. He told me that they were hoping to get in first so that they could buy the best souvenirs.

8. Once we were inside the place, I saw what he meant; T-shirts were hanging with thirty-five-dollar price tags, and every other kind of object with the group's name or picture on it was being bought by frantic fans.

9. I understood then why the tickets had been so inexpensive; as long as they brought the customers to the merchandise, they had done their job.

10. After three opening acts, my daughter's favorite group finally arrived on stage, overwhelmed the crowd with special effects, and left everyone with lots of souvenirs as memories.

REVIEW EXERCISE

To practice finding all of the sentence structures we have studied so far, mark the following paragraphs from John T. Malloy's 1970s self-help book *Dress for Success*. First, put parentheses around prepositional phrases, then underline subjects once and verbs or verb phrases twice. Finally put a broken line beneath dependent clauses. Begin by marking the first paragraph, then check your answers at the back of the book before going on to the next paragraph. (Remember that *ing* verbs alone and the *to*____ forms of verbs are never real verbs in sentences. We will learn more about them on p. 116.)

For business wear bow ties give off several negative effects. You will not be taken seriously when [you are] wearing one. The only positive use comes if you are too powerful a personality, in which case they can soften your image. But otherwise you will not be thought responsible if you wear a bow tie. Most people will not trust you with anything important. It is a death knell for anyone selling his services as a consultant or lawyer, etc. The number of people who will trust you at all, with anything, will be cut in half.

In general, I have found that people believe that a man in a bow tie will steal. It creates the impression of being unpredictable, thus some experienced trial lawyers who believe they have a good case will try to keep a man wearing a bow tie off a jury.

Bow ties are acceptable as sports attire, and if you do wear them for such occasions, stick to the same patterns recommended for all other ties.

Using Standard English Verbs

The next two discussions are for those who need practice in using Standard English verbs. Many of us grew up doing more speaking than writing. But in college and in the business and professional world, the use of Standard Written English is essential.

The following charts show the forms of four verbs as they are used in Standard Written English. These forms might differ from the way you use these verbs when you speak. Memorize the Standard English forms of these important verbs. The first verb *(talk)* is one of the regular verbs (verbs that all end the same way according to a pattern); most verbs in English are regular. The other three verbs charted here *(have, be,* and *do)* are irregular and are important because they are used not only as main verbs but also as helping verbs in verb phrases.

Don't go on to the exercises until you have memorized the forms of these Standard English verbs.

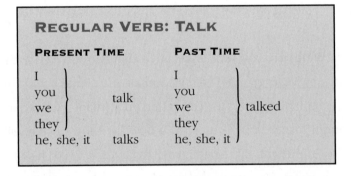

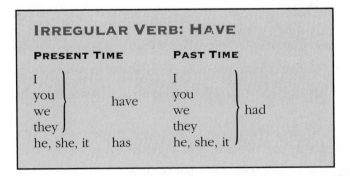

IRREGULAR VERB: BE

PRESENT TIME		PAST TIME	
I	am	I	was
you ⎫		we ⎫	
we ⎬	are	you ⎬	were
they ⎭		they ⎭	
he, she, it	is	he, she, it	was

IRREGULAR VERB: DO

PRESENT TIME		PAST TIME	
I ⎫		I ⎫	
you ⎪		you ⎪	
we ⎬	do	we ⎬	did
they ⎪		they ⎪	
he, she, it	does	he, she, it ⎭	

Sometimes you may have difficulty with the correct endings of verbs because you don't hear the words correctly. Note carefully the *s* sound and the *ed* sound at the end of words. Occasionally the *ed* is not clearly pronounced, as in *They tried to help,* but most of the time you can hear it if you listen.

Read the following sentences aloud, making sure that you say every sound.

1. He seems satisfied with his new job.

2. She likes saving money for the future.

3. It takes strength of character to control spending.

4. Todd makes salad for every potluck he attends.

5. I used to know all their names.

6. They supposed that they were right.

7. He recognized the suspect and excused himself from the jury.

8. Susan sponsored Dorothy in the school's charity event.

Now read some other sentences aloud from this text, making sure that you sound all the *s*'s and *ed*'s. Reading aloud and listening to others will help you use the correct verb endings automatically.

E X E R C I S E S

In these pairs of sentences, use the present form of the verb in the first sentence and the past form in the second. All the verbs follow the pattern of the regular verb *talk* except the irregular verbs *have*, *be*, and *do*. Keep referring to the tables if you're not sure which form to use. Correct your answers for each exercise before going to the next.

Exercise 1

1. (prepare)   She _____ people's taxes. She _____ my taxes last year.

2. (help)   I always _____ my roommate with the dishes. I _____ him with them yesterday.

3. (be)   They _____ happy with their new home. They _____ too crowded in their old home.

4. (have)   We _____ a lot of homework this weekend. We _____ no homework last weekend.

5. (do)   She _____ well on most quizzes. She _____ very well on yesterday's quiz.

6. (need)   My son _____ a new backpack. He _____ several new textbooks at the start of the semester.

7. (have)   Sue fixed up her car; now it _____ a sunroof and a CD player. It only _____ a cassette deck before.

8. (be)   He _____ a counselor at the summer camp. He _____ a lifeguard last year.

9. (work)   She _____ too hard. Last week, she _____ without a day off.

10. (be)   I _____ finally qualified to tutor other students. I _____ not qualified to tutor them before.

Exercise 2

1. (be)   They _____ college freshmen this semester. They _____ high school seniors last year.

2. (do)   He _____ his best writing at night. He _____ not do well on the first in-class essay.

3. (have)   She _____ two weeks left to write her transfer application letter. She originally _____ two months, but she has been putting it off.

4. (open)   He _____ a new restaurant every year. He even _____ one in my neighborhood recently.

5. (have)   I always _____ fun with my friend Norman. I _____ a great time in Las Vegas with him over spring break.

6. (count)   She _____ boxes at the factory part time. Yesterday she _____ boxes for six hours straight.

7. (be)   Many of us _____ left handed. We _____ unsure at first which hand to use when we played tennis.

8. (do)   They _____ everything to make their grandmother's life easier. They _____ her shopping and her laundry yesterday.

9. (look)   You _____ like an adult now. You _____ like a kid when your hair was longer.

10. (be)   At the moment, she _____ the fastest cashier in the store. She _____ the second-fastest cashier when Carl still worked there.

Underline the Standard English verb forms. All the verbs follow the pattern of the regular verb *talk* except the three irregular verbs *have, be*, and *do*. Keep referring to the tables if you are not sure which form to use.

Exercise 3

1. I recently (change, changed) my career plans; now I (want, wants) to be a chef.

2. Last year, I (have, had) my mind set on becoming a kindergarten teacher.

3. I (sign, signed) up for several childhood education classes, and they all (turn, turned) out to be disappointing.

4. The class work (was, were) often too easy, and the reading assignments (was, were) too hard.

5. We (does, did) spend part of the semester working in a real kindergarten class where we (was, were) able to observe just what the teacher (do, does).

6. The teacher that I (observes, observed) (have, had) twenty-seven children to look after.

7. I (watch, watched) her as she (help, helped) them learn their numbers and letters.

8. She (have, had) her students, their parents, and the school's administration to worry about all the time.

9. I never (imagine, imagined) that a kindergarten teacher (have, had) so many responsibilities.

10. A chef (need, needs) to worry about the food and the customers, and those (is, are) responsibilities that I (is, am) ready to take.

Exercise 4

1. My mother and I (watch, watches) the same game show every night.

2. She (watch, watches) it at her house, and I (watch, watches) it at my house.

3. I (is, am) better at answering the literature questions, and my mom (is, am) better at answering the questions on science and geography.

4. Mom and I (is, are) very competitive and proud of the information that we know.

5. But the show's final question usually (decide, decides) the outcome of our contest.

6. For that question, we (wager, wagers) all or part of our winnings so far.

7. After the show, we both (add, adds) up our scores, and then one of us (call, calls) the other to see who the champion (is, are).

8. We (love, loves) this tradition and (has, have) kept it going for eight years now.

9. Someday I (plan, plans) to try out for the show and surprise my mom one night.

10. She (like, likes) the show so much that she would probably faint if she saw me up there with the signaling button in my hand.

Exercise 5

Correct any of the following sentences that do not use Standard English verb forms.

1. Yesterday my English teacher assigns a narration essay.

2. Now we have one week to finish a rough draft.

3. Before the assignment, he showed us two sample narration essays.

4. They was about holiday traditions in different families.

5. In one essay, the writer explain the tradition of Thanksgiving at her house.

6. I likes the part about making pies for the adults and candy for the kids.

7. The second essay outline the steps another family goes through to prepare for Chinese New Year.

8. That one have even more details about food and gifts for the children.

9. My teacher asked us to write about a family ritual of our own.

10. I start my rough draft last night; it's about my dad's obsession with Halloween.

PROOFREADING EXERCISE

Correct any sentences in the following paragraph that do not use Standard English verb forms.

I have a new piano teacher, Mr. Stevensen, who talk very softly and play the piano beautifully. When he wants to teach me a new song, he start by showing me the sheet music. Then he ask me to look it over. I am always nervous if it show a new hand position or a new dynamic sign. But then he calm me down with his soothing voice and patient manner. Once I figure the piece out by looking at it, I plays it through slowly. Mr. Stevensen don't do any of the annoying things my other piano teachers did. I like him a lot.

SENTENCE WRITING

Write ten sentences about a problem in your neighborhood. Check your sentences to be sure that they use Standard English verb forms. Try exchanging papers with another student if possible.

Using Regular and Irregular Verbs

All regular verbs end the same way in the past form and when used with helping verbs. Here is a table showing all the forms of some regular verbs and the various helping verbs they are used with.

REGULAR VERBS				
BASE FORM	**PRESENT**	**PAST**	**PAST PARTICIPLE**	***ING* FORM**
(Use after can, may, shall, will, could, might, should, would, must, do, does, did.)			*(Use after have, has, had. Some can be used after forms of be.)*	*(Use after forms of be.)*
ask	ask *(s)*	asked	asked	asking
bake	bake *(s)*	baked	baked	baking
count	count *(s)*	counted	counted	counting
dance	dance *(s)*	danced	danced	dancing
decide	decide *(s)*	decided	decided	deciding
enjoy	enjoy *(s)*	enjoyed	enjoyed	enjoying
finish	finish *(s)*	finished	finished	finishing
happen	happen *(s)*	happened	happened	happening
learn	learn *(s)*	learned	learned	learning
like	like *(s)*	liked	liked	liking
look	look *(s)*	looked	looked	looking
mend	mend *(s)*	mended	mended	mending
need	need *(s)*	needed	needed	needing
open	open *(s)*	opened	opened	opening
start	start *(s)*	started	started	starting
suppose	suppose *(s)*	supposed	supposed	supposing
tap	tap *(s)*	tapped	tapped	tapping
walk	walk *(s)*	walked	walked	walking
want	want *(s)*	wanted	wanted	wanting

NOTE- When there are several helping verbs, the last one determines which form of the main verb should be used: they *should* finish soon; they should *have* finished an hour ago.

When do you write *ask, finish, suppose, use?* And when do you write *asked, finished, supposed, used?* Here are some rules that will help you decide.

Write *ask, finish, suppose, use* (or their *s* forms) when writing about the present time, repeated actions, or facts:

He *asks* questions whenever he is confused.

They always *finish* their projects on time.

I *suppose* you want me to help you move.

Birds *use* leaves, twigs, and feathers to build their nests.

Write *asked, finished, supposed, used*

1. **When writing about the past:**

   He *asked* the teacher for another explanation.

   She *finished* her internship last year.

   They *supposed* that there were others bidding on that house.

   I *used* to study piano.

2. **When some form of *be* (other than the word *be* itself) comes before the word:**

   He was *asked* the most difficult questions.

   She is *finished* with her training now.

   They were *supposed* to sign at the bottom of the form.

   My essay was *used* as a sample of clear narration.

3. **When some form of *have* comes before the word:**

   The teacher has *asked* us that question before.

   She will have *finished* all of her exams by the end of May.

   I had *supposed* too much without any proof.

   We have *used* many models in my drawing class this semester.

All the verbs in the chart on page 96 are regular. That is, they're all formed in the same way—with an *ed* ending on the past form and on the past participle. But many verbs are irregular. Their past and past participle forms change spelling instead of just adding an *ed*. Here's a chart of some irregular verbs. Notice that the base, present, and *ing* forms end the same as regular verbs. Refer to this list when you aren't sure which verb form to use. Memorize all the forms you don't know.

IRREGULAR VERBS				
BASE FORM	**PRESENT**	**PAST**	**PAST PARTICIPLE**	***ING* FORM**
(Use after can, may, shall, will, could, might, should, would, must, do, does, did.)			*(Use after have, has, had. Some can be used after forms of be.)*	*(Use after forms of be.)*
be	is, am, are	was, were	been	being
become	become *(s)*	became	become	becoming
begin	begin *(s)*	began	begun	beginning
break	break *(s)*	broke	broken	breaking
bring	bring *(s)*	brought	brought	bringing
build	build *(s)*	built	built	building
buy	buy *(s)*	bought	bought	buying
catch	catch *(es)*	caught	caught	catching
choose	choose *(s)*	chose	chosen	choosing
come	come *(s)*	came	come	coming
do	do *(es)*	did	done	doing
draw	draw *(s)*	drew	drawn	drawing
drink	drink *(s)*	drank	drunk	drinking
drive	drive *(s)*	drove	driven	driving
eat	eat *(s)*	ate	eaten	eating
fall	fall *(s)*	fell	fallen	falling
feel	feel *(s)*	felt	felt	feeling
fight	fight *(s)*	fought	fought	fighting
find	find *(s)*	found	found	finding
forget	forget *(s)*	forgot	forgotten	forgetting
forgive	forgive *(s)*	forgave	forgiven	forgiving
freeze	freeze *(s)*	froze	frozen	freezing
get	get *(s)*	got	got *or* gotten	getting
give	give *(s)*	gave	given	giving
go	go *(es)*	went	gone	going
grow	grow *(s)*	grew	grown	growing
have	have *or* has	had	had	having
hear	hear *(s)*	heard	heard	hearing
hold	hold *(s)*	held	held	holding
keep	keep *(s)*	kept	kept	keeping

BASE FORM	PRESENT	PAST	PAST PARTICIPLE	*ING* FORM
know	know *(s)*	knew	known	knowing
lay (to put)	lay *(s)*	laid	laid	laying
lead (like "bead")	lead *(s)*	led	led	leading
leave	leave *(s)*	left	left	leaving
lie (to rest)	lie *(s)*	lay	lain	lying
lose	lose *(s)*	lost	lost	losing
make	make *(s)*	made	made	making
meet	meet *(s)*	met	met	meeting
pay	pay *(s)*	paid	paid	paying
read (pron. "reed")	read *(s)*	read (pron. "red")	read (pron. "red")	reading
ride	ride *(s)*	rode	ridden	riding
ring	ring *(s)*	rang	rung	ringing
rise	rise *(s)*	rose	risen	rising
run	run *(s)*	ran	run	running
say	say *(s)*	said	said	saying
see	see *(s)*	saw	seen	seeing
sell	sell *(s)*	sold	sold	selling
shake	shake *(s)*	shook	shaken	shaking
shine (give light)	shine *(s)*	shone	shone	shining
shine (polish)	shine *(s)*	shined	shined	shining
sing	sing *(s)*	sang	sung	singing
sleep	sleep *(s)*	slept	slept	sleeping
speak	speak *(s)*	spoke	spoken	speaking
spend	spend *(s)*	spent	spent	spending
stand	stand *(s)*	stood	stood	standing
steal	steal *(s)*	stole	stolen	stealing
strike	strike *(s)*	struck	struck	striking
swim	swim *(s)*	swam	swum	swimming
swing	swing *(s)*	swung	swung	swinging
take	take *(s)*	took	taken	taking
teach	teach *(es)*	taught	taught	teaching
tear	tear *(s)*	tore	torn	tearing
tell	tell *(s)*	told	told	telling
think	think *(s)*	thought	thought	thinking
throw	throw *(s)*	threw	thrown	throwing
wear	wear *(s)*	wore	worn	wearing
win	win *(s)*	won	won	winning
write	write *(s)*	wrote	written	writing

Sometimes verbs from the past participle column are used after some form of the verb *be* (or verbs that take the place of *be* like *appear, seem, look, feel, get, act, become*) to describe the subject or to say something in a passive, rather than active, way.

She is contented.

You appear pleased. (You are pleased.)

He seems delighted. (He is delighted.)

She looked surprised. (She was surprised.)

I feel shaken. (I am shaken.)

They get bored easily. (They are bored easily.)

You acted concerned. (You were concerned.)

He was thrown out of the game. (Active: *The referee threw him out of the game.*)

They were disappointed by the news. (Active: *The news disappointed them.*)

Often these verb forms become words that describe the subject; other times they still act as part of the verb of the sentence. What you call them doesn't matter. The only important thing is to be sure you use the correct form from the past participle column.

E X E R C I S E S

Write the correct form of the verb. Refer to the tables and explanations on the preceding pages if you aren't sure which form to use after a certain helping verb. Check your answers after each exercise.

Exercise 1

1. (practice)   I must _____ my violin at least once a day, or I feel guilty.

2. (practice)   After I have _____ for a half an hour or so, I feel better.

3. (practice)   Sometimes when I am _____, I lose track of time.

4. (practice)   Then I can _____ for over an hour without realizing it.

5. (practice)   Once I had _____ for two hours, but it felt like only twenty minutes.

6. (practice)   My instructor says that he has similar experiences when he _____.

7. (practice)   I guess all musicians _____ in pretty much the same way.

8. (practice) It isn't easy to ignore someone who is _____ a musical instrument.

9. (practice) Especially when people are _____ the violin, their family and neighbors can become irritated.

10. (practice) That is why I always _____ when my family is away from home.

Exercise 2

1. (try) I must _____ to think of new ways to entertain my parrot, Rusty. If I don't keep him amused, then he _____ to run away.

2. (buy) My mom _____ Rusty for my eighteenth birthday even though she usually _____ me a new CD or a shirt or something simple like that.

3. (be) So I _____ really surprised when I saw a big green parrot sitting on a perch in my room when I got home from school on my birthday. I _____ not usually a big animal lover.

4. (think) Mom must have _____ that I needed a new responsibility, but I didn't _____ so.

5. (grow) Rusty has _____ a little since I got him. And I've _____ a lot since I've had to take care of him.

6. (leave) Before I _____ for school each day, I give Rusty fresh food, treats, and water. Once I _____ the window open by mistake and found him in the tree outside my room when I came back.

7. (watch) Parrots love to talk and be entertained, so Rusty _____ all the game shows and soap operas that are on TV during the day. Meanwhile I am _____ my teachers draw their notes on the chalkboard at school.

8. (hear) He _____ what the game show hosts and soap opera stars say, and then I _____ the same expressions all night long because he repeats them over and over again.

9. (speak) Sometimes Rusty _____ so clearly that it sounds exactly like words that are _____ by a human being.

10. (be)   At first, I _____ not sure I wanted Rusty, but now he _____ such a big part of my life that I can't imagine not having him.

Exercise 3

1. (take, suppose)   My sister Brenda _____ a day off last week even though she was _____ to be working.

2. (do, earn)   She _____ not feel sick exactly; she just felt that she had _____ a day of rest.

3. (call, tell, feel)   So Brenda _____ her office and _____ her boss that she did not _____ well enough to work that day.

4. (think, be)   She never _____ that she would get caught, but she _____ wrong.

5. (leave, drive, see)   Just as Brenda was _____ the house to buy some lunch, her coworker _____ by and _____ her.

6. (feel, know, tell)   She _____ such panic because she _____ that he would _____ their boss that she looked fine.

7. (try, go)   Brenda _____ to explain herself when she _____ back to the office the next day.

8. (be, undo)   The damage had _____ done, however, and nothing could _____ it.

9. (wish, take)   Now Brenda _____ that she could _____ back that day.

10. (use, call, do)   She _____ to have a great relationship with her boss, but since the day she _____ in sick, he _____ not trust her anymore.

Exercise 4

1. (use, put)   Many people _____ a direct deposit system that _____ their salary money directly into their bank accounts.

2. (do, do)

With such a system, the employer _____ not have to issue paychecks, and employees _____ not have to cash or deposit them.

3. (transfer, spend)

The employer's computer just _____ the money to the bank's computer, and the employee can _____ it as usual after that.

4. (be, like, choose)

Direct deposit _____ almost always optional, but so many people _____ the system that most people _____ it.

5. (do, want)

My dad _____ not trust such systems; he _____ to have complete control over his money.

6. (trust, be)

He barely even _____ banks to keep his money safe for him, so he _____ definitely suspicious of computers.

7. (imagine, make)

I can _____ him as a pioneer in an old western movie sleeping on a mattress stuffed with all of the money he has ever _____.

8. (talk, ask, worry)

I was _____ to my dad about money the other day, and I _____ him why he always _____ about it so much.

9. (look, say, understand)

He just _____ at me and _____ , "You'll _____ some day."

10. (trust, be)

I _____ my dad's experiences; he has never _____ wrong before.

Exercise 5

1. (lie, fall)

I was _____ out in the sun last Sunday, and I _____ asleep.

2. (be, do)

That _____ the worst thing I could have _____.

3. (wear, shield)

I was _____ a pair of big dark sunglasses, which _____ my eyes from the light.

4. (lie, wake, realize, happen)   I must have _____ there for over an hour before I _____ up and _____ what had _____.

5. (feel, start)   At first I _____ fine, but then my skin _____ to feel really tight and thin.

6. (pass, turn, begin)   As the minutes _____, my skin _____ bright red, and the pain _____.

7. (describe, experience)   I can't even _____ how much pain I _____.

8. (be, feel, see)   Almost worse than the pain _____ the embarrassment I _____ as I _____ my face in the mirror.

9. (look, tape, be, protect, wear)   Around my eyes, it _____ as if someone had _____ the shape of white glasses to my face, but that _____ just the skin that had been _____ by the sunglasses I was _____.

10. (have, feel)   The people at work _____ a big laugh the next day at my expense, but then they just _____ sorry for me.

PROGRESS TEST

This test covers everything you've learned in the Sentence Structure section so far. One sentence in each pair is correct. The other is incorrect. Read both sentences carefully before you decide. Then write the letter of the incorrect sentence in the blank. Try to name the error and correct it if you can.

1. ___ **A.** After taking a nap for several hours in the afternoon.

   B. I was able to work past midnight without stopping.

2. ___ **A.** We have taken many classes together.

   B. Last semester we enroll in the same math class.

3. ___ **A.** He likes every movie that we see.

   B. Whenever we go to see a new movie.

4. ___ **A.** Karen use to take the bus to school.

   B. Now she carpools with her friend.

5. ___ **A.** Their camping location was far into the mountains.

   B. Because Tim was driving his mother worried all night.

6. ___ **A.** I need to stop procrastinating.

   B. I will write in my journal every day, and will turn in all my work on time.

7. ___ **A.** My brother and I were suppose to help with the garage sale.

   B. He forgot to pick me up.

8. ___ **A.** He had already finish his dinner by the time I came home.

   B. I ate my dinner while I watched television alone.

9. ___ **A.** I looked everywhere for the plane tickets before I found them.

   B. They were laying on the dining room table.

10. ___ **A.** Packing for a long trip is difficult.

   B. Especially not knowing how hot or cold the weather will be.

Maintaining Subject/Verb Agreement

As we have seen, the subject and verb in a sentence work together, so they must always agree. Different subjects need different forms of verbs. When the correct verb follows a subject, we call it subject/verb agreement.

The sentences below illustrate the rule that *s* verbs follow most singular subjects but not plural subjects.

One turtle walks.	Three turtles walk.
The baby cries.	The babies cry.
A democracy listens to the people.	Democracies listen to the people.
One child plays.	Many children play.

And the following sentences show how forms of the verb *be (is, am, are, was, were)* and helping verbs *(be, have,* and *do)* are made to agree with their subjects.

This puzzle is difficult.	These puzzles are difficult.
I am amazed.	You are amazed.
He was sleeping.	They were sleeping.
That class has been canceled.	Those classes have been canceled.
She does not want to participate.	They do not want to participate.

The following words are always singular and take an *s* verb or the irregular equivalent *(is, was, has, does):*

("ONE" WORDS)	("BODY" WORDS)	
one	anybody	each
anyone	everybody	
everyone	nobody	
no one	somebody	
someone		

Someone feeds my dog in the morning.

Everybody was at the party.

Each does her own homework.

Remember that prepositional phrases often come between subjects and verbs. You should ignore these interrupting phrases, or you may mistake the wrong word for the subject and use a verb form that doesn't agree.

Someone from the apartments feeds my dog in the morning. *(Someone is the subject, not apartments.)*

Everybody on the list of celebrities was at the party. *(Everybody is the subject, not celebrities.)*

Each of the twins does her own homework. *(Each is the subject, not twins.)*

However, the words *some, any, all, none,* and *most* are exceptions to this rule of ignoring prepositional phrases. These words can be singular or plural, depending on the words that follow them in prepositional phrases.

Some of the *pie* is gone.

Some of the *cookies* are gone.

Is any of the paper still in the supply cabinet?

Are any of the pencils still in the supply cabinet?

All of her work has been published.

All of her poems have been published.

None of the jewelry is missing.

None of the clothes are missing.

On July 4th, most of the country celebrates.

On July 4th, most of the citizens celebrate.

When a sentence has more than one subject joined by *and,* the subject is plural:

The teacher and the tutors eat lunch at noon.

A glazed doughnut and an onion bagel were sitting on the plate.

However, when two subjects are joined by *or,* then the subject closest to the verb determines the verb form:

Either the teacher *or* the tutors eat lunch at noon.

Either the tutors *or* the teacher eats lunch at noon.

A glazed donut *or* an onion bagel was sitting on the plate.

In most sentences, the subject comes before the verb. However, in some cases, the subject follows the verb, and subject/verb agreement needs special attention. Study the following examples:

Over the building flies a solitary flag. (flag flies)

Over the building fly several flags. (flags fly)

There is a good reason for my actions. (reason is)

There are good reasons for my actions. (reasons are)

E X E R C I S E S

Underline the verbs that agree with the subjects of the following sentences. Remember to ignore prepositional phrases, unless the subjects are *some, any, all, none,* or *most.* Check your answers ten at a time.

Exercise 1

1. Tony Schwartz (collect, collects) sounds.

2. He (has, have) been recording ordinary sounds since he was a young man and (is, are) saving them for future generations.

3. In his collection (is, are) everything from the "ka-ching" of an old cash register bell to the voice of an elevator man calling out the merchandise available on the different floors of an old department store.

4. His assortment of sounds (include, includes) the various noises his dog made during its first year of life.

5. Schwartz's talent at recording sounds (has, have) helped him get many jobs over the years.

6. One of these jobs (was, were) recording the voices of child actors for advertisers in the 1950s and 1960s.

7. Schwartz's love of sounds (stem, stems) from a brief period of blindness that he went through as a teenager.

8. Now Schwartz (stay, stays) close to his home in Manhattan.

9. In his own neighborhood (is, are) enough sounds to keep him busy.

10. One of his most unusual recordings (was, were) of the burial of a little boy's pet turtle.

Source: People, 4 Oct. 1999

Exercise 2

1. There (is, are) new risks for kids in this technological age; these risks primarily (involve, involves) their wrists.

2. Many adults already (suffer, suffers) from carpal tunnel syndrome.

3. And now children (is, are) also coming down with similar conditions, called repetitive stress injuries (RSIs).

4. From the use of computers and video games (come, comes) unnatural body positions that (lead, leads) to health problems.

5. The child's wrists, neck, and back (start, starts) to hurt or feel numb after he or she (work, works) or (play, plays) on the computer for a long time.

6. The problem (start, starts) with computer furniture.

7. The chairs, desks, and screens (is, are) usually not at the proper height to be used comfortably by children.

8. Straining and repetition often (cause, causes) reduced circulation and even nerve damage.

9. Often RSI damage to the wrists (is, are) irreversible.

10. Experts in the field of RSI (warn, warns) parents to teach children how to avoid these injuries.

Source: U.S. News & World Report, 5 July 1999

Exercise 3

1. One night in the spring of 1998, several boys (was, were) playing basketball in Monahans, Texas, when they saw an object fall to earth nearby.

2. The bright object that the boys saw (was, were) a meteor.

3. Scientists at NASA (has, have) studied the meteor and (has, have) named it Monahans 1998.

4. Monahans 1998 (is, are) the first meteor to be found filled with water from outer space.

5. To the scientists' surprise, the small, cantaloupe-sized rock also (contain, contains) bubbles trapped in crystals within its center.

6. Of course, water (support, supports) living things, so Monahans 1998 (has, have) excited those who (is, are) searching for evidence of life in outer space.

7. As an explanation, at least one scientist (say, says) that water may be a normal occurrence in meteors, that NASA (was, were) just fortunate to get to Monahans 1998 before the water evaporated.

8. This scientist (believe, believes) that many meteors probably (has, have) water in them, but it (dry, dries) before anyone (find, finds) them.

9. After studying the water in Monahans 1998, NASA (has, have) found that it (date, dates) back to the beginning of our solar system.

10. All of the scientists (agree, agrees) that Monahans 1998 (is, are) a discovery that will continue to spark our imaginations.

Source: Newsweek, 6 Sept. 1999

Exercise 4

1. Everyone in my drawing class (is, are) supposed to finish a drawing a week.

2. But each of us (has, have) a different way of beginning.

3. One of my classmates always (start, starts) by humming and rocking back and forth in front of his easel.

4. Another one just (put, puts) dots in the places where she (want, wants) her figures to go.

5. Jennifer, my best friend, (like, likes) to draw really light circles wherever the faces will be.

6. In the past, I (has, have) usually started by drawing a continuous line until it (look, looks) like something.

7. In other words, I (let, lets) the drawing tell me what it (want, wants) to be.

8. But Jennifer and my other classmates (has, have) taught me something.

9. It (help, helps) to have a plan; their drawings often (turn, turns) out better than mine.

10. Either they or I (am, are) right, but I don't know which it (is, are) yet.

Exercise 5

1. When a person (picture, pictures) the state of Maine, a desert scene (do, does) not immediately come to mind.

2. But sand dunes (is, are) just what people find when they (visit, visits) a tourist attraction in Freeport, Maine, near Brunswick.

3. In the midst of the tree-filled Maine countryside (is, are) a huge patch of sand called the Desert of Maine.

4. These acres of sand (is, are) not artificially constructed but (has, have) resulted from a variety of natural factors over thousands of years.

5. There (was, were) glacier movements, repeated harvests of the same crop, and the continuous grazing of livestock.

6. All of these factors (has, have) contributed to the sandy piece of land that Carolyn and Sid Dobson bought in the 1980s.

7. The Dobsons (has, have) added exhibits to the Desert's overall appeal, including a collection of several hundred samples of sand from around the world.

8. Each summer, sand artists (create, creates) sand pictures and bottled sand sculptures for the Desert of Maine's guests.

9. Throughout the attraction's open season, groups of visitors (is, are) driven in trams past the Desert's landmark plastic camel for a unique photo opportunity.

10. Nowhere else (is, are) the lush hills of the northeast and the dry sands of the southwest combined in such an unusual sight as the Desert of Maine.

Source: America's Strangest Museums (Citadel, 1996)

PROOFREADING EXERCISE

Find and correct the ten subject/verb agreement errors in the following paragraph.

All of the students in my drama club has chosen the play *Cyrano de Bergerac* for our next production. There is actually two famous Cyrano de Bergeracs. One of them is the title character of the play, and the other is the real person who had that name. Both of these men is famous for their large noses and for their writing. But only the fictional Cyrano loves Roxane. The tragic story of Cyrano and Roxane were written by Edmond Rostand. In it, Cyrano believe that Roxane could never love an ugly man. She thinks that she love Christian, Cyrano's fellow soldier who is extremely handsome. But she really love Cyrano, who writes all of the love letters that Christian gives Roxane. In those letters are the soul that Roxane admire, but she finds out too late. It's a very sad and dramatic story, and I hope that either my friend Lisa or I gets the part of Roxane.

SENTENCE WRITING

Write ten sentences in which you describe the clothes you are wearing. Use verbs in the present time. Then go back over your sentences—underline your subjects once, underline your verbs twice, and be sure they agree.

Avoiding Shifts in Time

People often worry about using different time frames in writing. Let common sense guide you. If you begin writing a paper in past time, don't shift back and forth to the present unnecessarily; and if you begin in the present, don't shift to the past without good reason. In the following paragraph the writer starts in the present and then shifts to the past, then shifts again to the present:

In the novel *To Kill a Mockingbird,* Jean Louise Finch is a little girl who lives in the South with her father, Atticus, and her brother, Jem. Everybody in town calls Jean Louise "Scout" as a nickname. When Atticus, a lawyer, chose to defend a black man against the charges of a white woman, some of their neighbors turned against him. Scout protected her father by appealing to the humanity of one member of the angry mob. In this chapter, five-year-old Scout turns out to be stronger than a group of adult men.

All the verbs should be in the present:

> In the novel *To Kill a Mockingbird,* Jean Louise Finch is a little girl who lives in the South with her father, Atticus, and her brother, Jem. Everybody in town calls Jean Louise "Scout" as a nickname. When Atticus, a lawyer, chooses to defend a black man against the charges of a white woman, some of their neighbors turn against him. Scout protects her father by appealing to the humanity of one member of the angry mob. In this chapter, five-year-old Scout turns out to be stronger than a group of adult men.

This sample paragraph discusses only the events that happen within the novel's plot, so it needs to maintain one time frame—the present, which we use to write about literature and repeated actions.

However, sometimes you will write about the present, the past, and even the future together. Then it may be necessary to use these different time frames within the same paragraph, each for its own reason. For example, if you were to give biographical information about Harper Lee, author of *To Kill a Mockingbird,* within a discussion of the novel and its influence, you might need to use all three time frames:

> Harper Lee grew up in Alabama, and she based elements in the book on experiences from her childhood. Like the character Atticus, Lee's father was a lawyer. She wrote the novel in his law offices. *To Kill a Mockingbird* is Harper Lee's most famous work, and it received a Pulitzer Prize for fiction in 1960. Lee's book will be forty years old in the year 2000. It remains one of the most moving and compassionate novels in American literature.

This paragraph uses past *(grew, based, was, wrote, received)*, present *(is, remains),* and future *(will be)* in the same paragraph without committing the error of shifting. Shifting occurs when the writer changes time frames inconsistently or for no reason, confusing the reader (as in the first example given).

PROOFREADING EXERCISES

Which of the following student paragraphs shift *unnecessarily* back and forth between time frames? In those that do, change the verbs to maintain one time frame, thus making the entire paragraph read smoothly. (First, read the paragraphs to determine whether unnecessary shifting takes place. One of the paragraphs is correct.)

1. Melinda French majored in computer science at Duke University and later earned an MBA. Then she gets a job at Microsoft and starts making a good living of her own. But when Melinda French married Bill Gates in 1994, she no longer has to think about money. Bill and Melinda Gates bought a mansion worth seventy-five million dollars. In 1996, their daughter Jennifer was born, and in 1999 they had a son. They named him Rory. Together, the couple created the Bill and Melinda Gates Foundation, a fund of nearly twenty billion dollars to give to charities.

Source: Newsweek, 30 Aug. 1999

2. I watched a documentary on the Leaning Tower of Pisa last night. I was amazed to find out that the tower began leaning before it was even finished. Workers over several centuries adjusted their materials as they built the tower to compensate for its increasing angle. That's why the tower is actually shaped a little like a banana. I'm surprised that the famous landmark is still standing after everything people have done to it since it was finished. In the 1930s, for instance, Mussolini thought that it should be straightened. So he had workers drill holes in the foundation and pour tons of concrete beneath it. Others tried digging out the earth around the sunken part. But that just caused flooding because they went below the soil's water table. The narrator of the documentary said that every time anyone tries to correct the tower, it leans a little more to the south. Now scientists are using special drilling techniques to extract enough soil deep beneath the tower to reverse its angle a little. If successful, this most recent correction will add three hundred years to the life of the Tower of Pisa.

3. I really enjoyed my summer vacation this year. It isn't long enough, of course, but I made the most of the time I have. My geology club took a trip to Baja. We didn't pack enough to eat, but the beautiful scenery takes my breath away. Once I'm back home, I always play a lot of tennis with my roommates. One night we stayed at the tennis court until after it closes. We are just hitting volleys in the dark with only the moon for lighting. It was an unplanned thing, and we could barely see the ball. It's fun to goof off with my friends on a summer evening. Overall, the trip to Baja and the after-hours tennis match are the highlights of my summer vacation.

Recognizing Verbal Phrases

We know (from the discussion on p. 84) that a verb phrase is made up of a main verb and at least one helping verb. But sometimes certain forms of verbs are used not as real verbs but as some other part of a sentence. Verbs put to other uses are called *verbals*.

A verbal can be a subject:

Skiing is my favorite Olympic sport. *(Skiing is the subject, not the verb. The verb is is.)*

A verbal can be a descriptive word:

His *bruised* ankle healed very quickly. (*Bruised* describes the subject, ankle. *Healed* is the verb.)

A verbal can be an object:

I like *to read* during the summer. (*To read* is the object. *Like* is the verb.)

Verbals link up with other words to form *verbal phrases*. To see the difference between a real verb phrase and a verbal phrase, look at these two sentences:

I was bowling with my best friends. (*Bowling* is the main verb in a verb phrase. Along with the helping verb *was*, it shows the action of the sentence.)

I enjoyed *bowling* with my best friends. (Here the real verb is *enjoyed*. *Bowling* is not the verb; it is part of a verbal phrase—*bowling with my best friends*—which is what I enjoyed.)

THERE ARE THREE KINDS OF VERBALS

1. *ing* verbs used without helping verbs *(running, thinking, baking . . .)*
2. verb forms that often end in *ed, en,* or t *(tossed, spoken, burnt . . .)*
3. verbs that follow *to* _____ *(to walk, to eat, to cause . . .)*

Look at the following sentences using the previous examples in verbal phrases:

Running two miles a day is great exercise. (real verb = is)

She spent two hours *thinking of a title for her essay.* (real verb = spent)

We had such fun *baking those cherry vanilla cupcakes.* (real verb = had)

Tossed in a salad, artichoke hearts add zesty flavor. (real verb = add)

Spoken in Spanish, the dialogue sounds even more beautiful. (real verb = sounds)

The gourmet pizza, *burnt by a careless chef,* shrunk to half its normal size. (real verb = shrunk)

I like *to walk around the zoo by myself.* (real verb = like)

To eat exotic foods takes courage. (real verb = takes)

They actually wanted *to cause an argument.* (real verb = wanted)

E X E R C I S E S

Each of the following sentences contains at least one verbal or verbal phrase. Double underline the real verbs or verb phrases and put brackets around the verbals and verbal phrases. Remember to locate the verbal first *(running, wounded, to sleep . . .)* and include any word(s) that go with it *(running a race, wounded in the fight, to sleep all night).* Real verbs will never be inside verbal phrases. Complete the first set and check your answers before going on to the next.

Exercise 1

1. The idea of home schooling children has become more popular recently.

2. Many parents have decided to teach kids themselves instead of sending them off to public or private school classrooms.

3. There are many different reasons to choose home schooling.

4. In Hollywood, for instance, child actors often are forced to drop out of traditional schools due to their schedules.

5. The home schooling option allows for one of their parents, or a special teacher, to continue to instruct them on the set.

6. Other parents simply want to be directly involved in their child's learning.

7. Many school districts have special independent study "schools," offering parents the structure and materials that they need to provide an appropriate curriculum on their own.

8. Children do all of their reading and writing at home with their parents guiding them along the way.

9. The family meets with the independent study school's teacher regularly to go over the child's work and to clarify any points of confusion.

10. Many parents would like to have the time to home school their children.

Exercise 2

1. By 2003, a Japanese company called Matsushita expects to offer fully interactive houses operated by computer network.

2. Getting ready for work in the morning will be very different.

3. The electronic toilet-of-the-future is designed to take care of everything—weighing you, checking your health through various tests, and even sending the data to your doctor if necessary.

4. Talking into your television's remote control will turn on the space-age TV screens of the future positioned in almost every room of the house.

5. Using a cell phone with its own video screen from your desk at work, you'll be able to check the contents of your refrigerator before shopping for groceries.

6. And once you return home with the food, you can update the fridge's contents using voice commands.

7. Glancing at monitors set up in key areas, you can check the status of your laundry room, living room, and kitchen simultaneously.

8. The rooms themselves will respond to your movements through the use of infrared sensors—lighting up, cooling off, or heating up as necessary.

9. A security system will be used to take the picture of anyone approaching the front door and to store the snapshot for twelve months.

10. Needless to say, the fully wired Japanese house of the new millennium will be expensive, costing nearly five percent more than an ordinary, old-fashioned one.

Source: U.S. News & World Report, 7 June 1999

Exercise 3

1. Binney & Smith is a company headquartered in Easton, Pennsylvania.

2. The company is responsible for making one of the most treasured memories of many people's childhoods—Crayola crayons.

3. Company officials took a controversial step in 1990 by retiring eight old colors of crayons and replacing them with new, more modern hues.

4. Before Binney & Smith canceled the eight colors, they asked children to help them make the decision.

5. Grownups were very upset with the choices, forming groups with names like RUMPS (Raw Umber and Maize Preservation Society) and CRAYON (Committee to Reestablish All Your Old Norms).

6. These angry adults continued to write and call the company until a solution was found.

7. Binney & Smith opened a Crayola Hall of Fame at company headquarters, briefly reissuing crayon sets with the original colors intact.

8. Crayola Hall of Fame visitors now get to walk past five-foot-high statues of Crayolas in the eight retired colors.

9. Pushing a button by one of the statues activates a recording of children and adults' fond memories of the color.

10. For instance, a little girl's voice tells how important raw umber was to her; she explains that she used it to color her skin in the pictures she drew of herself.

Source: *America's Strangest Museums* (Citadel, 1996)

Exercise 4

1. It is very easy to give someone the bubonic plague these days—in tie form, that is.

2. A microscopic picture of the plague is just one of the "decorations" adorning the Infectious Awareables collection of ties sold by Roger Freeman.

3. Freeman was a dentist before becoming a tie salesman.

4. The diseased ties are just starting to become popular.

5. There are ties showing cholera, staph, ebola, and malaria, to name just a few.

6. Inventors decided to label the ties with information about the conditions pictured on their surfaces.

7. Freeman took over selling the stock of ties after being given a herpes tie as a present.

8. Freeman loves the disease patterns seen through a microscope.

9. Their vivid colors and abstract shapes make them perfect to use as tie designs.

10. The Infectious Awareables ties are priced reasonably, selling for around forty dollars a piece.

Source: *People,* 20 Sept. 1999

Exercise 5

1. John Steinbeck, author of *The Grapes of Wrath,* was the first native of California to receive the Nobel Prize for literature.

2. Calling his hometown of Salinas "Lettuceberg," Steinbeck's writing made the area famous.

3. At the time, not everyone liked the attention brought by his portrayals of life in *Cannery Row* and other works.

4. Steinbeck's father was the treasurer of Monterey County for ten years, working also for the Spreckels company.

5. John Steinbeck tried to find satisfaction in his birthplace, enrolling in and quitting his studies at Stanford University many times.

6. Finally, Steinbeck moved to New York, distancing himself from his California roots.

7. Steinbeck won the Nobel Prize in 1962, revealing the literary world's esteem for his work.

8. Not writing anything of the caliber of the Salinas stories while living in New York, Steinbeck did return to California before he died in 1968.

9. In 1972, the Salinas library changed its name, to be known thereafter as the John Steinbeck Library.

10. And the house Steinbeck was born in became a restaurant and then a full-fledged museum chronicling the life of Salinas' most celebrated citizen.

Source: California People (Peregrine Smith, 1982)

PARAGRAPH EXERCISE

Double underline the real verbs or verb phrases and put brackets around the verbals and verbal phrases in the following paragraph from the book *California People*, by Carol Dunlap.

Simon Rodia (Sam Rodia, 1879–1965). The southeastern L.A. neighborhood of Watts is known for two things, the 1965 epidemic of destruction called the Watts Riots and the unique act of creative construction known as the Watts Towers. Rodia was a loner, an Italian-born tile setter and all-around handyman who lived in the mixed Chicano and black neighborhood. . . . What is known is that he spent thirty years constructing an elaborate structure out of . . . scrap iron and metal, broken glass and crockery. Considered "highly significant" in the words of art history—"possibly the most significant structure ever created by one man alone"—the Watts Towers look something like an ornate oil derrick, a Gothic cathedral, and a jungle gym all in one. Rodia, a man whose acts spoke for themselves, deeded his property to a neighbor in 1954 and left. Five years later, the City of Los Angeles tried to demolish the towers as a public hazard. Then living in the Suisun Bay town of Martinez, Rodia remained silent. . . . The towers survived a stress test to become a remote outpost on the Los Angeles tourist circuit. . . . Rodia died a month before the riots which spared his corner of the old neighborhood.

SENTENCE WRITING

Write ten sentences that contain verbal phrases. Use the ten verbals listed here to begin your verbal phrases: *owning, taking, bowling, cutting, to get, to be, to cut, to respect, shaped, driven*. The last two are particularly difficult to use as verbals. There are sample sentences listed in the Answer Section at the back of the book. But first, try to write your own so that you can compare the two.

Correcting Misplaced or Dangling Modifiers

When we modify something, we change whatever it is by adding something to it. We might modify a car, for example, by adding special tires. In English we call words, phrases, and clauses modifiers when they add information to part of a sentence. To do its job properly, a modifier should be in the right spot—as close to the word it describes as possible. If we put new tires on the roof of the car instead of where they belong, they would be misplaced. In the following sentence, the modifier is too far away from the word it modifies to make sense. It is a misplaced modifier:

> Swinging from tree to tree, we watched the monkeys at the zoo.

Was it *we* who were swinging from tree to tree? That's what the sentence says because the modifying phrase *Swinging from tree to tree* is next to *we*. It should be next to *monkeys*.

> At the zoo, we watched the monkeys swinging from tree to tree.

The next example has no word at all for the modifier to modify:

> At the age of eight, my family finally bought a dog.

Obviously the family was not eight when it bought a dog. Nor was the dog eight. The modifier *At the age of eight* is dangling there with no word to attach itself to, no word for it to modify. We can get rid of the dangling modifier by turning it into a dependent clause. (See p. 60 for a discussion of dependent clauses.)

> When I was eight, my family finally bought a dog.

Here the clause has its own subject and verb—*I was*—and there's no chance of misunderstanding the sentence. Here's another dangling modifier:

> After a ten-minute nap, the plane landed.

Did the plane take a ten-minute nap? Who did?

> After a ten-minute nap, I awoke just as the plane landed.

E X E R C I S E S

Carefully rephrase any of the following sentences that contain misplaced or dangling modifiers. Some sentences are correct.

Exercise 1

1. After checking the time, my watch dropped on the floor.

2. I located my car walking around the parking lot several times.

3. We watched the 3-D movie with special glasses.

4. A day after taking the midterm, my instructor was absent.

5. Most of the cats in the show looked very happy in their kennels.

6. Our mail carrier slipped and fell on the ice in front of our house.

7. In our textbook, we read an essay about George Orwell's definition of *imperialism.*

8. Taking too many classes this semester, I am finding it hard to cope.

9. I purchased my first car with a sunroof, but I'll never do it again.

10. My cousin sent me a picture from our family reunion in a large envelope.

Exercise 2

1. We walked to our class together and met later in the quad.

2. I drank a cup of tea reading the newspaper.

3. Helping to advertise the event, a plane pulled a large banner across the sky.

4. After last week's weather, a sunny day would be a relief.

5. We arrived at the zoo without any money.

6. John, his sister, and their two dates rode to the prom in the same limousine.

7. Lying on my desk for two weeks, I finally finished the reading assignment.

8. We heard music coming from our neighbor's backyard.

9. My friends and I ate a whole bucket of popcorn waiting in the lobby.

10. Before calling the dentist, my tooth started to feel better.

Exercise 3

1. Travelers encountered delays flying from Los Angeles to New York.

2. Disappointed by the actor's performance, the critic wrote a negative review.

3. We watched the ballet dancers with binoculars.

4. He kicked his friend in the class by accident.

5. She found a few mistakes looking over her essay.

6. The valet parking attendant handed my mother the keys with a wink.

7. Loving the smell of fresh coffee, Starbucks is the perfect place for my brother to work.

8. They sent us an invitation to their wedding in a fancy envelope.

9. At the age of ten, we moved to Michigan.

10. The teacher will return our essays on smoking before the final exam.

Exercise 4

1. Getting a headache from the fumes, the small plane finally made it to our destination.

2. Full of empty calories, that carnival sold the best cotton candy I'd ever tasted.

3. Two months after moving, our old apartment is still empty.

4. She promised to return the library books in her e-mail message.

5. The students took the notes sitting in small groups.

6. Before saying goodnight, the porch light burned out.

7. Decorated beautifully, our hostess showed us her favorite room.

8. Scampering along the baseboards of the cabin, I saw a tiny gray mouse.

9. Trying to open my car door with a hanger, I stared at the keys dangling from the ignition.

10. All along the highway, volunteers planted trees wearing special T-shirts.

Exercise 5

1. Feeling the excitement of the first day of school, my backpack was left behind.

2. Full of surprises, we saw the new movie that everyone is talking about.

3. My cousins and I always wrapped our gifts in our pajamas on the night before the holiday.

4. Practicing for an hour a day, his tennis has improved.

5. The price of gasoline fluctuates, rising and falling several times a year.

6. Sitting on the beach all day, I made a decision.

7. They discovered a new trail hiking in the nearby mountains.

8. She felt the pressure of trying to get good grades from her parents.

9. I enjoy traveling to new places with my friends and even my family.

10. Written in green ink, the teacher's comments seemed positive even when pointing out a problem.

PROOFREADING EXERCISE

Find and correct any misplaced or dangling modifiers in the following paragraphs.

A man in Edinburgh, Scotland, has invented a device, hoping to become famous and wealthy. The device is a variation on the center-mounted brake light used in the design of many new cars, located just above the trunk and visible from behind. Instead of just a solid red brake light, however, this invention displays words to other drivers written in bold, red-lighted letters.

With simplicity in mind, the vocabulary the inventor gave the machine is limited to three words: "Sorry," "Thanks," and "Help." After making an aggressive lane change, the machine could apologize for us. Or after being allowed to go ahead of someone, the device could offer thanks to the considerate person responsible. Of course, at the sight of the "Help" display, we could summon fellow citizens for assistance.

And there is no need to worry about operating the device while driving. With three easy-to-reach buttons, the messages can be activated without taking our eyes off the road.

SENTENCE WRITING

Write five sentences that contain misplaced or dangling modifiers; then revise those sentences to put the modifiers where they belong. Use the examples in the explanations as models.

Following Sentence Patterns

Sentences are built according to a few basic patterns. For proof, rearrange each of the following sets of words to form a complete statement (not a question):

apples a ate raccoon the

the crashing beach were waves the on

your in am partner I life

been she school has to walking

you wonderful in look green

There are only one or two possible combinations for each due to English sentence patterns. Either *A raccoon ate the apples,* or *The apples ate a raccoon,* and so on. But in each case, the verb or verb phrase makes its way to the middle of the statement.

To understand sentence patterns, you need to know that verbs can do three things.

1. They can show actions:

    The raccoon ate the apples.

    The waves were crashing on the beach.

    She has been walking to school.

2. They can link subjects with descriptive words:

    I am your partner in life.

    You look wonderful in green.

3. They can help other verbs form verb phrases:

    The waves were crashing on the beach.

    She has been walking to school.

Look at these sentences for more examples:

    Mel grabbed a slice of pizza. (The verb *grabbed* shows Mel's action.)

    His slice was the largest one in the box. (The verb *was* links *slice* with its description as *the largest one.*)

    Mel had been craving pizza for a week. (The verbs *had* and *been* help the main verb *craving* in a verb phrase.)

Knowing what a verb does in a clause helps you gain an understanding of the three basic sentence patterns:

SUBJECT + ACTION VERB + OBJECT PATTERN

Some action verbs must be followed by a person or object that receives the action.

    S   AV   OBJ.
    Sylvia completed the difficult math test. (*Sylvia completed* makes no sense without being followed by the object that she completed—*test.)*

SUBJECT + ACTION VERB (+ NO OBJECT) PATTERN

At other times, the action verb itself finishes the meaning and needs no object after it.

S AV
She celebrated at home with her family. (*She celebrated* makes sense alone. The two prepositional phrases—*at home* and *with her family* are not needed to understand the meaning of the clause.)

SUBJECT + LINKING VERB + DESCRIPTION PATTERN

A special kind of verb that does not show an action but links a subject with a description is called a *linking verb*. It acts like an equal sign in a clause. Learn to recognize the most common linking verbs: *is, am, are, was, were, seem, feel, appear, become, look.*

S LV   DESC.
Sylvia was always an excellent student. (*Sylvia* equals *an excellent student.*)

S LV   DESC.
Sylvia has become very intelligent. (*Very intelligent* describes *Sylvia.*)

NOTE- We learned on page 84 that a verb phrase includes a main verb and its helping verbs. Helping verbs can be used in any of the sentence patterns.

S AV
Sylvia is going to Seattle for a vacation. (Here the verb *is* helps the main verb *going,* which is an action verb with no object followed by two prepositional phrases—*to Seattle* and *for a vacation.*)

The following chart outlines the patterns using short sentences that you should memorize:

THE THREE BASIC SENTENCE PATTERNS

S + AV + Obj.	S + AV
They hit the ball.	They ran (quickly) (around the bases).
	not objects

S + LV +	Desc.
They are	state champions.
They look	professional.

These are the three basic patterns of most of the clauses used in English sentences. Knowing them can help writers control their sentences and improve their use of words.

E X E R C I S E S

First, put parentheses around any prepositional phrases. Next, underline the subjects once and the verbs or verb phrases twice. Then mark the sentence patterns above the words. Remember that the patterns never mix together. For example, unlike an action verb, a linking verb will almost never be used alone (for example, "He seems."), nor will an action verb be followed by a description of the subject (for example, "She took tall."). And if there are two independent clauses, each one may have a different pattern. Check your answers after the first set of ten.

Exercise 1

1. My sister Belinda is allergic to many things.

2. She gets hives from mold and pollen.

3. Of course, milk upsets her stomach.

4. Strawberries and raspberries are many people's favorite fruits.

5. But they give Belinda a rash on her face and arms.

6. The doctor has made a list of Belinda's allergies.

7. Soon she'll be receiving allergy shots.

8. The shots should reduce Belinda's sensitivity to these substances.

9. Everyone in my family is hoping for the best.

10. With luck, Belinda will feel better soon.

Exercise 2

1. Scientists around the world are working toward a new technology.

2. It is a computer, of course.

3. It will translate one language into another instantly.

4. People will carry the device with them in their travels.

5. They will ask a question in English, and the device will repeat the question in French, Spanish, German, or Japanese.

6. The traveler will hear the translation over a pair of headphones.

7. But computers still have some trouble in recognizing people's speech.

8. Ordinary ramblings usually include numerous interruptions, such as "um" and "er."

9. Nobody has programmed totally accurate translating software yet.

10. But researchers are now closer than ever to using computers as translators.

Source: Discover, Nov. 1999

Exercise 3

1. Giuseppe Verdi's opera *A Masked Ball* is a classic, and performances of it are usually spectacular.

2. But two British men, Richard Jones and Anthony McDonald, staged a truly unique offering of Verdi's opera for the Bregenz Festival in Austria in the summer of 1999.

3. The most amazing part of the Austrian production was the stage, shaped like an open book.

4. The stage floated on a lake, and the audience watched the performance from seats on the shore.

5. This floating book was also huge; its surface covered more than eight thousand square feet.

6. Actors crossed a bridge to the stage and then walked great distances during the opera.

7. The size, shape, and location of the stage were unique enough.

8. Then Jones and McDonald stunned audiences with an eighty-foot prop next to the stage.

9. The prop was a human skeleton, and just one of its fingers was the same height as an actor on the stage.

10. During each performance, the towering skeleton moved and pushed one of the actors across the stage.

Source: People, 4 Oct. 1999

Exercise 4

1. In America, we love our pets.

2. We own more than one hundred million of them.

3. Almost sixty percent of the people in the United States live with pets.

4. Of these pet owners, thirty percent have chosen dogs as their favorites.

5. Twenty-seven percent prefer cats.

6. Pet food and supply companies are prospering at the moment.

7. Americans are even buying health insurance for their pets.

8. In the 1980s, the average cost for pet medical treatment was slightly more than two hundred dollars.

9. Now people will spend thousands for pet-care measures.

10. The pet-care industry makes more than eleven billion dollars a year.

Source: U.S. News & World Report, 17 May 1999

Exercise 5

1. One pet owner in Vermont demonstrates some people's devotion to their animals.

2. Richard Durgin had a schnauzer named Ben.

3. Ben developed kidney disease, and Durgin paid six thousand dollars in vet bills.

4. Then Ben suffered from injuries in a car accident, and Durgin spent even more on a new hip and a reconstructed paw for Ben.

5. When a vet suggested a five-thousand-dollar kidney transplant for the pet schnauzer, Durgin declined.

6. Ben's kidney problems finally took their toll.

7. Ben no longer runs around Durgin's house, but his memory lives on.

8. Durgin drinks his morning coffee from a specially made set of mugs.

9. One of the ingredients in the clay was Ben's ashes.

10. Ben was one beloved dog.

Source: U.S. News & World Report, 17 May 1999

PARAGRAPH EXERCISE

Label the sentence patterns in the following paragraphs. They are from a book by Paul Zelanski and Mary Pat Fisher titled, simply, *Color.* It helps to put parentheses around prepositional phrases first to isolate them from the words that make up the sentence patterns—the subjects, the verbs, and any objects after action verbs or any descriptive words after linking verbs (*is, was, were, seem, appear,* and so on).

Color is perhaps the most powerful tool at an artist's disposal. It affects our emotions beyond thought and can convey any mood, from delight to despair. It can be subtle or dramatic, capture attention or stimulate desire. Used more boldly and freely today than ever before, color bathes our vision with an infinite variety of sensations, from clear, brilliant hues to subtle, elusive mixtures. Color is the province of all artists, from painters and potters to product designers and computer artists.

SENTENCE WRITING

Write ten sentences describing the weather today and your feelings about it—make your sentences short and clear. Then go back and label the sentence patterns you have used.

Avoiding Clichés, Awkward Phrasing, and Wordiness

CLICHÉS

A cliché is an expression that has been used so often it has lost its originality and effectiveness. Whoever first said "light as a feather" had thought of an original way to express lightness, but today that expression is worn out. Most of us use an occasional cliché in speaking, but clichés have no place in writing. The good writer thinks up fresh new ways to express ideas.

Here are a few clichés. Add some more to the list.

the bottom line

older but wiser

last but not least

in this day and age

different as night and day

out of this world

white as a ghost

sick as a dog

tried and true

at the top of their lungs

the thrill of victory

one in a million

busy as a bee

easier said than done

better late than never

Clichés lack freshness because the reader always knows what's coming next. Can you complete these expressions?

the agony of . . .

breathe a sigh of . . .

lend a helping . . .

odds and . . .

raining cats and . . .

as American as . . .

been there . . .

worth its weight . . .

Clichés are expressions too many people use. Try to avoid them in your writing.

AWKWARD PHRASING

Another problem—awkward phrasing—comes from writing sentence structures that *no one* else would use because they break basic sentence patterns, omit necessary words, or use words incorrectly. Like clichés, awkward sentences might *sound* acceptable when spoken, but as polished writing, they are usually unacceptable.

AWKWARD

There should be great efforts in terms of the cooperation between coaches and their athletes.

CORRECTED

Coaches and their athletes should cooperate.

AWKWARD

During the experiment, the use of key principles was essential to ensure the success of it.

CORRECTED

The experiment was a success. *or* We did the experiment carefully.

AWKWARD

My favorite was when the guy fell all the way down the ship.

CORRECTED

In my favorite scene, a man fell all the way down the deck of the sinking ship.

WORDINESS

Good writing is concise writing. Don't say something in ten words if you can say it better in five. "In today's society" isn't as effective as "today," and it's a cliché. "At this point in time" could be "presently" or "now."

Another kind of wordiness comes from saying something twice. There's no need to write "in the month of August" or "9 a.m. in the morning" or "my personal opinion." August *is* a month, 9 a.m. *is* morning, and anyone's opinion *is* personal. All you need to write is "in August," "9 a.m.," and "my opinion."

Still another kind of wordiness comes from using expressions that add nothing to the meaning of the sentence. "The point is that we can't afford it" says no more than "We can't afford it."

Here is a sample wordy sentence:

The construction company actually worked on that particular building for a period of six months.

And here it is after eliminating wordiness:

The construction company worked on that building for six months.

WORDY WRITING	CONCISE WRITING
advance planning	planning
an unexpected surprise	a surprise
ask a question	ask
at a later date	later
basic fundamentals	fundamentals
but nevertheless	but (or nevertheless)
combine together	combine
completely empty	empty
down below	below
each and every	each (or every)
end result	result
fewer in number	fewer
free gift	gift
green in color	green
in order to	to
in spite of the fact that	although
just exactly	exactly
large in size	large
new innovation	innovation
on a regular basis	regularly
past history	history
rectangular in shape	rectangular
refer back	refer
repeat again	repeat
serious crisis	crisis
sufficient enough	sufficient (or enough)
there in person	there
two different kinds	two kinds
very unique	unique

EXERCISES

Exercise 1

Rewrite the following sentences to eliminate clichés and awkward phrasing.

1. I know that practice makes perfect, but I just can't seem to get behind the idea of practicing the piano.

2. I've been learning the ins and outs of piano playing for just about two years.

3. I thought it was a good idea at first, but in this day and age, it seems so old-fashioned to study all the notes and hand positions.

4. I mean, right now anyone can go into a store and buy keyboards that play music themselves.

5. That's what I did when I found out that owning a real piano is easier said than done.

6. I couldn't afford any of them; the prices were way over the top.

7. So I got one of the upright digital keyboards that is really close to the sound and feel of the real thing.

8. My music teacher has no idea that I spend hours not practicing my fingering but having my keyboard play the demo songs.

9. All I have to do is push the right button, and the theme from *Star Wars* fills the air.

10. Of course, the sad truth is that I'll probably never learn to play the piano myself.

Exercise 2

Cross out words or rewrite parts of each sentence to eliminate wordiness. Doing these exercises can almost turn into a game to see how few words you can use without changing the meaning of the sentence.

1. After a lot of advance planning, we were recently able to hold a reunion where everybody in the family came together to celebrate my grandmother's birthday.

2. Of course, we wanted it to be a surprise so that Grandma wouldn't know about it ahead of time; we couldn't wait to see the happy look of joy on her face when she saw us all there in person.

3. Each and every one of us had to travel some distance to reach the campground where we were having the reunion since we have all spread out across the state and even the country in order to make our livings.

4. In spite of the fact that we all had to travel to get there, we made it at the exact time that we needed to be there so that Grandma could walk up and find us all there together already before she walked up.

5. My cousin Jeff was the one who was chosen to distract Grandma before the reunion.

6. He decided to take her shopping with him at the mall; he told her that he needed a new coat and that she was the one that he trusted the most to help him choose the right one.

7. She was flattered that he trusted her judgment, so she went with him to buy the coat.

8. To make a long story short, while they were shopping for the coat at the mall, Jeff pretended to suddenly remember that he told a friend that he would go camping with him, so Jeff drove Grandma to the campground.

9. When they drove up, we all kind of hid behind trees and tables so that we wouldn't be seen, and then we all jumped out together and yelled "Surprise!"

10. We sat Grandma down in a big chair somebody had brought and made her feel like the queen of a country; we waited on her and entertained her and made her feel special.

Exercises 3, 4, and 5

Revise the sentences in the remaining exercises to eliminate any clichés, awkward phrasing, or wordiness.

Exercise 3

1. I just got finished reading an article that explains that the ancient Egyptians used what we now call makeup in a lot of different ways, not just for beauty.

2. First of all, they used makeup to paint their faces in an effort to make themselves more attractive to other human beings.

3. Egyptians seemed to be just as hung up on staying young and gorgeous looking as we modern folks do.

4. And it was a big eye-opener to me that the Egyptian men put makeup on their eyes and lips just like the Egyptian women.

5. French scientists and beauty experts have been studying the leftover contents that remain inside ancient vessels found inside the buried tombs of kings and queens of the Nile as far back in time as 2700 B.C.

6. From these leftover remains of ancient makeup, scientists have been able to identify the ingredients that the Egyptians used in their makeup concoctions.

7. The list of ingredients that the scientists discovered includes goose fat, lettuce, animal blood, crushed beetles, cinnamon, and some other ingredients that did not naturally occur in nature.

8. That means that the Egyptians had to know enough about chemistry to make artificial ingredients in the same way that we make artificial ingredients in this day and age.

9. Last but not least, the Egyptians seemed to have used makeup for medicinal rather than only cosmetic purposes.

10. Two of the substances that the Egyptians made artificially were laurionite and phosgenite, and these two ingredients may have helped to cure the eye problems that many Egyptians had due to the fact that the Nile river often flooded the valley and contained bacteria that commonly infected people's eyes.

Source: Discover, Sept. 1999

Exercise 4

1. I was as happy as a clam when I found out a few days ago that I will be getting a tax return of eight hundred dollars this year.

2. Before this, I used to do my own taxes myself.

3. I would wait for my W-2 forms to get here in the mail and then fill out the short form that lets me get the whole thing over with quick, even if I don't get a whole lot back from Uncle Sam.

4. Then my mom started giving me the old song and dance about that I'm getting old enough to do the right thing instead of taking the easy way out.

5. Well, that was all it took to make me wake up and smell the coffee.

6. I asked around at work to see if anyone knew a tax person to recommend, and my friend Jason said that he did, and he gave me her number.

7. I called the tax preparer that Jason used; her name was Helen.

8. After I went to see Helen, she explained to me that I should be the one to control the amount that gets taken out of my paycheck for taxes, not the other way around.

9. I never even had a clue that there was so much to know about being a "grownup," as my mom calls it.

10. And I bet I've just started to scratch the surface of what "real" grownups understand.

Exercise 5

1. One of the foods that Americans like the most is pizza, and we gobble it up like there's no tomorrow.

2. In fact, we eat nearly four hundred slices of pizza every single second to be specific.

3. There is an interesting story behind the name of one of the biggest pizza companies in America.

4. A pair of brothers named Frank and Dan Carney were growing up in Kansas in the late 1950s and going to a nearby state university.

5. Frank and Dan decided that it would be a good idea for them to start their own business, so they borrowed about five hundred dollars from their mom.

6. Then after they bought a bunch of used restaurant equipment and supplies, they opened up their own little pizza place.

7. The sign that they hired someone to make for their restaurant only had a little bit of space after the word *Pizza* to put another word.

8. They had only enough for about three letters, so they chose a short word—*hut*—and "Pizza Hut" was born.

9. Little did they know they would be so successful.

10. There are Pizza Huts all over the world now, close to ten thousand of them to be exact.

Source: Smithsonian, June 1997

PROOFREADING EXERCISE

Revise the sentences in the following paragraph to eliminate any clichés, awkward phrasing, or wordiness.

In my family, I don't think that you could call anybody in it "normal." In fact, every single member of my family is a bit of an oddball. The oddest one of all has to be my Uncle Crank. His real name is actually Frank, but ever since I was growing up, Uncle Frank told us kids to call him Uncle "Crank." That's because of his arm. Frank has an arm that is out of the ordinary because it doesn't bend the right way at the elbow. So you can go right up to it and turn it like a crank on an old car in the silent films. He is as proud as a peacock about the trick his arm can do. He is unique, all right, but I wish the doctors had fixed his elbow so that Uncle "Crank" could have been just a normal Uncle Frank. That way he wouldn't have to call attention to how different he is all the time.

SENTENCE WRITING

Go back to the sentences you wrote for the Sentence Writing exercise on p. 68 or p. 95 and revise them to eliminate any clichés, awkward phrasing, or wordiness.

Correcting for Parallel Structure

Your writing will be clearer and more memorable if you use parallel construction. That is, when you make any kind of list, put the items in similar form. If you write

My favorite coffee drinks are lattes, mochas, and the ones with espresso.

the sentence lacks parallel structure. The items don't all have the same form. But if you write

My favorite coffees are lattes, mochas, and espressos.

then the items are parallel. They are all single-word nouns. Or you could write

I like drinks blended with milk, flavored with chocolate, and made with espresso.

Again the sentence has parallel structure because all three descriptions are verbal phrases. Here are some more examples. Note how much easier it is to read the sentences with parallel construction.

LACKING PARALLEL CONSTRUCTION	HAVING PARALLEL CONSTRUCTION
I like to hike, to ski, and going sailing.	I like to hike, to ski, and to sail. (all "to____" verbs)
The office has run out of pens, paper, ink cartridges, and we need more toner, too.	The office needs more pens, paper, ink cartridges, and toner. (all nouns)
They decided that they needed a change, that they could afford a new house, and wanted to move to Arizona.	They decided that they needed a change, that they could afford a new house, and that they wanted to move to Arizona. (all dependent clauses)

The supporting points in an outline should always be parallel. In the following brief outlines, the supporting points in the left-hand column are not parallel in structure. Those in the right-hand column are parallel.

NOT PARALLEL	PARALLEL
Food Irradiation	Food Irradiation
I. How is it good?	I. Benefits
A. Longer shelf life	A. Extends shelf life
B. Using fewer pesticides	B. Requires fewer pesticides
C. Kills bacteria	C. Kills bacteria
II. Concerns	II. Concerns
A. Nutritional value	A. Lowers nutritional value
B. Consumers are worried	B. Alarms consumers
C. Workers' safety	C. Endangers workers

Using parallel construction will make your writing more effective. Note the effective parallelism in these well-known quotations:

A place for everything and everything in its place.

Isabella Mary Beeton

I have been poor and I have been rich. Rich is better.

Sophie Tucker

Ask not what your country can do for you; ask what you can do for your country.

John F. Kennedy

We hold these truths to be self-evident, that all men are created equal, that they are endowed by their creator with certain unalienable rights, that among these are Life, Liberty, and the pursuit of Happiness.

Thomas Jefferson

E X E R C I S E S

Most—but not all—of the following sentences lack parallel structure. In some, you will be able to cross out the part that is not parallel and write the correction above. Other sentences will need complete rephrasing.

Exercise 1

1. Nearly anyone who has grown up in America during the last century remembers putting a baby tooth under a pillow and the result of a quarter or two in its place in the morning.

2. The tradition of leaving a tooth for the Tooth Fairy and its significance are hard to trace.

3. One person who is trying to understanding the myth and collects everything to do with it is Dr. Rosemary Wells.

4. Dr. Wells runs the Tooth Fairy Museum in Deerfield, Illinois, and knows as much as anyone else about the elusive tooth taker.

5. Wells' interest in the legend of the Tooth Fairy started in the early 1970s when one of her dental students asked where it came from.

6. Since then Wells has gathered books, written essays, has an art collection, and receives gifts about the Tooth Fairy.

7. One of the most intriguing things about the story is that, unlike Santa Claus, the Tooth Fairy does not have any specific "look," and people don't think of the Tooth Fairy's gender.

8. Wells has discovered a few ancient rituals having to do with lost teeth, such as tossing the tooth into the air or that you should pitch it at a rat.

9. Both children in Europe and Mexican children have the story of the "Tooth Mouse" that comes to take away discarded baby teeth.

10. This story and the fairy stories brought over from England, Ireland, and Scotland probably melded together to form the legend of the Tooth Fairy.

Source: America's Strangest Museums (Citadel, 1996)

Exercise 2

1. The use of bar codes has a clear past but a future that is uncertain.

2. The bar code scanner was first used on June 26, 1974, and the first product that it scanned was a pack of chewing gum.

3. That took place at one supermarket in Ohio, but since then the same company's bar-code business has grown to scan more than a billion items a day around the country.

4. The bar codes themselves had been used on products all the way back to the 1960s, but they were not used to add up a customer's bill at the checkout counter until that day in 1974.

5. Now the bar code idea is spreading to other areas of item control.

6. Prisons track inmates, shipping companies scan railroad cars, hospitals verify blood samples, and even some cows are bar-coded by cattle ranchers to identify them.

7. Some people worry about the future use of bar codes and their possible misuse.

8. Several years ago, there was a rumor that the government was going to put bar codes on people's foreheads and then officials could keep track of these people for the rest of their lives.

9. Such a paranoid idea and one that is so far-fetched is usually not true.

10. But the possibilities of bar codes do make people wonder about how they will be used, where they will be used, and the reasons for their use in the years to come.

Source: New York Times, 27 June 1999, and Wall Street Journal, 19 Apr. 1999

Exercise 3

1. I was washing my car two weeks ago, and that's when I noticed a few bees buzzing around the roof of my garage.
2. I didn't worry about it at the time, but it was something that I should have worried about.
3. As I drove into my driveway a week later, a whole swarm of bees flew up and down in front of my windshield.
4. The swarm wasn't that big, but the bees flying tightly together looked really frightening.
5. They flew in a pattern as if they were riding on a roller coaster or almost like waves.
6. I was glad that my wife and kids were away for the weekend.
7. There was nothing I could do but to wait in my car until they went away.
8. Finally, the bees flew straight up into the air and then disappeared.
9. Once inside my house, I opened the phone book and started to call a bee expert.
10. The bees had made a hive out of part of my garage roof, the expert said, but once I replace the lumber in that area, I should not be bothered with bees anymore.

Exercise 4

1. The Smithsonian's National Museum of Natural History is older than many other Smithsonian branches and has more visitors than many other branches too.
2. The museum began serving the country in 1910, and since then having continued to add objects of interest to its collections.
3. Visitors to the Natural History museum can view its huge assortment of gemstones, minerals, and artifacts from different cultures and learn more about them at the same time.

4. According to Smithsonian officials, the National Museum of Natural History is working toward three different goals simultaneously, and it hopes to achieve them all.

5. The museum's primary goal is to increase its already gigantic collection of natural history objects; these items are of global significance as well as allowing scientists to study historical evidence from hundreds of millions of years ago.

6. The second goal is to teach young people to appreciate how important the study of natural history is and also the benefits of knowing natural history.

7. The museum is especially proud of its plans for interactive children's exhibits, such as an Insect Zoo, Africa Hall, and something called the Discovery Room.

8. The final goal for the museum is to satisfy the needs of researchers and preparing them to solve the problems of the future.

9. The museum's three goals will all come together as it begins two new programs.

10. Both focus on mammals and reach out to middle school students and the general public; one is already underway in several school districts, and the other will soon show up in airports, malls, and public libraries around the country.

Source: Smithsonian, Jan. 1999

Exercise 5

Make the sentences in the following list parallel.

1. To cut down on fuel bills while cooking, consider the following energy-saving hints.

2. Avoid preheating your oven unless it is electric.

3. You should always cover pots when cooking.

4. Don't open the oven door to check on food.

5. You can use the oven light instead.

6. Many people use a flame that extends past the bottom of the pan, but don't do that; it's wasteful.

7. Follow the directions given in a recipe for the time of cooking and what temperature to cook at.

8. Prepare your whole meal in the oven or on top of the stove, not both.

9. It's very important to check all the burners and be sure they are off after use.

10. If you follow these suggestions, you will save money on your energy bills and you probably will also cook better meals.

PROOFREADING EXERCISE

Proofread the following paragraph about Shirley Temple, the famous child star of the 1930s, and revise it to correct any errors in parallel structure.

Shirley Temple was born in 1928. In 1931, when she was just three years old, someone discovered her natural talent at a dance lesson, and she was asked to be in movies. She starred in many films that are still popular today. Among them are *Heidi*, *Rebecca of Sunnybrook Farm*, and *Curly Top* was one of her earliest. Directors loved Shirley's acting style and the fact that she was able to do a scene in only one take, but not everyone trusted Shirley Temple. Graham Greene was sued when he claimed that Shirley was about thirty years old and in reality was a dwarf. Little Shirley's parents helped with her career, and they also earned money for their efforts. In the early days, the studios paid her mother several hundred dollars a week to put fifty-six curlers in Shirley's hair each night. That way, her famous ringlets would always be perfect, and her hair looked the same each time. Shirley's father managed her money, so much money that at one point Shirley Temple was among the ten highest paid people in America. It was 1938, and she was only ten years old.

Source: California People (Peregrine Smith, 1982)

SENTENCE WRITING

Write ten sentences that use parallel structure. You may choose your own subject, or you may describe the process of studying for an important test. Be sure to include pairs and lists of objects, actions, locations, or ideas.

Using Pronouns

Nouns name people, places, things, and ideas—such as *students, school, computers,* and *cyberspace.* Pronouns take the place of nouns to avoid repetition and to clarify meaning. Look at the following two sentences. Nouns are needlessly repeated in the first sentence, but the second uses pronouns.

> The boy's mother felt that the children at the party were too loud, so the boy's mother told the children that the party would have to end if the children didn't calm down.

> The boy's mother felt that the children at the party were too loud, so *she* told *them* that *it* would have to end if *they* didn't calm down.

In the second sentence, *she* replaces *mother,* *they* and *them* replace *children,* and *it* takes the place of *party.*

Of the many kinds of pronouns, the following cause the most difficulty because they include two ways of identifying the same person (or people), but only one form is correct in a given situation:

SUBJECT GROUP	OBJECT GROUP
I	me
he	him
she	her
we	us
they	them

Use a pronoun from the Subject Group in two instances:

1. Before a verb as a subject:

He is my cousin. (*He* is the subject of the verb *is.)*

He is taller than *I.* (The sentence is not written out in full. It means "*He* is taller than *I* am." *I* is the subject of the verb *am.)*

Whenever you see *than* in a sentence, ask yourself whether a verb has been left off the end of the sentence. Add the verb, and then you'll automatically use the correct pronoun. In both speaking and writing, always add the verb. Instead of saying, "She's smarter than (I, me)," say, "She's smarter than I *am.*" Then you will use the correct pronoun.

2. After a linking verb (is, am, are, was, were) as a pronoun that renames the subject:

The one who should apologize is *he.* (*He* is *the one who should apologize.* Therefore the pronoun from the Subject Group is used.)

The winner of the lottery was *she.* (*She* was *the winner of the lottery.* Therefore the pronoun from the Subject Group is used.)

Modern usage allows some exceptions to this rule, however. For example, *It's me* or *It is her* (instead of the grammatically correct *It is I* and *It is she*) may be common in spoken English.

Use pronouns from the Object Group for all other purposes. In the following sentence, *me* is not the subject, nor does it rename the subject. It follows a preposition; therefore, it comes from the Object Group.

My boss went to lunch with Jenny and *me.*

A good way to tell whether to use a pronoun from the Subject Group or the Object Group is to leave out any extra name (and the word *and*). By leaving out *Jenny and,* you will say, *My boss went to lunch with me.* You would never say, *My boss went to lunch with I.*

My father and *I* play chess on Sundays. (*I* play chess on Sundays.)

She and her friends rented a video. (*She* rented a video.)

We saw Kevin and *them* last night. (We saw *them* last night.)

The teacher gave *us* students certificates. (Teacher gave *us* certificates.)

The coach asked Craig and *me* to wash the benches. (Coach asked *me* to wash the benches.)

Pronoun Agreement

Just as subjects and verbs must agree, pronouns should agree with the words they refer to. If the word referred to is singular, the pronoun should be singular. If the noun referred to is plural, the pronoun should be plural.

Each classroom has its own chalkboard.

The pronoun *its* refers to the singular noun *classroom* and therefore is singular.

Both classrooms have their own chalkboards.

The pronoun *their* refers to the plural noun *classrooms* and therefore is plural.

The same rules that we use to maintain the agreement of subjects and verbs also apply to pronoun agreement. For instance, ignore any prepositional phrases that come between the word and the pronoun that takes its place.

The *box* of chocolates has lost *its* label.

Boxes of chocolates often lose *their* labels.

A *player* with the best concentration usually beats *her or his* opponent.

Players with the best concentration usually beat *their* opponents.

When a pronoun refers to more than one word joined by *and,* the pronoun is plural:

The *teacher* and the *tutors* eat *their* lunches at noon.

The *salt* and *pepper* were in *their* usual spots at noon.

However, when a pronoun refers to more than one word joined by *or,* then the word closest to the pronoun determines its form:

Either the *teacher* or the *tutors* eat *their* lunches in the classroom.

Either the *tutors* or the teacher eats *her* lunch in the classroom.

Today many people try to avoid gender bias by writing sentences like the following:

If anyone wants help with the assignment, he or she can visit me in my office.

If anybody calls, tell him or her that I'll be back soon.

Somebody has left his or her pager in the classroom.

But those sentences are wordy and awkward. Therefore some people, especially in conversation, turn them into sentences that are not grammatically correct.

If anyone wants help with the assignment, they can visit me in my office.

If anybody calls, tell them that I'll be back soon.

Somebody has left their pager in the classroom.

Such ungrammatical sentences, however, are not necessary. It just takes a little thought to revise each sentence so that it avoids gender bias and is also grammatically correct:

Anyone who wants help with the assignment can visit me in my office.

Tell anybody who calls that I'll be back soon.

Somebody has left a pager in the classroom.

Probably the best way to avoid the awkward *he or she* and *him or her* is to make the words plural. Instead of writing, "Each actor was in his or her proper place on stage," write, "All the actors were in their proper places on stage," thus avoiding gender bias and still having a grammatically correct sentence.

PRONOUN REFERENCE

A pronoun replaces a noun to avoid repetition, but sometimes the pronoun sounds as if it refers to the wrong word in a sentence, causing confusion. Be aware that when you write a sentence, *you* know what it means, but your reader may not. What does this sentence mean?

The students tried to use the school's computers to access the Internet, but they were too slow, so they decided to go home.

Who or what was too slow, and who or what decided to go home? We don't know whether the two pronouns (both *they*) refer to the students or to the computers. One way to correct such a faulty reference is to use singular and plural nouns:

The students tried to use a school computer to access the Internet, but it was too slow, so they decided to go home.

Here's another sentence with a faulty reference:

Sharon told her mother that she needed a haircut.

Who needed the haircut—Sharon or her mother? One way to correct such a faulty reference is to use a direct quotation:

Sharon told her mother, "You need a haircut."

Sharon said, "Mom, I need a haircut."

Or you could always rephrase the sentence completely:

Sharon noticed her mother's hair was sticking out in odd places, so she told her mother to get a haircut.

Another kind of faulty reference is a *which* clause that appears to refer to a specific word, but it doesn't really.

I wasn't able to finish all the problems on the exam, which makes me worried.

The word *which* seems to replace exam, but it isn't the exam that makes me worried. The sentence should read

I am worried that I wasn't able to finish all the problems on the exam.

The pronoun *it* causes its own reference problems. Look at this sentence, for example:

When replacing the ink cartridge in my printer, it broke, and I had to call the technician to come and fix it.

Did the printer or the cartridge break? Here is one possible correction:

The new ink cartridge broke when I was putting it in my printer, and I had to call the technician for help.

EXERCISES

Exercise 1

Underline the correct pronoun. Remember the trick of leaving out the extra name to help you decide which pronoun to use. Use the correct grammatical form even though an alternate form may be acceptable in conversation.

1. My sister Maggie and (I, me) went shopping over the weekend.

2. I usually enjoy shopping more than (she, her).

3. This time, however, both (she and I, her and me) enjoyed ourselves.

4. Since Maggie is less style conscious than (I, me), she doesn't normally want to shop in certain stores.

5. Every time (she and I, her and me) have been shopping before, Maggie has just waited outside the trendy stores while I looked around.

6. But the one who was the most daring this weekend was (she, her).

7. Maggie may be more conservative than (I, me) most of the time, but she needed an impressive outfit for her upcoming high school reunion.

8. Just between (you and me, you and I), I think she found it.

9. Maggie was thrilled when a salesperson came right up to (she and I, her and me) and said, "You're looking for the perfect outfit, aren't you?"

10. Instead of ignoring Maggie's clothing advice in the future, I will start listening to (she, her).

Exercise 2

Underline the pronoun that agrees with the word the pronoun replaces. If the correct answer is *his or her/her or his,* revise the sentence to eliminate the need for this awkward expression. Check your answers as you go through the exercise.

1. I live a long way from the city center and don't own a car, so I use public transportation and rely on (its, their) stability.

2. Based on my experiences, I'd say the city's system of buses has (its, their) problems.

3. Each of the bus routes that I travel on my way to work falls behind (its, their) own schedule.

4. Many of the other passengers also transfer on (his or her, their) way to work.

5. One day last week, each of the passengers had to gather (his or her, their) belongings and leave the bus, even though it had not reached a scheduled stop.

6. Both the driver and the mechanic who came to fix the bus offered (his, their) apologies for making us late.

7. Once the bus was fixed, the passengers were allowed to bring (his or her, their) things back on board.

8. Everyone did (his or her, their) best to hide (his or her, their) annoyance from the driver because he had been so nice.

9. As every passenger stepped off the bus at the end of the line, the driver thanked (him or her, them) for (his or her, their) patience and under-standing.

10. Sometimes it is the people within a system that makes (it, them) work after all.

Exercise 3

Underline the correct pronoun. Again, if the correct answer is *his or her/her or his,* revise the sentence to eliminate the need for this awkward expression.

1. A rental car agency must be very competitive in (its, their) pricing.

2. The one blamed for the incident was (she, her).

3. Each of the new employees has (his or her, their) own locker in the employee lounge.

4. The debate teams from each school will continue (its, their) tournament tomorrow.

5. Every member of the audience had (his or her, their) opinion of the play and expressed it in the volume of (his or her, their) applause.

6. When it comes to Beanie Babies, no one know more than (he, him).

7. The teacher gave my fellow students and (I, me) a few suggestions.

8. (You and he, You and him) are similar in many ways.

9. My mother is actually younger than (she, her).

10. All of the customers at the supermarket shopped for (his or her, their) groceries at different speeds.

Exercise 4

Most—but not all—of the sentences in the next two sets aren't clear because we don't know what word the pronoun refers to. Revise such sentences, making the meaning clear. Since there are more ways than one to rewrite each sentence, yours may be as good as the ones at the back of the book. Just ask yourself whether the meaning is clear.

1. Mr. Martin told his student that he didn't understand him.

2. As we were arranging the sign on the easel, it fell over.

3. Our hamster escapes from its cage at least once a year, which frustrates us all.

4. Tracy asked her old roommate why she wasn't invited to the reunion.

5. They printed new raffle tickets and sold them for one dollar each.

6. I finished washing my car, turned off the hose, and drove it into the garage.

7. Janice told her sister that there was a kite on top of her roof.

8. We arrived early at the theater, which made it possible to relax a little.

9. Ken's boss let him take his laptop computer to night school with him.

10. When I cooked a potato in the microwave, it blew up.

Exercise 5

1. The Howells purchased new lawn chairs, but they were too fancy for them.

2. The teacher ordered a new textbook, and it arrived the next week.

3. I initialed the changes on the contract, put the top back on my pen, and handed it to the real estate agent.

4. When students join study groups, they help a lot.

5. As we placed the jars in pans of boiling water, they shattered.

6. Whenever I receive good news, I enjoy it.

7. Phone companies offer different prices for their handling of long-distance calls.

8. Dan's tutor asked him to rewrite his essay.

9. Many people visit amusement parks for their thrilling rides.

10. The committee members interviewed the applicants in their offices.

PROOFREADING EXERCISE

The following paragraph contains errors in the use of pronouns. Find and correct the errors.

My friend Kevin and me went out the other day. We saw a movie at the new theater complex down the block. After the cashier handed Kevin and I our tickets, we went into the lobby and were impressed with their decorations. Old movie posters lined the hallways to the theaters, and they were in really fancy gold frames. After the movie, I asked Kevin if he liked it. He said that it was the worst one he had ever been to. He told me that the parking was impossible, the screen was too small, and the seats were uncomfortable. He said that he would rather go to the place where we saw our last movie. At least it had a full-size screen and good sound, even if it wasn't as pretty as the new one.

SENTENCE WRITING

Write ten sentences about a conversation between you and someone else. Then check that your pronouns are grammatically correct, that they agree with the words they replace, and that references to specific nouns are clear.

Avoiding Shifts in Person

To understand the meaning of "person" when using pronouns, imagine a conversation between two people about a third person. The first person speaks using "I, me, my . . ."; the second person would be called "you"; and when the two of them talked of a third person, they would say "he, she, they. . . ." You should never forget the idea of "person" if you remember it as a three-part conversation.

First person—*I, me, my, we, us, our*

Second person—*you, your*

Third person—*he, him, his, she, her, hers, they, them, their, one, anyone*

You may use all three of these groups of pronouns in a paper, but don't shift from one group to another without good reason.

Wrong: Few people know how to manage *their* time. *One* need not be an efficiency expert to realize that *one* could get a lot more done if *he* budgeted *his* time. Nor do *you* need to work very hard to get more organized.

Better: *Everyone* should know how to manage *his or her* time. *One* need not be an efficiency expert to realize that *a person* could get a lot more done if *one* budgeted *one's* time. Nor does *one* need to work very hard to get more organized.(Too many *one*'s in a paragraph make it sound overly formal, and they lead to the necessity of avoiding sexism by using *s/he* or *he or she*, etc. Sentences can be revised to avoid using either *you* or *one*.)

Best: Many of *us* don't know how to manage *our* time. *We* need not be efficiency experts to realize that *we* could get a lot more done if *we* budgeted *our* time. Nor do *we* need to work very hard to get more organized.

Often students write *you* in a paper when they don't really mean *you, the reader.*

You wouldn't believe how many times I saw that movie.

Such sentences are always improved by getting rid of the *you.*

I saw that movie many times.

PROOFREADING EXERCISES

Which of the following student paragraphs shift *unnecessarily* between first-, second-, and third-person pronouns? In those that do, revise the sentences to eliminate such shifting, thus making the entire paragraph read smoothly. (First, read the paragraphs to determine whether unnecessary shifting takes place. One of the paragraphs is correct.)

1. I read an article about the first cloned sheep named Dolly. Dolly was cloned in 1996 from a six-year-old sheep, and now scientists are studying Dolly to see if she is aging any differently than a "normal" sheep. So far, they have found that she seems to be getting older faster than an uncloned animal, but the differences are only visible on a molecular level. From the outside, Dolly seems perfectly average. She has had many babies of her own already, but they reveal that nature may correct itself after cloning takes place. Some of Dolly's babies have her "older" molecules, and some have only brand new ones. The future of cloning will be affected by continued studies of Dolly and her offspring.

Source: U.S. News & World Report, 7 June 1999

2. Communicating through e-mail has made people lose their manners. You used to get a letter with a polite salutation at the top, such as "Dear Sirs" or even "To whom it may concern," and with a signature or printed name at the bottom to tell us who sent it. And an old-fashioned letter had not only the sender's address but also your address on it too. Then there was the postmark to tell what town the letter was mailed from. Now, with different people using the same e-mail accounts and sending them from all over the world, you never know where your electronic mail comes from unless the person follows the old rules of correspondence. But many people writing e-mail don't include salutations or signatures. I miss the old days when people took more time on their correspondence.

3. Christopher Wolfe will always have a reason to be proud, and I bet you'll never guess what it is. When he was seven years old, Christopher discovered a new dinosaur, and scientists named it after him. They called it *Zuniceratops christopheri*. This unknown species of dinosaur had two horns, one over each eye. You might have heard of other discoveries of dinosaurs with horns, but the one whose bones

Christopher found lived twenty million years earlier than any others. Christopher's father, Douglas Wolfe, was with him when he spotted the fossil in the Arizona/New Mexico desert. Douglas, a paleontologist, knew right away that his son's find was genuine. However, the kids at school had a hard time believing Christopher when he came in the next school day and told his classmates that he had discovered a new dinosaur species.

Source: People, 2 Nov. 1998

REVIEW OF SENTENCE STRUCTURE ERRORS

One sentence in each pair contains an error. Read both sentences carefully before you decide. Then write the letter of the *incorrect* sentence in the blank. Try to name the error and correct it if you can. You may find any of these errors:

awk	awkward phrasing
cliché	overused expression
dm	dangling modifier
frag	fragment
mm	misplaced modifier
pro	incorrect pronoun
pro agr	pronoun agreement error
pro ref	pronoun reference error
ro	run-on sentence
s/v agr	subject/verb agreement error
wordy	wordiness
//	not parallel

1. ___ **A.** I am sick and tired of news programs that report only gossip.

   B. We heard two different lectures on the death penalty.

2. ___ **A.** Each of the pieces of cake were the same size.

   B. The teacher gave Jane and me extra credit for the results of our Internet research.

3. ___ **A.** When the blizzard struck, all flights into the area were canceled.

    B. After a quick phone call, the dog next door was quiet.

4. ___ **A.** For lunch, we ate tuna sandwiches and potato chips.

    B. One of my ankles was sore after playing tennis all afternoon.

5. ___ **A.** The customers filled out suggestion cards they contained some good ideas.

    B. I can't imagine Sigmund Freud at an amusement park.

6. ___ **A.** The thing is, I never really wanted to choose a major.

    B. The weather should be perfect in March.

7. ___ **A.** I still have trouble knowing when to use commas and semicolons.

    B. Everyone at the party brought their swimsuits.

8. ___ **A.** I enjoy watching videos at home because you can stop the tape and eat a snack whenever you want.

    B. Shopping over the Internet is easier now than it ever was.

9. ___ **A.** The last one to get home that night was she.

    B. We stared at a tank of goldfish waiting for a table at the new restaurant.

10. ___ **A.** The combination to my art locker is a secret between the art department and me.

    B. I wouldn't take that class if it were the last class on earth.

11. ___ **A.** We applied for a scholarship, a loan, and to be accepted into the honors program.

    B. Few people know how to reduce stress.

12. ___ **A.** Many people wondering about what appears to be the shape of a face found on Mars.

    B. Many employees who use computers believe that their e-mail should be private.

13. ___ **A.** Two girls and a boy were playing at the sink when I began my observation.

    B. These studies of children's behavior has to be done carefully.

14. ___ **A.** Trading collectible cards and toys is a new hobby for many young people.

B. It is very difficult to know just what is and is not valuable, however.

15. ___ **A.** Either the students or the tutor is correct.

B. Either the students or the tutor are correct.

PROOFREADING EXERCISE

Find and correct the sentence structure errors in the following essay.

Mother Tells All

The most memorable lessons I have learned about myself have come from my own children. A mother is always on display she has nowhere to hide. And children are like parrots. Whatever they hear her say will be repeated again. If I change my mind about anything, you can be sure they will repeat back every word I uttered out of my mouth.

For example, last summer I told my kids that I was going to go to an exercise class and lose about forty pounds. Well, I lost some of the weight, and I did go to that exercise class. But as soon as I lost weight, I felt empty like a balloon losing air. I felt that I did not want to lose any more weight or do exercise anymore. I thought that my children would accept what I had decided.

When I stopped, the first thing one of my sons said was, "Mom, you need to go back to exercise class." Then they all started telling me what to eat all the time and I felt horrible about it. I had given up these things because I wanted to, but my words were still being repeated to me like an alarm clock going off without stopping. Finally, my kids ran out of steam and got bored with the idea of my losing weight. Once in a while, one of them still make a joke about my "attempt" to lose weight it hurts me that they don't understand.

The lesson that I have learned from this experience is that, if I am not planning on finishing something, I won't tell my children about it. They will never let me forget.

Punctuation and Capital Letters

Period, Question Mark, Exclamation Point, Semicolon, Colon, Dash

Every mark of punctuation should help the reader. Here are the rules for six marks of punctuation. The first three you have known for a long time and probably have no trouble with. The one about semicolons you learned when you studied independent clauses (p. 76). The ones about the colon and the dash may be less familiar.

Put a period (.) at the end of a sentence and after most abbreviations.

> The students elected Ms. Daniels to represent the class.

> Tues.   etc.   Jan.   sq. ft.   lbs.

Put a question mark (?) after a direct question but not after an indirect one.

> Will the midterm be an open-book or a closed-book test? (direct)

> I wonder if the midterm will be an open-book or a closed-book test. (indirect)

Put an exclamation point (!) after an expression that shows strong emotion. Use it sparingly.

> I can't believe I did so well on my first exam!

Put a semicolon (;) between two independent clauses in a sentence *unless* they are joined by one of the connecting words *for, and, nor, but, or, yet, so.*

> My mother cosigned for a loan; now I have my own car.

Some careers go in and out of fashion; however, people will always need doctors.

To be sure that you are using a semicolon correctly, see if a period and capital letter can be used in its place. If they can, you are putting the semicolon in the right spot.

My mother cosigned for a loan. Now I have my own car.

Some careers go in and out of fashion. However, people will always need doctors.

Put a colon (:) after a complete statement that introduces something: one item, a list, or a quotation that follows.

The company announced its Employee-of-the-Month: Lee Jones. (The sentence before the colon introduces the name that follows.)

In London, we plan to visit the following famous sites: the Tower of London, Piccadilly Circus, and Madame Tussaud's Wax Museum. (Here *the following famous sites* ends a complete statement and introduces the list that follows, so a colon is used.)

In London, we plan to visit the Tower of London, Piccadilly Circus, and Madame Tussaud's Wax Museum. (Here *we plan to visit* does not end a complete statement, so no colon is used.)

Thoreau had this to say about time: "Time is but the stream I go a-fishin in." (*Thoreau had this to say about time* is a complete statement. Therefore, a colon comes after it before adding the quotation.)

Thoreau said, "Time is but the stream I go a-fishin in."(*Thoreau said* is not an introductory statement. Therefore, a colon does not come after it.)

Use a dash (—) to indicate an abrupt change of thought or to emphasize what follows. Use it sparingly.

I found out today—or was it yesterday?—that I have inherited a fortune.

We have exciting news for you—we're moving!

E X E R C I S E S

Add to these sentences the necessary punctuation (periods, question marks, exclamation points, semicolons, colons, and dashes). The commas used within the sentences are correct and do not need to be changed.

Exercise 1

1. Wasn't the weather beautiful today ?
2. I wonder when the autumn breezes will start to blow .
3. It still felt like summer at least while the sun was shining .
4. At sunset the white, wispy clouds turned pink then the blue sky behind them started to turn gold .
5. It was breathtaking !
6. The only hint of fall came ; after the sun went down the temperature dropped about twenty degrees in an hour
7. I have always thought of summer as my favorite season ; however, today may have convinced me to switch to fall .
8. I never noticed that the leaves are so beautiful even after they have dropped from the trees .
9. I walked through the park and collected a bouquet of huge autumn leaves it was fun .
10. I hope tomorrow will be as pretty as today !

Exercise 2

1. Nancy Cartwright is a well-known actress on television ; however, we never see her when she is acting .
2. Cartwright is famous for playing one part : the voice of Bart Simpson
3. Besides her career as the most mischievous Simpson, Cartwright is married and has children of her own a boy and a girl .
4. Wouldn't it be strange if your mother had Bart Simpson's voice ?
5. Cartwright admits that she made her own share of trouble in school .
6. But the similarities between her and her famous character end there .
7. Bart is perpetually ten years old Cartwright is in her forties .
8. Bart is a boy Cartwright is obviously a woman .
9. It's no surprise that Cartwright is very popular with her children's friends .

10. When they yell for her to "Do Bart Do Bart" she declines with Bart's favorite saying "No way, man".

Source: People, 14 Dec. 1998

Exercise 3

1. I have just discovered the fun of fondue.

2. The story of the invention of fondue goes this way a farmer's wife accidentally dropped a chunk of cheese on the warming pan near the fire, and after mopping up the liquefied cheese with a piece of bread, she popped the morsel in her mouth and decided to make a meal of it

3. Since its discovery, fondue has always been a process rather than a product there are special pans to melt the cheese, fuel to keep it warm, and forks to hold the bread or meat to dip in it

4. I now understand why fondue was especially popular in the 1960s and 1970s

5. People then probably enjoyed the ritual of sitting down together and participating in a meal eaten from one pot

6. And the ingredients of bread and cheese couldn't be simpler, could they

7. There is also a rule that we might find distasteful now but thirty years ago must have seemed like fun according to the book *Fabulous Fondues*, the person who lost a piece of bread in the fondue pot had to pay a forfeit

8. The forfeits were listed as follows if a man lost the cube of bread, he owed the hostess a bottle of wine however, if a woman lost the cube of bread, she had to give one of the men at the table a kiss

9. Of course, other foods can be substituted for the traditional chunks of bread boiled potatoes, celery sticks, pretzels, crackers, mushrooms, and even nuts

10. I plan to have a fondue party as soon as I possibly can

Exercise 4

1. Other nations have given America gifts that have become part of our national landscape; for example, France gave us the Statue of Liberty.

2. In 1912, Japan sent the United States three thousand cherry trees as a goodwill gesture.

3. The Japanese wanted to share their own tradition of Sakura Matsuri; that is the spring celebration of the beauty of the cherry blossoms.

4. During cherry blossom time, there are picnics and field trips; wherever the cherry trees are blooming in Japan.

5. Of the three thousand cherry trees that Japan sent to America, only one hundred and twenty five remain they bloom in Washington, DC, every spring.

6. Thanks to the National Park Service, the lost Japanese trees have been replaced with ones grown in America; however, the original gift trees are the most prized of all.

7. New technology has allowed scientists to take clippings from the original Japanese cherry trees and grow new ones; consequently, the gift will live on.

8. Every spring in Washington, DC, thousands of people come to join in the Japanese enjoyment of cherry blossom time; in America it's called the Cherry Blossom Festival.

9. And beginning in 2001, the first five hundred offspring of the gift trees will be planted; they will continue to grow next to the originals.

10. The Statue of Liberty stands in New York Harbor; the cherry trees bloom in the capital both were gifts from other nations that add to the beauty of our own.

Source: U.S. News & World Report, 5 Apr. 1999

Exercise 5

1. In 1999 Nancy Mace did something no woman had ever done before, she graduated from the Citadel.

2. The South Carolina military academy had been in the news before, however, the news had not been good.

3. Six years before Mace graduated from there, the Citadel admitted its first female cadet Shannon Faulkner.

4. But Faulkner met with unrelenting resistance and hostility from her classmates.

5. Faulkner left the Citadel without finishing a term, nevertheless, other women enrolled there, including Nancy Mace.

6. Mace took an extra heavy load of classes to finish her studies in just three years.

7. She received some of the same treatment as Faulkner, however, Mace was prepared for it.

8. She also had a Brigadier General in her family, in fact, he handed her the diploma at the Citadel's graduation ceremony.

9. Mace was the first woman to graduate from the last class of the twentieth century at the Citadel.

10. There are currently dozens of female cadets at the Citadel, many more will probably follow.

Source: U.S. News & World Report, 17 May 1999

PROOFREADING EXERCISE

Can you find the five errors in this student paragraph?

The ingredients you will need for a lemon meringue pie are: lemon juice, eggs, sugar, cornstarch, flour, butter, water, and salt. First you combine flour, salt, butter, and water for the crust and bake until lightly brown then you mix and cook the lemon juice, egg yolks, sugar, cornstarch, butter, and water for the filling. Once the filling is poured in the cooked crust, you whip the meringue. Meringue is made of egg whites and sugar. Pile the meringue on top of the lemon filling, place the pie in the hot oven for a few minutes, and you'll have the best lemon meringue pie you've ever tasted.

SENTENCE WRITING

Write ten sentences of your own that use periods, question marks, exclamation points, semicolons, colons, and dashes correctly. Imitate the examples used in the explanations if necessary. Write about an interesting assignment you have done for a class, or choose your own topic.

Comma Rules 1, 2, and 3

Commas and other pieces of punctuation guide the reader through your sentence structures in the same way that signs guide drivers on the highway. Imagine what effects misplaced or incorrect road signs would have. Yet students often randomly place commas in their sentences. Try not to use a comma unless you know there is a need for it. Memorize this rhyme about comma use: *When in doubt, leave it out.*

Among all of the comma rules, six are most important. Learn these six rules, and your writing will be easier to read. You have already studied the first rule on page 77.

1. Put a comma before *for, and, nor, but, or, yet, so* (remember them as the *fanboys*) when they connect two independent clauses.

> The neighbors recently bought a minivan, and now they go everywhere together.

> We wrote our paragraphs in class today, but the teacher forgot to collect them.

> She was recently promoted, so she has moved to a better office.

If you use a comma alone between two independent clauses, the result is an error called a ***comma splice.***

> The ice cream looked delicious, it tasted good too. (comma splice)

> The ice cream looked delicious, and it tasted good too. (correct)

Before using a comma, be sure such words do connect two independent clauses. The following sentence is merely one independent clause with one subject and two verbs. Therefore, no comma should be used.

> The ice cream looked delicious and tasted good too.

2. Use a comma to separate three or more items in a series.

> Students in the literature class are reading short stories, poems, and plays.

> On Saturday I did my laundry, washed my car, and cleaned my room.

Occasionally, writers leave out the comma before the *and* connecting the last two items of a series, but it is more common to use it to separate all the items equally. Some words work together and don't need commas between them even though they do make up a kind of series.

> The team members wanted to wear their brand new green uniforms.

> The bright white sunlight made the room glow.

To see whether a comma is needed between words in a series, ask yourself whether *and* could be used naturally between them. It would sound all right to say *short stories and poems and plays;* therefore, commas are used. But it would not sound right to say *brand and new and green uniforms* or *bright and white sunlight;* therefore, no commas are used.

> If an address or date is used in a sentence, put a comma after every item, including the last. (No comma comes between the month and day in a date.)

> My father was born on August 19, 1941, in Mesa, Arizona, and grew up there.

> She lived in St. Louis, Missouri, for two years.

When only the month and year are used in a date, no commas are needed.

> She graduated in May 1985 from Indiana University.

3. Put a comma after an introductory expression (it may be a word, a phrase, or a dependent clause) or before a comment or question that is tacked on at the end.

Finally, he was able to get through to his insurance company.

During her last performance, the actress fell and broke her foot.

Once I have finished my homework, I will call you.

He said he needed to ruminate, whatever that means.

The new chairs aren't very comfortable, are they?

E X E R C I S E S

Add commas to the following sentences according to the first three comma rules. Some sentences may not need any commas, and some may need more than one. Any other punctuation already in the sentences is correct. Check your answers after the first set.

Exercise 1

1. For the first time in my life I feel like an adult.

2. I am taking general education classes in college and I am getting good grades.

3. Even though I receive some financial aid I mostly support myself.

4. I have a job a car and an apartment of my own.

5. When I am ready I plan to transfer to a university.

6. After I complete the course work at community college my parents will be proud of me but they will be even prouder when I get my degree.

7. I know that my father wants me to major in business yet my mother wants me to be a teacher.

8. Eventually it will be my decision.

9. Although I don't see myself in front of a class full of students I have always loved the school environment.

10. And it's easier to see myself there than in front of a room full of salespeople.

Exercise 2

1. When the government issued the Susan B. Anthony dollar coin it met with some disapproval.

2. People didn't dislike the person on the coin but they did dislike the size and color of the coin.

3. It was nearly the same size as a quarter had a rough edge like a quarter's and was the same color as a quarter.

4. It differed from a quarter in that it was faceted around the face was lighter in weight and was worth four times as much.

5. Due to these problems the Susan B. Anthony dollar has been replaced by a new dollar coin.

6. Like the Anthony dollar the new coin holds the image of a famous American woman.

7. She was the young Native American guide and interpreter for the Lewis and Clark expedition and her name was Sacagawea.

8. The story of Sacagawea's life tells of hardship suffering and illness but it also tells of incredible knowledge courage and strength.

9. While the men on the famous expedition had only themselves to worry about Sacagawea assisted the men and made the treacherous journey from North Dakota to the Pacific with her baby strapped to her back.

10. Although the same size as the previous dollar coin the Sacagawea dollar has a smooth wide edge and it is gold.

Source: U.S. News & World Report, 17 May 1999

Exercise 3

1. There are more than 3,700 colleges and universities in the country and they have all chosen names for their mascots.

2. What surprises people are the choices some of them have made.

3. You have your traditional Knights Lancers Spartans and Raiders.

4. Then there are the Rams Bulls Mustangs Gators and Razorbacks.

5. In the animal category a few odd choices are the Gila Monsters of Eastern Arizona College the Horned Frogs of Texas Christian University and the Slugs of the University of California at Santa Cruz.

6. The clergy are represented as mascots with the Battling Bishops and the Fighting Parsons.

7. In an effort to include female mascot names with their previously male-only counterparts some schools have added the Women of Troy to the Trojans Yeowomen to the Yeomen and Ladybraves to the Scalping Braves.

8. In the polite category there are the Gentlemen and Ladies of Centenary College in Louisiana and the Lords and Ladies of Kenyon College in Ohio.

9. At the extreme end of this inclusive trend are the Lumberjacks and Lumberjills the Vikings and Vi Queens and the Wildcat and Kittens.

10. The most esoteric are the Lights and Skylights of Montana State University-Northern in Havre Montana and the most edible are the Artichokes of Scottsdale Community College.

Source: Smithsonian, October 1998

Exercise 4

1. People used to think that emeralds had magical powers.

2. They were supposed to cure disease lengthen life and protect innocence.

3. Part of their appeal was how rare they are for emeralds are even rarer than diamonds.

4. Geologists have been mystified by emeralds because they are produced through a unique process—the blending of chromium vanadium and beryllium.

5. These are substances that almost never meet nor do they often combine—except in emeralds.

6. In South Africa Pakistan and Brazil emeralds were created by intrusions of granite millions to billions of years ago.

7. These areas are known for their beautiful gems but emeralds from Columbia are larger greener and more sparkling.

8. Scientists believe that the difference lies in the makeup of the sedimentary rock in Columbia.

9. Instead of the granite found in other emerald-rich countries the predominant substance in Columbia is black shale.

10. Even though these lustrous green gems can now be synthesized a real emerald always contains a trapped bubble of fluid and this minuscule natural imperfection is known in the gem business as a "garden."

Source: Discover, May 1999

Exercise 5

1. If you're ever in Palo Alto California you must visit the Barbie Hall of Fame there.

2. What you'll find are more than fifteen thousand examples of Barbie and all the companions and accessories that have been sold along with her for over forty years.

3. Barbie was born in the late 1950s but she remains ageless at the Barbie Hall of Fame.

4. The Barbie museum's founder and curator is Evelyn Burkhalter and she knows everything about Barbie.

5. She knows that Mattel has sold more than five hundred million Barbies since the doll was introduced.

6. Barbie has served in the army the air force and the marines.

7. She has worked as a doctor a ballerina and an astronaut.

8. She has driven a Volkswagen a Mercedes and a limo.

9. She has figure-skated for Olympic medals has managed a fast-food restaurant and has run her own beauty salon.

10. Evelyn Burkhalter's Barbie collection is worth close to a million dollars and it includes every Barbie product with the exception of half a dozen outfits that have eluded her so far.

Source: America's Strangest Museums (Citadel, 1996)

PROOFREADING EXERCISE

Apply the first three comma rules to the following paragraph.

When Niels Rattenborg studied the brains of mallard ducks he made an interesting discovery. Rattenborg wondered how ducks protected themselves as they slept. The ducks slept in rows and these rows were the secret to their defense. To his surprise Rattenborg found that the two ducks on the ends of the row did something special with the sides of their heads facing away from the row. Instinctively the ducks on the edge kept one eye open and one half of their brains awake as they slept. The rest of the ducks slept with both eyes closed and both sides of their brains inactive. The two guard ducks were able to frame the ducks in the middle watch for danger and sleep almost as soundly as their neighbors.

Source: Discover, May 1999

SENTENCE WRITING

Combine the following sets of sentences in different ways using all of the first three comma rules. You may need to reorder the details and change the phrasing.

I am taking an archery class.

It's more fun than I expected it to be.

I get home from school.

I do my homework.

I eat dinner.

I watch a little television.

I go to sleep.

Grant and Gretchen don't know what to do.

They are getting married.

Grant's last name is Ketchem.

Gretchen doesn't want to be known as Gretchen Ketchem.

She might keep her maiden name instead.

Comma Rules 4, 5, and 6

The next three comma rules all involve using a pair of commas to enclose information that is not needed in a sentence—information that could be taken out of the sentence without affecting its meaning. Two commas are used—one before and one after—to signal unnecessary words, phrases, and clauses.

4. Put commas around the name of a person spoken to.

> Did you know, Danielle, that you left your backpack at the library?

> We regret to inform you, Mr. Davis, that your policy has been canceled.

5. Put commas around expressions that interrupt the flow of the sentence (such as *however, moreover, therefore, of course, by the way, on the other hand, I believe, I think*).

> I know, of course, that I have missed the deadline.

> They will try, however, to use the rest of their time wisely.

> Today's exam, I think, is only a practice test.

Read the preceding sentences aloud, and you'll hear how those expressions interrupt the flow of the sentence. But sometimes such expressions flow smoothly into the sentence and don't need commas around them.

> Of course he checked to see if their plane had been delayed.

> We therefore decided to stay out of it.

> I think you made the right decision.

Remember that when one of the previous words like *however* joins two independent clauses, that word needs a semicolon before it. It may also have a comma after it, especially if there seems to be a pause between the word and the rest of the sentence. (See p. 76.)

> The bus was late; *however,* we still made it to the museum before it closed.

> I am improving my study habits; *furthermore,* I am getting better grades.

> She was interested in journalism; *therefore,* she took a job at a local newspaper.

> I spent hours studying for the test; *finally,* I felt prepared.

Thus words like *however* or *therefore* may be used in three ways:

1. as an interrupter (commas around it)

2. as a word that flows into the sentence (no commas needed)

3. as a connecting word between two independent clauses (semicolon before and often a comma after)

6. Put commas around additional information that is not needed in a sentence.

Such information may be interesting, but the subject and main idea of the sentence would be clear without it. In the following sentence

Maxine Taylor, who organized the fundraiser, will introduce the candidates.

the clause *who organized the fundraiser* is not needed in the sentence. Without it we still know exactly who the sentence is about and what she is going to do: Maxine Taylor will introduce the candidates. Therefore, the additional information is set off from the rest of the sentence by commas to show that it could be left out. But in the following sentence

The woman who organized the fundraiser will introduce the candidates.

The clause *who organized the fundraiser* is needed in the sentence. Without it the sentence would read: The woman will introduce the candidates. We would have no idea which woman. The clause *who organized the fundraiser* couldn't be left out because it tells us which woman. Therefore, commas are not used around it. In this sentence

Hamlet, Shakespeare's famous play, has been made into a movie many times.

the additional information *Shakespeare's famous play* could be left out, and we would still know the main meaning of the sentence: *Hamlet* has been made into a movie many times. Therefore, the commas surround the added material to show that it could be omitted. But in this sentence

Shakespeare's famous play *Hamlet* has been made into a movie many times.

the title of the play is necessary. Without it, the sentence would read: Shakespeare's famous play has been made into a movie many times. We would have no idea which of Shakespeare's famous plays was being discussed. Therefore, the title couldn't be left out, and commas are not used around it.

The trick in deciding whether additional information is necessary is to say, "If I don't need it, I'll put commas around it."

E X E R C I S E S

Add any necessary commas to these sentences according to Comma Rules 4, 5, and 6. Any commas already in the sentences follow Comma Rules 1, 2, and 3. Some sentences may be correct.

Exercise 1

1. This year's Thanksgiving dinner I think was better than last year's.
2. I think this year's Thanksgiving dinner was better than last year's.
3. It was certainly more entertaining this year.
4. Certainly it was more entertaining this year.
5. The guest who brought the apple pie sang karaoke with our mom after dinner.
6. My sister's new boyfriend who brought the apple pie sang karaoke with our mom after dinner.
7. The person responsible for basting the turkey Uncle Ken did a great job; it was moist and delicious.
8. The person who was responsible for basting the turkey did a great job; it was moist and delicious.
9. The gravy however was better last year.
10. However the gravy was better last year.

Exercise 2

1. We trust of course that people who get their driver's licenses know how to drive.
2. Of course we trust that people who get their driver's licenses know how to drive.
3. The people who test drivers for their licenses make the streets safer for all of us.
4. Mr. Kraft who tests drivers for their licenses makes the streets safer for all of us.
5. We may therefore understand when we fail the driving test ourselves.

6. Therefore we may understand when we fail the driving test ourselves.

7. The driver's seat we know is a place of tremendous responsibility.

8. We know that the driver's seat is a place of tremendous responsibility.

9. We believe that no one should take that responsibility lightly.

10. No one we believe should take that responsibility lightly.

Exercise 3

1. The writing teacher Ms. Gonzales has published several of her own short stories.

2. The Ms. Gonzales who teaches writing is not the Ms. Gonzales who teaches history.

3. My daughter's friend Harry doesn't get along with her best friend Jenny.

4. My daughter's best friend Jenny doesn't get along with one of her other friends Harry.

5. The tiger which is a beautiful and powerful animal symbolizes freedom.

6. The tiger that was born in September is already on display at the zoo.

7. The students who helped set up the chairs were allowed to sit in the front row.

8. Kim and Teresa who helped set up the chairs were allowed to sit in the front row.

9. My car which had a tracking device was easy to find when it was stolen.

10. A car that has a tracking device is easier to find if it's stolen.

Exercise 4

1. Frozen "TV" dinners which were first sold by Swanson & Sons in 1954 had only one original variety—turkey on cornbread with sweet potatoes, peas, and gravy.

2. The company sold its original three-part dinner trays for ninety-nine cents a piece.

3. Campbell Soup Company seeing the success of the TV dinner concept bought the Swanson brand in 1955.

4. The need for frozen foods began after women started to hold jobs of their own during WWII, so Swanson offered frozen chicken and frozen meat pies.

5. These women's families who had been used to complete home-cooked meals needed a fast alternative.

6. Clarke Swanson who inherited his father's business brought the TV dinner concept to life.

7. He interviewed women who were shopping at supermarkets and asked them questions about packages and preferences.

8. Clarke Swanson is the one responsible for the eye-catching package that the first TV dinners came in.

9. The front of the package looked like a TV screen surrounded by the image of a wooden TV cabinet complete with knobs and the featured meal on the screen.

10. The frozen TV dinner which was born in the 1950s lives on as a billion-dollar industry today.

Source: Frozen Food Age, Mar. 1994

Exercise 5

1. Zippo lighters the only domestic lighters that can still be refilled are highly useful tools and highly prized collectibles.

2. A Zippo that was made in 1933 and that has the "Patent Pending" mark on it could sell for as much as ten thousand dollars even though it cost less than two dollars when it was made.

3. The value of Zippo lighters is well known in Guthrie, Oklahoma home of the National Lighter Museum.

4. Zippos have always been special to soldiers who often had to rely on the flame from their Zippo to warm food or light a fire.

5. There are even those who claim that a Zippo in their pocket saved their lives by deflecting bullets aimed at them during battle.

6. There have been many special edition Zippos made to celebrate an event the first moon landing, for example.

7. Eric Clapton famed guitarist and songwriter used a clicking Zippo as an instrument in a song he wrote for the movie *Lethal Weapon 2*.

8. George G. Blaisdell the man responsible for distributing, naming, and refining the Zippo as we know it died in the late 1970s, but he cared about his customers.

9. All Zippo lighters come with a lifetime guarantee which covers the lighters' inner workings but not the outer finish.

10. The Zippo Repair Clinic which fixes around a thousand lighters a day refunds any money sent by the customer.

Source: Smithsonian, Dec. 1998

PROOFREADING EXERCISE

Insert the necessary commas into this paragraph according to Comma Rules 4, 5, and 6.

There are many NASA facilities spread throughout the United States. The most well known of the centers in California is the Jet Propulsion Laboratory located in Pasadena home of the annual Tournament of Roses Parade. The parade itself is not a NASA project however. Another of California's facilities is the Ames Research Center where NASA scientists use massive wind tunnels in their research. There are also NASA facilities in Texas, Virginia, Alabama, New York, New Mexico, and Maryland to name a few. The most famous center of all of course has to be the John F. Kennedy Space Center. No doubt everyone has seen the live image of a spacecraft lifting off the launching pad at Cape Canaveral. It is a sight I believe that a person never forgets.

Source: Discover, Apr. 1999

SENTENCE WRITING

Combine the following sets of sentences in different ways using Comma Rules 4, 5, and 6. Try to combine each set in a way that needs commas and in a way that doesn't need commas. You may reorder the details and change the phrasing.

Las Vegas is a city famous for its casinos.

Las Vegas also has lots of little chapels.

Some people choose to get married there.

I think.

She has a black belt in Karate.

My roommate received scholarship money.

Her name is Barbara.

She thought that she had to pay the scholarship money back.

REVIEW OF THE COMMA

SIX COMMA RULES

1. Put a comma before *for, and, nor, but, or, yet, so* when they connect two independent clauses.

2. Put a comma between three or more items in a series.

3. Put a comma after an introductory expression or before an after-thought.

4. Put commas around the name of a person spoken to.

5. Put commas around an interrupter, like *however* or *therefore*.

6. Put commas around unnecessary additional information.

PROOFREADING EXERCISE

Add the missing commas, and identify which one of the six comma rules applies in the brackets at the *end* of each sentence. Each of the six sentences illustrates a different rule.

I'm writing you this reminder Tracy to be sure that you don't forget our plans to visit the zoo this Saturday. [ ] I know we're good friends but lately you have let our plans slip your mind. [ ] When we were supposed to go to the flea market last week you forgot all about it. [ ] I'm taking this opportunity therefore to refresh your memory. [ ] I can't wait to see the polar bears the gorillas the giraffes and the elephants. [ ] And I have made special plans for a behind-the-scenes tour of several of the exhibits by Max Bronson the zoo's public relations officer. [ ] See you Saturday!

SENTENCE WRITING

Write at least one sentence of your own to demonstrate each of the six comma rules.

Quotation Marks and Underlining/*Italics*

Put quotation marks around a direct quotation (the exact words of a speaker) but not around an indirect quotation.

The officer said, "Please show me your driver's license." (a direct quotation)

The officer asked to see my driver's license. (an indirect quotation)

If the speaker says more than one sentence, quotation marks are used before and after the entire speech.

> She said, "One of your brake lights is out. You need to take care of the problem right away."

If the quotation begins the sentence, the words telling who is speaking are set off with a comma unless, of course, a question mark or an exclamation point is needed.

> "I didn't even know it was broken," I said.
>
> "Do you have any questions?" she asked.
>
> "You mean I can go!" I yelled.
>
> "Yes, consider this just a warning," she said.

Each of the preceding quotations begins with a capital letter. But when a quotation is broken, the second part doesn't begin with a capital letter unless it's a new sentence.

> "If you knew how much time I spent on the essay," the student said, "you would give me an A."
>
> "A chef might work on a meal for days," the teacher replied. "That doesn't mean the results will taste good."

Put quotation marks around the titles of short stories, poems, songs, essays, TV program episodes, or other short works.

> I couldn't sleep after I read "The Lottery," a short story by Shirley Jackson.
>
> My favorite Woodie Guthrie song is "This Land Is Your Land."
>
> We had to read George Orwell's essay "A Hanging" for my speech class.
>
> Jerry Seinfeld's troubles in "The Puffy Shirt" episode are some of the funniest moments in TV history.

Underline titles of longer works such as books, newspapers, magazines, plays, record albums or CDs, movies, or the titles of TV or radio series.

> The Color Purple is a novel by Alice Walker.
>
> I read about the latest discovery of dinosaur footprints in Newsweek.
>
> Gone with the Wind was re-released in movie theaters in 1998.
>
> My mother listens to The Writer's Almanac on the radio every morning.

You may choose to *italicize* instead of underlining if your word processor gives you the option. Just be consistent throughout any paper in which you use underlining or italics.

The Color Purple is a novel by Alice Walker.

I read about the latest discovery of dinosaur footprints in *Newsweek*.

Gone with the Wind was re-released in movie theaters in 1998.

My mother listens to *The Writer's Almanac* on the radio every morning.

E X E R C I S E S

Punctuate quotations, and underline or put quotation marks around titles used in the following sentences. Punctuation already within the sentences is correct.

Exercise 1

1. Do you need any help my sister asked.

2. In her book Gift from the Sea, Anne Morrow Lindbergh wrote The beach is not the place to work; to read, write or think. . . . One should lie empty, open, choiceless as a beach—waiting for a gift from the sea.

3. Sir Laurence Olivier had this to say about Shakespeare's most famous work: Hamlet is pound for pound . . . the greatest play ever written.

4. In 1999, singer Weird Al Yankovic released a parody of The Phantom Menace; it was sung to the tune of American Pie.

5. Civility costs nothing and buys everything observed Lady Mary Wortley Montagu (1689–1762).

6. Forrest Gump made many sayings famous, but Life is like a box of chocolates is the most memorable.

7. My teacher wrote Good Work! at the top of my essay.

8. The first time a contestant won a million dollars on the television quiz show Who Wants To Be a Millionaire? was in November 1999.

9. Karen asked Where will you be at noon?

10. My family subscribes to Newsweek, and we all enjoy reading it.

Exercise 2

1. We are reading the book Dibs in Search of Self in my English class.

2. I can't decide whether to call my narration essay A Day at the Beach or The Day I Made Waves.

3. I love to watch Nova, a series of nature programs on public television.

4. My favorite program in the series so far has been The Life of Birds.

5. There is nothing either good or bad but thinking makes it so, Hamlet says to Rosencrantz and Guildenstern.

6. Daddy is a famous poem by Sylvia Plath.

7. Plath also wrote a children's book called The It-Doesn't-Matter Suit.

8. Martha Stewart publishes her own magazine called Martha Stewart Living.

9. I've heard the expression Living well is the best revenge.

10. Indira Ghandi said You cannot shake hands with a clenched fist.

Exercise 3

1. In his play The Cherry Orchard, physician and playwright Anton Chekhov wrote When a lot of remedies are suggested for a disease, that means it can't be cured.

2. George Orwell, author of Animal Farm and 1984, felt that At 50, everyone has the face he deserves.

3. On the power of clear writing, Orwell said Good prose is like a window pane.

4. The assignment for Tuesday is to read the essay What Is Poverty?

5. I have read Kate Chopin's novel The Awakening and her short stories The Story of an Hour and The Storm.

6. Letters to the editor of the New York Times are good sources for research papers; I'm using one titled Time for Irradiation and another that shows the opposing view, Food Irradiation Holds Too Many Risks.

7. The title of my essay will be Pass the Ketchup: The Two Sides of the Food Irradiation Controversy.

8. The cruelest lies said Robert Louis Stevenson are often told in silence.

9. What color they all asked is your new car?

10. Sir Laurence Olivier felt this way about playing the part of Hamlet Once you have played it, it will devour and obsess you for the rest of your life. It has me. I think each day about it.

Exercise 4

1. George Sterling described San Francisco as the cool, grey city of love.

2. One of the most famous actresses of the early twentieth century was Mary Pickford; movie producer Samuel Goldwyn had this to say about working with her It took longer to make Mary's contracts than it did her pictures.

3. Goldwyn himself was no easier to get along with He would not acknowledge rejection according to one biographer He could not be insulted. He could not be deterred. He could not be withstood.

4. When someone suggested that Walt Disney run for mayor of Los Angeles following the success of Disneyland, Disney declined, saying I'm already king.

5. Disney knew what it meant to succeed; having dropped out of high school and having moved to Los Angeles with less than fifty dollars in his pocket, he empathized with Mickey Mouse, a character he described as a little fellow doing the best he could.

6. Mark Twain said of California It's a great place to live, but I wouldn't want to visit there.

7. There is a French expression *L'amour est aveugle; l'amitié ferme les yeux*, which translates as follows Love is blind; friendship closes its eyes.

8. Let's keep our voices down the librarian said as we left the study room.

9. Box-Car Bertha, renowned woman of the rails, suggested that Nobody can hurt you but yourself. Every experience you have makes you all the more fit for life.

10. Pain is inevitable said M. Kathleen Casey Suffering is optional.

Exercise 5

1. P. L. Travers wrote the book Mary Poppins about a magical English nanny who defies the laws of physics and alters the lives of everyone she meets.

2. Asked about the character of Mary Poppins, Travers said I never for one moment believed that I invented her. Perhaps she invented me.

3. Travers believed that A writer is only half a book—the reader is the other half.

4. Travers never felt comfortable in the spotlight following the success of Mary Poppins. I never talk about personal matters she said only ideas.

5. And Travers had firm ideas about the audience for her stories [T]hey were never in the first place written for children, but for everybody—or maybe to ease my own heart.

6. When Mary Poppins was made into a movie that differed in many ways from the book, Travers felt extremely uneasy.

7. The characters are entrusted to you Travers responded I don't want it ever to be possible that somebody could take [Mary Poppins] and write a story about her that wasn't mine.

8. Travers also found it difficult to convey to Mary Shepard, the illustrator of the original Mary Poppins books, just exactly how Mary Poppins should look.

9. Finally Travers explained I went out and found a little Dutch doll and showed it to her. But even then there were disagreements.

10. In an essay titled Lively Oracles, which Travers wrote for the journal

Parabola, she shared her thoughts about time Where the center holds and the end folds into the beginning there is no such word as farewell.

Source: The Horn Book Magazine, Sept./Oct. 1996

PROOFREADING EXERCISE

Punctuate quotations, and underline or put quotation marks around titles used in the following paragraph.

I've been reading the book How Children Fail by John Holt. I checked it out to use in a research paper I'm doing on education in America. Holt's book was published in the early 1960s, but his experiences and advice are still relevant today. In one of his chapters, Fear and Failure, Holt describes intelligent children this way Intelligent children act as if they thought the universe made some sense. They check their answers and their thoughts against common sense, while other children, not expecting answers to make sense, not knowing what is sense, see no point in checking, no way of checking. Holt and others stress the child's self-confidence as one key to success.

SENTENCE WRITING

Write ten sentences that list and discuss your favorite songs, TV shows, characters' expressions, movies, books, and so on. Be sure to punctuate titles and quotations correctly. Refer to the rules at the beginning of this section if necessary.

Capital Letters

CAPITALIZE

1. The first word of every sentence.

Peaches taste best when they are cold.

2. The first word of every direct quotation.

She said, "I've never worked so hard before."

"I have finished most of my homework," she said, "but I still have a lot to do." (The *but* is not capitalized because it does not begin a new sentence.)

"I love my speech class," she said. "Maybe I'll change my major." (*Maybe* is capitalized because it begins a new sentence.)

3. The first, last, and every important word in a title. Don't capitalize prepositions (such as *in, of, at, with*), short connecting words, the *to* in front of a verb, or *a, an,* or *the.*

I saw a copy of Darwin's *The Origin of Species* at a yard sale.

The class enjoyed the essay "How to Write a Rotten Poem with Almost No Effort."

Shakespeare in Love is a comedy based on Shakespeare's writing of the play *Romeo and Juliet.*

4. Specific names of people, places, languages, races, and nationalities.

Rev. Jesse Jackson	China	Caesar Chavez
Ireland	Spanish	Japanese
Ryan White	Philadelphia	Main Street

5. Names of months, days of the week, and special days, but not the seasons.

March	Fourth of July	spring
Tuesday	Easter	winter
Valentine's Day	Labor Day	fall

6. A title of relationship if it takes the place of the person's name. If *my* (or *your, her, his, our, their*) is in front of the word, a capital is not used.

I think Dad wrote to her.   *but*   I think my dad wrote to her.

She visited Aunt Sophie.   *but*   She visited her aunt.

We spoke with Grandpa.   *but*   We spoke with our grandpa.

7. Names of particular people or things, but not general terms.

I admire Professor Walters.   *but*   I admire my professor.

We saw the famous Potomac River. *but*   We saw the famous river.

Are you from the South?   *but*   Is your house south of the
                                            mountains?

I will take Philosophy 4 and   *but*   I will take philosophy and
English 100.   English.

She graduated from Sutter High   *but*   She graduated from high school.
School.

They live at 119 Forest St.   *but*   They live on a beautiful street.

We enjoyed the Monterey Bay   *but*   We enjoyed the aquarium.
Aquarium.

E X E R C I S E S

Add all of the necessary capital letters to the sentences that follow.

Exercise 1

1. i have always wanted to learn another language besides english.

2. right now i am taking english 410 in addition to my writing class.

3. the course title for english 410 is Basic Grammar.

4. english 410 is a one-unit, short-term class designed to help students with their verb forms, parts of speech, phrases, and clauses.

5. i hope that learning more about english grammar will help me understand the grammar of another language more easily.

6. now i must decide whether i want to take spanish, french, italian, or chinese.

7. i guess i could even take a class in greek or russian.

8. when i was in high school, i did take french for two years, but my clearest memory is of the teacher, mrs. gautier.

9. she was one of the best teachers that hillside high school ever had.

10. unfortunately, i did not study hard enough and can't remember most of the french that she taught me.

Exercise 2

1. sir laurence olivier was one of the most famous british actors of the twentieth century.

2. he was well known for playing the leading roles in shakespeare's plays.

3. he performed in london, on such stages as the old vic theatre and st. james's theatre, and for several years, he was director of the national theatre.

4. of course, olivier also played to audiences in cities around the world, such as new york, los angeles, moscow, and berlin.

5. among olivier's most celebrated roles were henry V, othello, richard III, and king lear.

6. though we can no longer see him on stage, we can still watch the film versions of his classic performances.

7. olivier also directed many plays and some of his own films.

8. he directed the 1948 black-and-white film version of <u>hamlet</u> and received the academy award for best actor for his performance in the title role.

9. one of olivier's most treasured memories was of a single live performance of <u>hamlet</u> in elsinore, denmark; it was scheduled to have been played outside but had to be moved inside at the last minute, causing all the actors to be especially brilliant under pressure.

10. american audiences might remember sir laurence olivier best for his portrayal of the tempestuous heathcliff in the movie <u>wuthering heights</u>, but he was a shakespearean actor at heart.

Source: Laurence Olivier on Acting (Simon, 1986)

Exercise 3

1. my mom and dad love old movie musicals.

2. that makes it easy to shop for them at christmas and other gift-giving occasions.

3. for mom's birthday last year, i gave her the video of gilbert and sullivan's comic opera <u>the pirates of penzance</u>.

4. it isn't even that old; it has kevin kline in it as the character called the pirate king.

5. i watched the movie with her, and i enjoyed the story of a band of pirates who are too nice for their own good.

6. actually, it is funnier than i thought it would be, and kevin kline sings and dances really well!

7. dad likes musicals, too, and i bought him tickets to see the revival of <u>chicago</u> on stage a few years ago.

8. he loves all those big production numbers and the bob fosse choreography.

9. there aren't many musicals made these days, but my folks did say that they would like a copy of the 1997 movie <u>evita</u>, starring madonna.

10. <u>evita</u> is the andrew lloyd webber musical about the first lady of argentina, eva peron.

Exercise 4

1. jodie foster was born as alicia christian foster on november 19, 1962.

2. jodie was raised by her mother, brandy, who worked for a film producer in hollywood.

3. at the age of three, jodie accompanied her older brother buddy to an audition and got her first job acting in a tv commercial.

4. she was the little girl with a dog nipping at her swimsuit in the coppertone tanning lotion commercials.

5. there were other tv ads before jodie acted in tv shows such as <u>the partridge family</u>, <u>gunsmoke</u>, and <u>the courtship of eddie's father</u>.

6. as a movie actress, jodie foster's credits include the following films: <u>taxi driver</u>, <u>bugsy malone</u>, <u>the accused</u>, and—of course—<u>silence of the lambs</u>.

7. she has won two best actress academy awards, which she keeps by her bathtub.

8. foster attended yale university in the early 1980s, earning a degree in literature.

9. in the late 1990s, yale awarded foster an honorary phd in fine arts, and she was nominated for a golden globe award for her role as an astronomer in the movie <u>contact</u>.

10. jodie foster became a mother in 1998; she had a boy and named him charles.

Source: Biography Magazine, Oct. 1998

Exercise 5

1. in 1999, new york's american museum of natural history featured an extremely popular exhibit.

2. the title of the exhibit was "*the endurance:* shackleton's legendary antarctic expedition."

3. *the endurance* was a british ship that set sail for antarctica in 1914.

4. ernest shackleton was the ship's captain, and frank hurley was the photographer shackleton took along to document the expedition's success.

5. shackleton and his crew were attempting to be the first to cross antarctica on foot and to claim this accomplishment for britain.

6. having nearly reached its landing site, *the endurance* got stuck in the ice, and the crew lived on the ice-bound ship for nearly a year before it was crushed by the ice and sunk.

7. the crew escaped the sinking ship but were forced to live on the ice and eventually to travel to an uninhabited island.

8. realizing that they could not survive much longer on their supplies, shackleton took five men with him in a lifeboat named *the james caird* and covered eight hundred miles before they reached another ship.

9. shackleton made it back to rescue the crew members he left behind, and all of them returned home safely.

10. the new york exhibit's displays, which included *the james caird* itself and frank hurley's pictures, brought the voyage of *the endurance* and the heroic efforts of shackleton and his crew to life for all of the visitors who saw them.

Source: U. S. News & World Report, 31 May 1999

REVIEW OF PUNCTUATION AND CAPITAL LETTERS

Punctuate these sentences. They include all the rules for punctuation and capitalization you have learned. Compare your answers carefully with those at the back of the book. Sentences may require several pieces of punctuation or capital letters.

1. The golden gate bridge is a famous landmark in the city of san francisco

2. Have you ever seen woody allens early films such as bananas or take the money and run

3. Theyve remodeled their house and now theyre ready to sell it

4. How much will the final exam affect our grades the nervous student asked

5. We have reviewed your policy mr martin and will be sending you a refund soon

6. The two students who earn the most points for their speeches will face each other in a debate

7. Ms thomas the new english 4b teacher recently received a national poetry award

8. Even though I enjoy my french class I believe should have taken spanish first

9. You always remember valentines day and our anniversary but you forget my birthday

10. The most memorable saying from the original toy story movie is when buzz lightyear exclaims to infinity and beyond

11. My sister subscribes to architectural digest magazine and my whole family loves to look through it when shes finished reading it

12. Finding low air fares takes time patience and luck

13. My friend is reading the novel thousand pieces of gold in her english class

14. I wonder how much my art history textbook will cost

15. Bill gates founder of microsoft is one of the richest people in the world

COMPREHENSIVE TEST

In these sentences you'll find all the errors that have been discussed in the entire text. Try to name the error in the blank before each sentence, and then correct the error if you can. You may find any of these errors:

awk	awkward phrasing
apos	apostrophe
c	comma needed
cap	capitalization
cliché	overused expression
cs	comma splice
dm	dangling modifier
frag	fragment
mm	misplaced modifier
p	punctuation
pro	incorrect pronoun
pro agr	pronoun agreement
pro ref	pronoun reference
ro	run-on sentence
shift	shift in time or person
sp	misspelled word
s/v agr	subject/verb agreement
wordy	wordiness
ww	wrong word
//	not parallel

A perfect—or almost perfect—score will mean you've mastered the first part of the text.

1. _____ She asked her sister if she could go to the store.

2. _____ Instructors break their classes up into groups when they wanted the students to learn on their own.

3. _____ I wonder if the real estate agent has called yet?

4. _____ A mans' overcoat lay on the back of the bus stop near my house until someone finally took it away.

5. _____ The teacher's lecture had an affect on all of us.

6. _____ We don't know which of the events occured first.

7. _____ There are several problems with the parking situation in the campus lots.

8. _____ My favorite high school teacher moved to arizona when she retired.

9. _____ The school awarded scholarships to my roommate and I, and we're both so happy.

10. _____ Cranberries can be harvested dry or another way is to gather them wet off the top of flooded bogs.

11. _____ The dishes need to be done and the trash needs to be taken out before you leave the cabin.

12. _____ Children can learn about dinosaurs going to museums.

13. _____ Since the room required a deposit but my check had not arrived.

14. _____ I haven't finished my term paper, the library has been closed for the long weekend.

15. _____ Each of the branches are covered with lights.

16. _____ After a long vacation, our house didn't seem as small as it did when we left.

17. _____ The hills were steeper than we thought none of us had worn the right shoes.

18. _____ From time to time, I get in the habit of eating too much junk food.

19. _____ I returned the book back to the library; it had been overdue for a long time.

20. _____ Everyone in town turned their porch lights on in support of the proposition.

P A R T   4

Writing

Aside from the basics of spelling, sentence structure, and punctuation, what else do you need to understand to write better? Just as sentences are built according to accepted patterns, so are other "structures" of English—paragraphs and essays for example.

Think of writing as including levels of structure, beginning small with words connecting to form phrases, clauses, sentences—and then sentences connecting to form paragraphs and essays. Each level has its own set of "blueprints." Words must be spelled correctly. A sentence needs a subject, a verb, and a complete thought. Paragraphs must be indented and should contain a main idea and valid support. And an essay should explore a topic in several paragraphs, usually including an introduction, body, and conclusion. These consistent structures comfort beginning writers as patterns that they can learn to use themselves.

Not everyone approaches writing as structure, however. One can write better without thinking about structure at all. A good place to start might be to write what you care about and care about what you write. You can make an amazing amount of progress by simply being genuine, being who you are naturally. No one has to tell you to be yourself when you speak, but beginning writers often need encouragement to be themselves in their writing.

Writing is almost never done without a reason. The reason may come from an experience, such as fighting an unfair parking ticket, or from a requirement in a class. And when you are asked to write, you often receive guidance in the form of an assignment: tell a story to prove a point, paint a picture with your words, summarize an article, compare two subjects, share what you know about something, explain why you agree with or disagree with an idea.

Learning to write well is important, one of the most important things you will do in your education. Confidence is the key. The writing sections will help you build confidence, whether you are expressing your own ideas or summarizing and responding to the ideas of others. Like the sentence structure sections, the writing sections are best taken in order. However, each one discusses an aspect of writing that can be reviewed on its own at any time.

What Is the Least You Should Know about Writing?

"Unlike medicine or the other sciences," William Zinsser points out, "writing has no new discoveries to spring on us. We're in no danger of reading in our morning newspaper that a breakthrough has been made in how to write [clearly]. . . . We may be given new technologies like the word processor to ease the burdens of composition, but on the whole we know what we need to know."

One thing we know is that we learn to write by *writing*—not by reading long discussions about writing. Therefore the explanations and instructions is this section are as brief as they can be, followed by samples from student and professional writers.

Understanding the basic structures and learning the essential skills covered in this section will help you become a better writer.

BASIC STRUCTURES	WRITING SKILLS
I. The Paragraph	**III.** Writing in Your Own Voice
II. The Essay	**IV.** Finding a Topic
	V. Organizing Ideas
	VI. Supporting with Details
	VII. Revising Your Papers
	VIII. Presenting Your Work
	IX. Writing about What You Read

Basic Structures

I. THE PARAGRAPH

A paragraph is unlike any other structure in English. Visually, it has its own profile: the first line is indented about five spaces, and sentences continue to fill the space between both margins until the paragraph ends (which may be in the middle of the line):

_____

_____

_____

_____

_____

_____ .

Beginning writers often forget to indent their paragraphs, or they break off in the middle of a line within a paragraph, especially when writing in class. You must remember to indent whenever you begin a new paragraph and fill the space between the margins until it ends. (Note: In business writing, paragraphs are not indented but double-spaced in between.)

Defining a Paragraph

A typical paragraph centers on one idea, usually phrased in a topic sentence from which all the other sentences in the paragraph radiate. The topic sentence does not need to begin the paragraph, but it most often does, and the other sentences support it with specific details. (For more on topic sentences and organizing paragraphs, see p. 217.) Paragraphs usually contain several sentences, though no set number is required. A paragraph can stand alone, but more commonly paragraphs are part of a larger composition, such as an essay. There are different kinds of paragraphs, based on the jobs they are supposed to do.

Types of Paragraphs

SAMPLE PARAGRAPHS IN AN ESSAY

Introductory paragraphs begin essays. They provide background information about the essay's topic and usually include the thesis statement or main idea of the essay. (See p. 215 for information on how to write a thesis statement.) Here is the introductory paragraph of a student essay entitled "Really Understanding":

> I was so excited when my parents told me that I could join them in America. Four years earlier, they left China to open a Chinese fast food restaurant in Los Angeles. After my parents asked me to help them in the restaurant, I started to worry about my English because I knew only a few words that I learned in China. They told me not to worry, that I would quickly grasp the language once I heard it every day. Soon after I joined them, I made a big mistake because of my lack of English skills and my conceit. From this experience, I learned the importance of really understanding.

In this opening paragraph, the student leads up to the main idea—"the importance of really understanding"—with background information about her family's restaurant and "a big mistake" that she made.

Body paragraphs are those in the middle of essays. Each body paragraph contains a topic sentence and presents detailed information about one subtopic or idea that relates directly to the essay's thesis. (See p. 217 for more information on organizing body paragraphs.) Here are the body paragraphs of the same essay:

> My mistake happened during my second week at the restaurant. Usually my mom and I stayed in front, dishing out the food and keeping the tables

clean, and my father cooked in the kitchen. If I needed any help or if some-one asked a question in English, my mom took care of it. However, that day my mom was sick, so she stayed home. My father and I went to work. He went straight to the kitchen, and I wiped those six square tables. By noon, my father had put big steaming trays of food on the counter. There was orange chicken, chicken with mushrooms, sweet and sour pork, kong bao chicken, and B.B.Q. pork. People came in, ordering their favorite foods.

After I took care of the lunch rush, it was 2:00, but my favorite customer had not arrived. He was an old, kind, educated man who came in almost every day at 12:00. Why hadn't he come for the last two days? Was he sick? I looked at his favorite dish and started to worry about him. As I was wondering, he walked through the door. I smiled to see him. He ordered "the usual"— chicken with mushrooms and steamed rice—and sat down at the table in the left corner. I wanted to ask him why he came late to show that I cared about him, but more customers came in, and I had to serve them. They ordered all the chicken with mushrooms left in the tray, so I called to my father to cook more. The old man finished his food and walked toward me. He looked at that tray of newly cooked chicken with mushrooms for a second, and then he asked me something. I only understood the word *yesterday*. Since he had not been in yesterday, I guessed that he said "Were you open yesterday?" I quickly answered, "Oh, yes!" He looked at me, and I could see that he didn't believe my answer, so I said "Yes" again. He just turned and walked away.

I did not understand what had happened. Two days passed, and he did not return. I thought about what he could have asked me and stared at the chicken and mushrooms for a minute. Suddenly, I realized what must have happened. He had come in two hours later than usual, at 2:00 that day, but the dish had been cooked at 12:00. Fast food cooked two hours earlier would not taste as fresh as if it were just prepared. He must have asked me "Was this *cooked* yesterday?" How could I have answered "Yes" not once but twice? He must have felt so bad about us. "He will never come back," I told myself.

Notice that each of the three body paragraphs discusses a single stage of the experience that taught her the value of really understanding.

Concluding paragraphs are the final paragraphs in essays. They bring the discussion to a close and share the writer's final thoughts on the subject. (See p. 229 for more about concluding paragraphs.) Here is the conclusion of the sample essay:

Four years have passed since then, and my favorite customer has not come back. It still bothers me. Why didn't I ask him to say the question again? If I had not been so conceited, I would have risked looking foolish for a moment. Now I am so repentant. I will never answer a question or do any-thing before I really understand what it means.

In this concluding paragraph, the student describes the effects of her experience—the regret and the lesson she learned.

SAMPLE OF A PARAGRAPH ALONE

Single-paragraph writing assignments may be given in class or as homework. They test the beginning writer's understanding of the unique structure of a paragraph. They may ask the writer to answer a single question, perhaps following a reading, or to provide details about a limited topic. Look at this student paragraph, the result of a homework assignment asking students to report on a technological development in the news:

> I just read that scientists are trying to breed or clone an extinct animal, just the way they did in the movie *Jurassic Park*. Only this is real. A group of Japanese biologists have the idea of bringing the woolly mammoth back to life. The woolly mammoth was an elephant-like beast with huge tusks and long hair. It stood about fourteen feet high. Now thousands of years after the last mammoth walked the earth, reproductive science might allow frozen mammoth remains to be used to generate a new woolly mammoth. I think that if the scientists are doing it to be able to save current animals from becoming extinct, then it's worthwhile. But if they are just doing it to say they can, I think they should watch *Jurassic Park* again.
>
> *Source: Discover*, Apr. 1999

These shorter writing assignments help students practice presenting information within the limited structure of a paragraph.

The assignments in the upcoming Writing Skills section will sometimes ask you to write paragraphs. Remember that you may review the previous pages as often as you wish until you understand the unique structure of the paragraph.

II. THE ESSAY

Like the paragraph, an essay has its own profile, usually including a title and several paragraphs.

Title

_____

_____
_____
_____
_____ .

_____
_____

_____
_____
_____ .
_____
_____
_____
_____
_____
_____
_____
_____
_____ .
_____
_____
_____
_____
_____
_____
_____
_____ .
_____
_____
_____
_____
_____
_____ .

While the paragraph is the single building block of text used in almost all forms of writing (letters, novels, newspaper stories, and so on), an essay is a more complex structure.

The Five-Paragraph Essay and Beyond

On pp. 201–202 you read a five-paragraph student essay illustrating the different kinds of paragraphs within essays. Many people like to include five paragraphs in an essay: an introductory paragraph, three body paragraphs, and a concluding paragraph. Three is a comfortable number of body paragraphs—it is not two, which makes an essay seem like a comparison even when it isn't; and it is not four, which may be too many subtopics for the beginning writer to organize clearly.

However, as writers become more comfortable with the flow of their ideas and gain confidence in their ability to express themselves, they are free to create essays of many different shapes and sizes. As in all things, learning about writing begins with structure and then expands to include all possibilities.

Defining an Essay

There is no such thing as a typical essay. Essays may be serious or humorous, but the best of them are thought-provoking and—of course—informative. Try looking up the word *essay* in a dictionary right now. Some words used to define what an essay is might need to be explained themselves:

An essay is *prose* (meaning it is written in the ordinary language of sentences and paragraphs).

An essay is *nonfiction* (meaning it deals with real people, factual information, actual opinions and events).

An essay is a *composition* (meaning it is created in parts that make up the whole, several paragraphs that explore a single topic).

An essay is *personal* (meaning it shares the writer's unique perspective, even if only in the choice of topic, method of analysis, and details).

An essay is *analytical* and *instructive* (meaning it examines the workings of a subject and shares the results with the reader).

A Sample Essay

For an example of a piece of writing that fits the previous definition, read the following essay about a museum devoted to the Salem witch trials (from the book *America's Strangest Museums*, by Sandra Gurvis).

The Salem Witch Museum

On the surface, Salem, Massachusetts, seems like an ordinary little town, replete with shopping malls, frozen yogurt shops, and fancy restaurants. But look a little closer and, along with historic homes, a quaint commons, and other points of interest befitting one of America's oldest settlements, you'll find symbols of witches on everything from street signs to T-shirts. For a real spook-out, among other sights, there's the Salem Witch Museum.

Housed in an eerie stone church in historic Washington Square, the museum offers a half-hour multisensory presentation with (appropriately) thirteen diorama stage settings. Each scene is lit up and narrated in the three-story nave, or center, of the church. "Along with depicting the full course and aftermath of the Salem witch trials, we try to provide an idea of what life was like in 1692," explains Patty MacLeod. There's a circle with the names of the executed in the nave; informational signs are scattered throughout. . . .

What exactly happened in the town of Salem over three hundred years ago? The apparently simple facts belie the complexity of events: More than two hundred people were accused of witchcraft, and of the twenty-three convicted, nineteen were hanged. Those who "confessed" were spared, while others who maintained their innocence went to their deaths. According to legend, two dogs were also hanged on Gallows Hill as witches (apparently they didn't confess either). . . .

"What many people today don't understand was that in the 1600s, everyone was very superstitious, believing in magic and the devil," MacLeod continues. . . . Eventually cooler heads prevailed, and by the early 1700s legal procedures against witches were declared unlawful by the governor of Massachusetts. But thanks to the Salem Witch Museum and others, it looks like "witchcraft" has settled in for a spell.

Now that you have learned more about the basic structures of the paragraph and the essay, you are ready to practice the skills necessary to write them.

Writing Skills

III. WRITING IN YOUR OWN VOICE

All writing "speaks" on paper, and the person "listening" is the reader. Some beginning writers forget that writing and reading are two-way methods of communication, just like spoken conversations between two people. When you write, your reader listens; when you read, you also listen.

When speaking, you express a personality in your choice of phrases, your movements, your tone of voice. Family and friends probably recognize your voice messages on their answering machines without your having to identify yourself. Would they also be able to recognize your writing? They would if you extended your "voice" into your writing.

Writing should not sound like talking, necessarily, but it should have a "personality" that comes from the way you decide to approach a topic, to develop it with details, to say it your way.

The beginning of this book discusses the difference between spoken English (following looser patterns of speaking) and Standard Written English (following accepted patterns of writing). Don't think that the only way to add "voice" to your writing is to use the patterns of spoken English. Remember that Standard Written English does not have to be dull or sound "academic." Look at this example of Standard

Written English that has a distinct voice, part of the book *You Can't Show Kids in Underwear and Other Little-Known Facts about Television,* by Barbara Seuling:

> When you think about it, it's kind of a miracle. You turn [it on], and within seconds you have another part of the world in your living room, talking, moving, and alive.
>
> This miracle-in-a-box, called television, happened about [seventy-five] years ago . . . and in that short time, it has grown into the most influential means of communication the world has ever known.
>
> Television has changed our behavior, saved lives, taught us, been companion to the lonely, and entertained and informed vast masses of people. It has shown us the moon, close up, and brought Olympic stadiums into our homes. It has made us witnesses to murder, and let us share rare moments with the great people of the world. It has recorded the extraordinary happenings of our time as history has never been recorded before. The possibilities of the tube seem endless.

Seuling's exerpt illustrates Standard Written English at its best—from its solid sentence structures to its precise use of words. But more important, Seuling's clear voice speaks to us and involves us in her world, in her amazement at the power of television. Students can involve us in their writing too, when they let their own voices through. Writing does not need to be about something personal to have a voice. Here is an example of a student writing about computer hackers:

> Some mischievous hackers are only out to play a joke. One of the first examples was a group who created the famous "Cookie Monster" program at Massachusetts Institute of Technology. Several hackers programmed MIT's computer to display the word "cookie" all over the screens of its users. In order for users to clear this problem, they had to "feed" the Cookie Monster by entering the word "cookie" or lose all the data on their screens.

Notice that both the professional and the student writer tell stories (narration) and paint pictures (description) in the sample paragraphs. Narration and description require practice, but once you master them, you will gain a stronger voice and will be able to add interest and clarity to even the most challenging academic writing assignments.

Narration

Narrative writing tells the reader a story, and since most of us like to tell stories, it is a good place to begin writing in your own voice. An effective narration allows readers to experience an event with the writer. Since we all see the world differently and feel unique emotions, the purpose of narration is to take readers with us through an experience. As a result, the writer gains a better understanding of what happened, and readers get to live other lives momentarily. Listen to the "voice" of this student writer telling the story of a humorous lesson he learned in his childhood:

A Sticky Situation

About thirty-two years ago when I was only six, my sister Renee—who was older and wiser—gave me some advice. She told me to chew gum all day and keep it in my mouth all night. That way, she said, I would never have to brush my teeth again. Of course, I listened to her. From then on, day and night, I had a wad of gum in my mouth. Bubble gum was my favorite, and as the flavor of each piece faded, I unwrapped a fresh pink rectangle of Bazooka and added it to the chunk already in my mouth. Looking back, I should have noticed that Renee didn't follow her own advice, and I should have realized that she was tricking me.

A few days into my new round-the-clock gum routine, I awoke with a pain on my head, not in my head but *on* my head. I got out of bed and went to the mirror. Back in those days, we boys had either a Beatlemania hairdo or a big goofy Afro. I had the typical Beatlemania hairdo, with one added feature—a shapeless clump of Bazooka plastered to the front of it.

Discovering the clump was just the start of my troubles. Getting it out was worse. My mom pulled and yanked and tweezed at every piece of hair with gum on it. But I had a better idea. After my mom had given up, I went to the bathroom and got the scissors. I still remember my six-year-old face in the mirror looking up cross-eyed to get every last bit of gum stuck to my hair. When I was finished, it looked as if a beaver had taken a bite out of my bangs.

The reason that I remember an event that happened so long ago is that the next day was "Picture Day" at school. And for over thirty years my family has kept the results in a frame on the piano. It shows me, a smiling six-year-old, missing two front teeth and wearing a bowl-shaped haircut with a perfect square cut out of the front. The missing teeth and the missing hair matched up perfectly. It's always been Renee's favorite picture of me.

I can't say that I learned just one lesson from this experience; I think I learned two. One is never to listen to your older brother or sister, especially your sister. The other lesson was never, never cut your own hair.

Description

Descriptive writing paints word pictures with details that appeal to the reader's five senses—sight, sound, touch, taste, and smell. The writer of description often uses comparisons to help readers picture one thing by imagining something else, just as the writer of "A Sticky Situation" compares the shape of his missing hair to a beaver bite. In the following paragraph, a student uses vivid details to bring the place she loves best to life:

> Fort Baker is located across the bay from San Francisco, almost under the Golden Gate Bridge. When I lived there as a child, nature was all I saw. Deer came onto our porch and nibbled the plants; raccoons dumped the trash cans over; skunks sprayed my brother because he poked them with a stick, and little field mice jumped out of the bread drawer at my sister when she opened it. Behind the house was a small forest of strong green trees; the dirt actually felt soft, and tall grassy plants with bright yellow flowers grew all around. I don't know the plants' real name, but my friend and I called it "sour grass." When we chewed the stems, we got a mouth full of sour juice that made our faces crinkle and our eyes water.

Here is another example, an essay by Roy Sorrels. In it he describes the process of gathering a special collection that he literally stumbled upon as he walked the streets of New York City. As we read Sorrels' piece, we can visualize his card collection glued to the wall and hear the "monte man" (sidewalk card gambler) and his rhyming expressions to attract customers.

Crazy? No, Just One Card Shy of a Full Deck

The first cards in my collection came from a three-card monte man on 14th Street in Lower Manhattan. Queen of hearts, queen of spades and queen of clubs. "Follow the red, follow the black," he chanted. "Find the red, Fred, you make some bread, Fred—choose the black, Jack, can't give no money back!" A lookout cried, "Cop!" and the man hurriedly pocketed the cash, kicked over his cardboard boxes and ran off. He left behind the three cards. I palmed them into my pocket.

It was the beginning of my yearlong hunt for one full deck of found playing cards. I created the rules. I had to find the cards on the sidewalks or streets of the city of New York, any borough. I could take no more than three cards at a time.

I loved my game. I brought my cards home and began to glue them together in a fan-shaped mandala on the wall over my desk. At first my friends were amused at me, on my hands and knees on sidewalks and streets at all hours, picking up cards. I asked around and nobody knew anybody who'd ever collected a deck of cards from the streets of New York. I had become what every New Yorker secretly longs to be, a harmless, amusing eccentric.

But then my friends began to be annoyed. They asked why I was doing this, exactly. At first, I scrambled for an answer, but the truth was I didn't know. . . .

I want to spend at least part of my time doing things that don't make sense. Perhaps it's my way of rebelling against a world in which everything must be useful. I need in my life something mysterious that can't easily be explained.

Finally, after a full year, I had all but the three of clubs. I continued to find cards, plenty of them, but weeks passed and still no three of clubs. I became melancholy, desperate. I needed the three of clubs. The city was holding out on me; fate was toying with me.

Then one day I was back on 14th Street. The same three-card monte man was juking and jiving. "Follow the red, not the black . . . find the red, Fred, you make some bread, Fred." I stopped 20 feet away from him and yelled "Cop!" He kicked over the boxes and ran.

The three cards fell on the sidewalk, facedown. I walked to where they lay. Spades you lose, hearts, you lose, but my man, my man, you got to choose. On my hands and knees, I turned over the cards.

Everyone ignored me, just another guy kneeling on a New York sidewalk, crying and kissing, for his own sweet reasons, the three of clubs.

Source: Reprinted with permission of the author. Originally appeared in *Smithsonian* (Apr. 1999).

You may have noticed that all of the examples in this section use both narration and description. In fact, most effective writing—even a good resume or biology lab report—calls for clear storytelling and the creation of vivid word pictures for the reader.

Writing Assignments

The following two assignments will help you develop your voice as a writer. For now, don't worry about topic sentences or thesis statements or any of the things we'll consider later. Narration and description have their own logical structures. A story has a beginning, a middle, and an end. And we describe things from top to bottom, side to side, and so on.

Assignment 1

NARRATION: FAMOUS SAYINGS

The following is a list of well-known expressions. No doubt you have had an experience that proves at least one of these to be true. Write a short essay that tells a story from your own life that relates to one of these sayings. (See if you can tell which of the sayings fits the experience narrated in the student essay "A Sticky Situation" on p. 208.) You might want to identify the expression you have chosen in your introductory paragraph. Then tell the beginning, middle, and end of the story. Be sure to use vivid details to bring the story to life. Finish with a brief concluding paragraph in which you share your final thoughts on the experience.

The grass is always greener on the other side of the fence.

Absence makes the heart grow fonder.

Practice makes perfect.

A picture is worth a thousand words.

Success is the best revenge.

When you have your health, you have everything.

Assignment 2

DESCRIPTION: A VALUABLE OBJECT

Describe an object that means a lot to you. It could be a gift that you received, an object you purchased for yourself, an heirloom in your family, or a memento from your childhood. Your goal is to make the reader visualize the object. Try to use details and comparisons that appeal to the reader's senses in some way. Look back at the examples for inspiration. Be sure the reader knows—from your choice of details—what the object means to you.

IV. Finding a Topic

You will most often be given a topic to write about, perhaps based on a reading assignment. However, when the assignment of a paper calls for you to choose your own topic without any further assistance, try to go immediately to your interests.

Look to Your Interests

If the topic of your paper is something you know about and—more important—something you *care* about, then the whole process of writing will be smoother and more enjoyable for you. If you ski, if you are a musician, or even if you just enjoy watching a lot of television, bring that knowledge and enthusiasm into your papers.

Take a moment to think about and jot down a few of your interests now (no matter how unrelated to school they may seem), and then save the list for use later when deciding what to write about. One student's list of interests might look like this:

> surfing the Internet
>
> playing video games with friends
>
> boogie boarding in summer
>
> collecting baseball cards

Another student's list might be very different:

> playing the violin
>
> going to concerts
>
> watching old musicals on video
>
> drawing caricatures of my friends

While still another student might list the following interests:

> going to the horse races
>
> reading for my book club
>
> traveling in the summer
>
> buying lottery tickets

These students have listed several worthy topics for papers. And because they are personal interests, the students have the details needed to support them.

With a general topic to start with, you can use several ways to gather the details you will need to support it in a paragraph or an essay.

Focused Free Writing (or Brainstorming)

Free writing is a good way to begin. When you are assigned a paper, try writing for ten minutes putting down all your thoughts on one subject—watching old movies on video, for example. Don't stop to think about organization, sentence structures, capitalization, or spelling—just let details flow onto the page. Free writing will help you see what material you have and will help you figure out what aspects of the subject to write about.

Here is an example:

When my friends and I went to Sea World in San Diego last summer, we saw an amazing bird show. The birds weren't in cages or tied to perches. Instead they flew freely down out of the sky and out of windows in a phony town that surrounded the stage. And they didn't just have parrots and cockatoos like all the other bird shows I've ever seen before. In those shows the birds just did tricks for treats. But Sea World's show had eagles and falcons and really tall cranes with feathers that looked like ladies' hats on their heads. It was really amazing.

Now the result of this free writing session is certainly not ready to be typed and turned in as a paragraph. But what did become clear in it was that the student could probably compare the two types of bird shows she has seen—the species of birds used and how they were presented.

Clustering

Clustering is another way of thinking a topic through on paper before you begin to write. A cluster is more visual than free writing. You could cluster the topic of "flea markets," for instance, by putting it in a circle in the center of a piece of paper and then drawing lines to new circles as ideas or details occur to you. The idea is to free your mind from the limits of sentences and paragraphs to generate pure details and ideas. When you are finished clustering, you can see where you want to go with a topic.

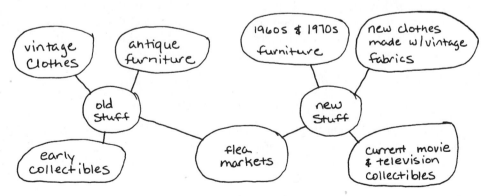

This cluster shows that the student has found two main categories of merchandise at flea markets. This cluster might lead to another where the student chooses one category—collectibles, for instance—and thinks of more details about them.

Talking with Other Students

It may help to talk to others when deciding on a topic. Many teachers break their classes up into groups at the beginning of an assignment. Talking with other students helps you realize that you see things just a little differently. Value the difference—it will help your written voice that we discussed earlier emerge.

Assignment 3
LIST YOUR INTERESTS

Make a list of four or five of your own interests. Be sure that they are as specific as the examples listed on p. 212. Keep the list for later assignments.

Assignment 4
DO SOME FREE WRITING

Choose one of your interests, and do some focused free writing about it. Write for ten minutes with that topic in mind but without stopping. Don't worry about anything such as spelling or sentence structures while you are free writing. The results are meant to help you find out what you have to say about the topic *before* you start to write a paper about it. Save the results for a later assignment.

Assignment 5
TRY CLUSTERING IDEAS

Choose another of your interests. Put it in the center of a piece of paper, and draw a cluster of details and ideas relating to it following the sample on page 213. Take the cluster as far as it will go. Then choose one aspect to cluster again on its own. This way you will arrive at specific, interesting details and ideas—not just the first ones that come to mind. Save the results of all your efforts.

V. Organizing Ideas

The most important thing to keep in mind, no matter what you are writing, is the idea you want to get across to your reader. Whether you are writing a paragraph or an essay, you must have in mind a single idea that you want to express. In a paragraph, such an idea is called a topic sentence; in an essay it's called a thesis statement, but they mean the same thing—an idea you want to get across. We will begin with a discussion of thesis statements.

Thesis Statements

Let's choose one of the students' interests listed on p. 212 as a general topic. "Surfing the Internet" by itself doesn't make any point. What about it? What does it do for you? What point about surfing the Internet would you like to present to your reader? You might write

> Surfing the Internet is a good way to discover new things.

But this is a vague statement, not worth developing. You might move into more specific territory and write

> I have improved my reading and writing skills by surfing the Internet.

Now you have said something specific. *When you write in one sentence the point you want to present to your reader, you have written a thesis statement.*

All good writers have a thesis in mind when they begin to write, or the thesis may well evolve as they write. Whether they are writing essays, novels, poems, or plays, they eventually have in mind an idea they want to present to the reader. They may develop it in various ways, but behind whatever they write is their ruling thought, their reason for writing, their thesis.

For any writing assignment, after you have done some free writing or clustering to explore your topic, the next step is to write a thesis statement. As you write your thesis statement, keep two things in mind:

1. A thesis statement must be a sentence *with a subject and a verb* (not merely a topic).

2. A thesis statement must be *an idea that you can explain or defend* (not simply a statement of fact).

Exercise 1

THESIS OR FACT?

Which of the following are merely topics or facts, and which are thesis statements that you could explain or defend? In front of each one that could be a thesis statement, write THESIS. In front of each one that is a fact, write FACT. Check your answers with those at the back of the book.

1. _____ I bought a new car last week.

2. _____ Someone tried to auction off a human organ on the Internet.

3. _____ E-mail has affected the way people write.

4. _____ We all shed about forty pounds of skin over our lifetimes.

5. _____ My life changed for the better when I quit smoking.

6. _____ Americans eat a lot of fast food.

7. _____ Los Angeles is working on its smog problem.

8. _____ Many people worried about the effects of Y2K.

9. _____ New possessions bring new responsibilities.

10. _____ Older people are finding it difficult to keep up with technology.

Assignment 6

WRITE A THESIS STATEMENT

Use your free writing or clustering results from Assignments 4 and 5 (p. 214) and write at least one thesis statement based on one of your interests. Be sure that the thesis you write is phrased as a complete thought that can be defended or explained in an essay.

Organizing an Essay

Once you have written a good thesis and explored your topic through discussion with others or by free writing and clustering, you are ready to organize your essay.

First you need an introductory paragraph. It should catch your reader's interest, provide necessary background information, and either include or suggest your thesis statement. (See p. 201 and p. 208 for two examples of student writers' introductory paragraphs). In your introductory paragraph, you may also list supporting points, but a more effective way is to let them unfold paragraph by paragraph rather than to give them all away in the beginning of the essay. Even if your supporting points don't appear in your introduction, your reader will easily spot them later if your paper is clearly organized.

Your second paragraph will present your first supporting point—everything about it and nothing more.

Your next paragraph will be about your second supporting point—all about it and nothing more.

Each additional paragraph will develop another supporting point.

Finally, you'll need a concluding paragraph. In a short paper, it isn't necessary to restate all your points. Your conclusion may be brief; even a single sentence to round out the paper may do the job. Remember that the main purpose of a concluding paragraph is to bring the paper to a close by sharing your final thoughts on the subject. (See p. 202 and p. 209 for two examples of concluding paragraphs.)

Learning to write this kind of paper will teach you to distinguish between the parts of an essay. Then when you're ready to write a longer paper, you'll be able to organize it clearly and elaborate on its design and content.

Topic Sentences

A topic sentence does for a paragraph what a thesis statement does for an essay—it states the main idea. Like thesis statements, topic sentences must be phrased as complete thoughts to be proven or developed through the presentation of details. But the topic sentence introduces an idea or subtopic that is the right size to cover in a paragraph. The topic sentence doesn't have to be the first sentence in a paragraph. It may come at the end or even in the middle, but putting it first is most common.

Each body paragraph should contain only one main idea, and no detail or example should be allowed to creep into the paragraph if it doesn't support the topic sentence. (See p. 203 and pp. 206–210 for more examples of body paragraphs within essays and of paragraphs alone.)

Organizing Body Paragraphs (or Single Paragraphs)

A single paragraph or a body paragraph within an essay is organized in the same way as an entire essay only on a smaller scale. Here's the way you learned to organize an essay:

Thesis: stated or suggested in introductory paragraph

First supporting paragraph

Second supporting paragraph

Additional supporting paragraphs

Concluding paragraph

And here's the way to organize a paragraph:

Topic sentence

First supporting detail or example

Second supporting detail or example

Additional supporting details or examples

Concluding or transitional sentence

You should have several details to support each topic sentence. If you find that you have little to say after writing the topic sentence, ask yourself what details or examples will make your reader believe that the topic sentence is true for you.

Transitional Expressions

Transitional expressions within a paragraph and between paragraphs in an essay help the reader move from one detail or example to the next and from one supporting point to the next. When first learning to organize an essay, you might start each supporting paragraph in a paper with a transitional expression.

There are transitions to show addition:

Also

Furthermore

Another (example, point, step, etc. . . .)

In addition

There are transitions to show sequence:

First	One reason	One example
Second	Another reason	Another example
Finally	Most important	In conclusion

There are transitions to show contrast:

However	On the other hand	In contrast

Exercise 2

ADDING TRANSITIONAL EXPRESSIONS

Place the appropriate transitional expressions into the blanks in the following paragraph to make it read smoothly. Check your answers with those in the back of the book.

First	Finally	However	In conclusion	Next

I have been planning to take a cruise with my husband and maybe my kids for several years now. _____, I haven't decided what kind of cruise to go on yet. _____, there are the romantic couple cruises to the Caribbean. But then I might worry about my children while we're away. _____, there are the breathtaking sights of Alaskan cruises. I've seen pictures of cruise ships passing right next to glaciers, although that seems a little dangerous. _____, there are the family cruises that cater to everyone's desire for adventure and fun. While the kids play one of the numerous supervised activities, the adults can relax and enjoy each other's company. _____, I think I've talked myself into a cruise for the whole family this summer!

Assignment 7

WOULD YOU LIKE TO BE CLONED?

New scientific methods are laying the groundwork for human cloning. Without considering the philosophical questions—in other words, *practically* speaking— would you like to be cloned? Why or why not? Write a long paragraph or a short essay in which you briefly answer this question. Your answer will be your main idea, and the reasons and details that support it should be your own opinions. Try free writing, clustering, or discussing the subject with others to find out how you feel about the topic before you begin to write.

VI. Supporting with Details

Now you're ready to support your main ideas with subtopics and specific details. That is, you'll think of ways to convince your reader that what you say in your thesis is true. How could you convince your reader that surfing the Internet has improved your reading and writing skills? You might write

My reading and writing skills have improved since I began surfing the Internet. (because)

1. The computer won't respond to sloppy spelling and punctuation.

2. I read much more on screen than I ever did on paper, and much faster.

3. I write e-mail to friends and family, but I never wrote real letters to them before.

NOTE- Sometimes if you imagine a *because* at the end of your thesis statement, it will help you write your reasons or subtopics clearly and in parallel form.

Types of Support

The subtopics developing a thesis and the details presented in a paragraph are not always reasons. Supporting points may take many forms based on the purpose of the essay or paragraph. They may be

examples (in an illustration)

steps (in a how-to or process paper)

types or kinds (in a classification)

meanings (in a definition)

similarities and/or differences (in a comparison/contrast)

effects (in a cause-and-effect analysis)

Whatever they are, supporting points should develop the main idea expressed in the thesis or topic sentence and prove it to be true.

Here is the final draft of a student essay about a challenging assignment. Notice how the body paragraphs map out the stages of the assignment. And all of the details within the body paragraphs bring the experience to life.

Drawing a Blank

On the day my drawing class started to learn about self-portraits last year, each of us had to bring a mirror to class. In backpacks and purses were make-up mirrors, dressing table mirrors—large and small mirrors of every shape and kind. I was nervous about drawing a self-portrait, so I brought only a tiny plastic pocket mirror. That way if I didn't do a good job, it would be my mirror's fault. I should have known I could do it if I tried.

I had never done well on human figure drawing. First our teacher, Ms. Newman, demonstrated the proportion of a human figure; she explained that a human body measures about seven times a human head. She used a tiny piece of chalk to draw on the board while she was talking. Then she showed how to sketch the face, from eyebrows to eyes, nose, mouth, and ears. After her lecture, she told us to begin drawing our self-portraits.

We all set up our mirrors. The ceiling danced with the reflections they made as we got to work. I looked down at my little square of scratched-up plastic and started to draw gingerly on my paper. I tried to put the eyes, nose, and mouth I had seen on the paper. When I finished, I wondered, "Who the heck is this?" The drawing didn't look anything like me. I was frustrated and sank down in my chair. After a minute, I told myself, "Try again." I drew another one, and it was a little better. But I could not really call it a self-portrait because it didn't look exactly like me.

   I asked Ms. Newman for help. She glanced at my previous attempts and said, "A good self-portrait doesn't just look like you, it also shows your personality and your feelings." She did not see any of these in my other drawings. So I tried again. I borrowed my friend's big glass mirror and stared into it; I was not only looking at my face, but also deep inside my face. This time, I freely sketched the shape of my face. Then I roughly placed my eyebrows, eyes, nose, mouth, and ears. I looked into the mirror again and drew the expression I saw there.

   When my portrait was finished, I wondered at the amazing work I had done. Even though it did not perfectly look like me, it really showed my personality and emotions through the contrast of light and dark. When Ms. Newman saw it, she applauded. Not only did I get an A on this project, it also became one of the strongest pieces in my portfolio. I realized that few things can be done successfully the first time. If I had given up after my first try, I would never have captured the real me.

(Note: See p. 222 for a rough draft of the above essay, before its final revisions.)

Learning to support your main ideas with vivid details is perhaps the most important thing you can accomplish in this course. Many writing problems are not really *writing* problems but *thinking* problems. Whether you're writing a term paper or merely an answer to a test question, if you take enough time to think, you'll be able to write a clear thesis statement and support it with paragraphs loaded with meaningful details.

Assignment 8

WRITE AN ESSAY ON ONE OF YOUR INTERESTS

Return to the thesis statement you wrote about one of your interests for Assignment 6 on p. 216. Now write a short essay to support it. You can explain the allure of your interest, its drawbacks or its benefits (such as the one about the Internet improving the student's reading and writing skills). Don't forget to use any free writing or clustering you may have done on the topic beforehand.

Assignment 9
A MISTAKE

Like the student writer of the essay "Really Understanding" (pp. 201–202), we all make mistakes. And these mistakes often affect other people. Write an essay about a mistake you have made or a mistake someone else made that had an effect on you.

VII. Revising Your Papers

Great writers don't just sit down and write a final draft. They write and revise. You may have heard the expression, "Easy writing makes hard reading." True, it is *easier* to turn in a piece of writing the first time it lands on paper. But you and your reader will be disappointed by the results. Try to think of revision as an opportunity instead of a chore, as a necessity instead of a choice.

Whenever possible, write the paper several days before the first draft is due. Let it sit for a while. When you reread it, you'll see ways to improve the organization or to add more details to a weak paragraph. After revising the paper, put it away for another day, and try again to improve it. Save all of your drafts along the way to see the progress that you've made or possibly to return to an area left out in later drafts but that fits in again after revision.

Don't call any paper finished until you have worked it through several times. Revising is one of the best ways to improve your writing.

Take a look at an early draft of the student essay you read on page 220 on the assignment to draw a self-portrait. Notice that the student has revised her rough draft by crossing out some parts, correcting word forms, and adding new phrasing or reminders for later improvement.

Drawing a Blank

~~If at First You Don't Succeed . . . Try, Try Again~~

On the day ~~that~~ my drawing class started to learn about self-portraits last year, each of us had to bring a
In backpacks and purses
mirror to class. ~~There~~ were make-up mirrors, dressing table mirrors—large and small mirrors of every shape and

kind. I was nervous about drawing a self-portrait, so I brought only a tiny plastic pocket mirror. That way if I didn't do a good job, it would be my mirror's fault. *Add a thesis

First, Ms. Newman, our teacher, demonstrated the proportion of a human figure; she explained that a human body measures about seven times a human head. She used a tiny piece of chalk to draw on the board while she was talking. Then she showed how to sketch the face, from eyebrows to eyes, nose, mouth and ears. After her lecture, she told us to begin our self-portraits. We all set up our mirrors, and the ceiling danced with the reflections they made as we got to work. I looked down at my little square of scratched-up plastic and started to draw gingerly on my paper. I tried to put the eyes, nose, and mouth I had seen on the paper. When I finished, I wondered, "Who the heck is this?" The drawing didn't look anything like me. I was so frustrated and sank down in my chair. After a minute, I told myself, "Try again." I drew another one, and it was a little better. But I could not really call it a self-portrait because it did not look exactly like me.

I asked Ms. Newman for help. She glanced at my previous attempts and said, "A good self-portrait doesn't just look like you, it also shows your personality and your feelings." She did not see any of these in my other drawings. So I tried again. I borrowed my friend's

big glass mirror and stared into it; I was not only looking
at my face, but also deep inside my face. This time,
I freely sketched ~~out~~ the shape of my face ~~, shape first.~~ Then, roughly I
placed my eyebrows, eyes, nose, mouth, and ears. ~~And~~ I
looked ~~at~~ into the mirror ~~, seeing my reflection closely. I~~ again and
drew ~~what I felt to be like in the mirror.~~ the expression I saw there.
   When my ~~drawing~~ Portrait was finished, I wondered at ~~what an~~ the
amazing work I had done. Even though it did not perfectly
look like me, it really showed my ~~characteristics~~ personality and emotions through
the contrast of ~~light~~ and dark. When ~~my teacher~~ Ms. Newman saw it, she applauded.
~~my drawing and she really liked it.~~ Not only did I get an
A ~~in~~ on this project; it also became one of the strongest
pieces in my portfolio. I ~~recognized~~ realized that ~~nothing could~~ few things can
be done successfully the first time. If I ~~gave~~ had given up after
my first try, I would never have ~~known I could have done~~ captured the real me.
~~such a great job. Now I know I will succeed no matter how~~
~~many times I must try.~~

Can you see why each change was made? Analyzing the reasons for the changes will help you improve your own revision skills.

Assignment 10

A COLLECTION

Roy Sorrels writes about his collection of playing cards that he found on the streets of New York City ("Crazy?" p. 210). Write about a collection you or someone you know has. How did the collection come about? What are the reasons for assembling the collection? Are there any special requirements the things must have to be in the collection?

   Write a rough draft of the paper and then set it aside. When you finish writing about the collection, reread your paper to see what improvements you can make to your rough draft. Use the following checklist to help guide you through this or any other revision.

REVISION CHECKLIST

Here's a checklist of revision questions. If the answer to any of these questions is no, revise that part of your paper until you're satisfied that the answer is yes.

1. Does the introductory paragraph introduce the topic clearly and suggest or include a thesis statement that the paper will explain or defend?

2. Does each of the other paragraphs support the thesis statement?

3. Does each body paragraph contain a clear topic sentence and focus on only one supporting point?

4. Do the body paragraphs contain enough details, and are transitional expressions well used?

5. Do the final thoughts expressed in the concluding paragraph bring the paper to a smooth close?

6. Does your (the writer's) voice come through?

7. Do the sentences read smoothly and appear to be correct?

8. Are the spelling and punctuation consistent and correct?

Exchanging Papers

This checklist could also be used when you exchange papers with another student in your class. Since you both have written a response to the same assignment, you will understand what the other writer went through and learn from the differences between the two papers.

Proofreading Aloud

Finally, read your finished paper *aloud*. If you read it silently, you will see what you *think* is there, but you are sure to miss some errors. Read your paper aloud slowly, pointing to each word as you read it to catch omissions and errors in spelling and punctuation. Reading a paper to yourself this way may take fifteen minutes to half an hour, but it will be time well spent. There are even word processing programs that will "speak" your text in a computer's voice. Using your computer to read your paper to you can be fun as well as helpful. If you don't like the way something sounds, don't be afraid to change it! Make it a rule to read each of your papers *aloud* before handing it in.

Here are four additional writing assignments to help you practice the skills of writing and revising.

Assignment 11

ARE YOU A TECHNOPHILE OR A TECHNOPHOBE?

On a scale of one to ten, how comfortable are you with all of the newest technologies? Make sure you clarify the scale, your position on it, and the technologies you are including in your discussion. Organize your results into the structure of a brief essay.

Assignment 12

WHAT IS FREEDOM?

Freedom is something many people take for granted. It is an abstract word—like *love*—that means different things to different people. How do you define the word *freedom*? Do you have it—if so, what kind? Write a brief essay in which you help the reader understand what you mean by "freedom." Be sure to give examples.

Assignment 13

THE BEST ADVICE

What was the best advice you ever received? What prompted the advice? Who gave it to you, and why was it so valuable? Organize your responses to these questions into the structure of a brief essay.

Assignment 14

A QUOTATION

Look through the quotations in Exercises 1–4 on pp. 185–188. Does one of them apply to you? Could you profit from following one of them? Write a short paper in which you react to or offer an explanation of one of the quotations and then support your reaction or explanation with examples from your own experiences.

VIII. PRESENTING YOUR WORK

Part of the success of a paper could depend on how it looks. The same paper written sloppily or typed neatly might even receive different grades. It is human nature to respond positively when a paper has been presented with care. Here are some general guidelines to follow.

Paper Formats

Your paper should be typed or written on a computer, double-spaced, or copied neatly in ink on 8 1/2-by-11-inch paper on one side only. A one-inch margin should be left around the text on all sides for your instructor's comments. The beginning of each paragraph should be indented five spaces.

Most instructors have a particular format for presenting your name and the course material on your papers. Always follow such instructions carefully.

Titles

Finally, spend some time thinking of a good title. Just as you're more likely to read a magazine article with an interesting title, so your readers will be more eager to read your paper if you give it a good title. Which of these titles from student papers would make you want to read further?

An Embarrassing Experience	Super Salad?
Falling into The Gap	Buying Clothes Can Be Depressing
Hunting: The Best Sport of All?	Got Elk?

Remember these three things about titles:

1. Only the first letter of the important words in a title should be capitalized.

   A Night at the Races

2. Don't put quotation marks around your own titles unless they include a quotation or title of an article, short story, or poem within them.

   "To Be or Not to Be" Is Not for Me

3. Don't underline (or *italicize*) your own titles unless they include the title of a book, play, movie, or magazine within them.

   Still Stuck on *Titanic*

A wise person once said, "Haste is the assassin of elegance." Instead of rushing to finish a paper and turn it in, take the time to give your writing the polish it deserves.

IX. WRITING ABOUT WHAT YOU READ

Reading and writing are related skills. The more you read, the better you will write. When you are asked to prepare for a writing assignment by reading a newspaper story, a magazine article, a professional essay, or part of a book, there are many ways to respond in writing. Among them, you may be asked to write your reaction to a reading assignment or a summary of a reading assignment.

Writing a Reaction

Reading assignments become writing assignments when your teacher asks you to share your opinion about the subject matter or to relate the topic to your own experiences. In a paragraph, you would have enough space to offer only the most immediate impressions about the topic. However, in an essay you could share your personal reactions, as well as your opinions on the value of the writer's ideas and support. Of course, the first step is always to read the selection carefully, looking up unfamiliar words in a dictionary.

SAMPLE REACTION PARAGRAPH

Here is a sample paragraph-length response following the class's reading of an essay called "What Is Intelligence?" by Isaac Asimov. In the essay, Asimov explains that there are other kinds of intelligence besides just knowledge of theories and facts. This student shares Asimov's ideas about intelligence, and she uses her own experiences to support her statements.

> I totally agree with Isaac Asimov. Intelligence doesn't only belong to Nobel Prize winners. I define "intelligence" as being able to value that special skill that a person has been born with. Not everyone is a math genius or a brain surgeon. For example, ask a brain surgeon to rotate the engine in your car. It isn't going to happen. To be able to take that certain skill that you've inherited and push it to its farthest limits I would call "intelligence." Isaac Asimov's definition is similar to mine. He believes that academic questions are only correctly answered by academicians. He gives the example of a farmer. A farming test would only be correctly answered by a farmer. Not everyone has the same talent; we are all different. When I attend my math classes, I must always pay attention. If I don't, I end up struggling with what I missed. On the other hand, when I'm in my singing class, I really do not have to struggle because the musical notes come to me with ease. This is just one example of how skills and talents differ from each other. I would rather sing a song than do math any day. We are all made differently. Some people are athletic, and some people are brainy. Some people can sing, and some can cook. It really doesn't matter what other people can do. If they have a talent—that's a form of intelligence.

If this had been an essay-length response, the student would have included more details about her own and other people's types of intelligence. And she may have wanted to quote and discuss Asimov's most important points.

Assignment 15

WRITE A REACTION PARAGRAPH

The following is an article by Megan Rooney in which she describes the "spotlight effect." Write a paragraph in which you respond thoughtfully to Rooney's topic and to the details she uses to support it.

In the Spotlight

Ever feel that you're Truman Burbank, with every eye trained on your every action, especially your blunders and shortcomings? Psychologists call the familiar feeling that the whole world is watching you the "spotlight effect." Thankfully (to everyone except narcissists), that social searchlight is turning out not to be as large or as bright as we fear. "We think that people notice us much more than they do," says Kenneth Savitsky, Ph.D., associate professor of psychology at Williams College, who has studied the phenomenon extensively with researchers from Williams, Cornell, and Northwestern.

In one experiment, a student wearing a Barry Manilow T-shirt was sent into a room filled with peers. Though the student was convinced that the "embarrassing" clothing would be noticed by at least half of the people, follow-up interviews found that less than 50% of the group recalled the shirt. In another semester-long experiment, dubbed the "Bad Hair Day Study," students rated their classmates on whether they looked better or worse than usual. The results show that the raters were less aware of variations in appearance than were the students they scored. Most people just don't notice when we're not looking our best or worst.

Why not? Simple egocentrism, declares Savitsky. Since we're focused on ourselves, we assume that others pay close attention to us, too, but everyone else is concerned with their own problems. "The truth is," says Cornell graduate student Justin Kruger, "we're just not as interesting to other people as we are to ourselves."

Source: Reprinted with permission from *Psychology Today* magazine.
Copyright © 1998 (Sussex Publishers, Inc.).

Before starting your reaction paragraph, *read the selection again carefully*. Be sure to use a dictionary to look up any words you don't know. You can also use the free writing and clustering techniques explained on pages 213–214. Or your instructor may want you to discuss the reading in groups.

Coming to Your Own Conclusions

Often you will be asked to come to your own conclusions based on a reading that simply reports information. In other words, you have to think about and write about what it all means.

Read the following "Police and Sheriff's Log," reprinted from the July 2, 1999, issue of *The Carmel Pine Cone* in Carmel, California. These are *real* police log entries, recorded by the Carmel-by-the-Sea Police Department and the Monterey

County Sheriff's Department, which the *Pine Cone* publishes once a week as a service to the community.

Sunday, June 20

Carmel-by-the-Sea: Fifth Avenue resident reported hearing sounds outside her window. Area check was negative.

Carmel-by-the-Sea: Tourist advised about camping in his vehicle. He departed from the area.

Carmel-by-the-Sea: Man was attempting to remove his dog from his vehicle when it bit his hand. Refused any medical assistance or a bite report. . . .

Carmel-by-the-Sea: Citizen flag-down regarding underage drinking. People were contacted—three were found to be underage. Turned over to the military authorities.

Carmel-by-the-Sea: Man was left behind by his alleged girlfriend after she discovered an adult magazine in his belongings. Taxi called to transport him to Monterey, to the Greyhound station.

Carmel-by-the-Sea: Report of loud engine noise at a Mission Street location. The engine was turned off.

Carmel-by-the-Sea: Report of construction work in progress at a Crespi residence. Contact made with the sub-contractor who was doing some prep work on wood forms. Warning given to the party involved.

Monday, June 21

Carmel-by-the-Sea: Casanova resident thought she heard strange noises outside her window. An area check showed nothing unusual.

Carmel-by-the-Sea: Junipero resident was feeling depressed about several personal issues. Provided a transport to CHOMP [nearby hospital] for him at his request.

Carmel-by-the-Sea: Three male juveniles located and reunited with their grandmother. . . .

Carmel-by-the-Sea: Report of a discarded umbrella near the roadway of 11th and Torres. The item was retrieved and later disposed of, since it was damaged.

Carmel-by-the-Sea: Man reported that someone had broken off a hasp lock set from a wooden tool box left on a job site. He did not know if anything was taken. He will verify.

Pebble Beach: A copper BB struck the rear sliding glass patio door of a Sunset Lane residence. The damage was not known until the next morning. A half-inch diameter chunk of glass fractured into the living room.

Carmel Valley: Woman reported unknown person(s) stole 45 recently planted plants from the driveway of the Chateau Julien Winery sometime during the night.

Carmel Valley: Punta Del Monte resident complained of noise coming from road construction at the Robles Del Rio Lodge. He said the construction was occurring too late in the day.

Carmel area: Person reported a disturbance at the Mission Ranch bar. A man had a verbal disagreement with employees at the bar. The person who reported the incident did not want criminal charges filed. The man was transported home.

Carmel area: Man reported that he may have left his cell phone on his work truck in the Carmel Woods area. After realizing what he had done, he returned. However, he was unable to locate the phone.

Tuesday, June 22

Carmel-by-the-Sea: Report of a possible fight near a taxi cab at San Carlos and Fifth. Upon arrival, contacted the subjects, who were intoxicated. There was a brief struggle between the two and no injuries were sustained. They did not want to talk about the matter and agreed to leave in separate taxis.

Carmel-by-the-Sea: Report of a loud party near Ocean and Casanova. Resident contacted and the party was quieted. . . .

Carmel area: Man reported unknown subject(s) had broken the hydraulics on the front gate at the entrance to the Palo Corona Ranch. Damage estimated at $400.

Wednesday, June 23

Carmel-by-the-Sea: Report of night-time construction at Ocean and San Carlos. Advised of CMC [municipal code] and shut down for the night.

Carmel-by-the-Sea: Hit and run at Carpenter and First. A general description was put out. Area check made, located suspect car at Camino del Monte. Acquired suspect information—he was driving on a suspended license. Information supplied to the district attorney's office.

Carmel-by-the-Sea: Man arrived at the station for a court-ordered booking. He was booked, photographed and printed for petty theft.

Carmel-by-the-Sea: Torres resident reported hearing voices outside her home. Nothing found in the area.

Carmel-by-the-Sea: Man found sleeping in his car. He got off work at a local restaurant and was too tired to drive home. This information was verified by the people at the neighboring business. Employees at another business allowed him to stay in their lot. He was advised of codes.

Carmel-by-the-Sea: Woman called to report that her ex-employer refused to pay her for 19 days worked, and also slapped her when she asked for the money owed to her. The ex-employer admitted making a mistake on her pay but denied slapping her. A witness of the confrontation said there was no physical confrontation. A check for the money owed was given to the woman.

Carmel-by-the-Sea: Assisted a woman with questions about marauding raccoons.

Carmel-by-the-Sea: Report of juveniles throwing rocks at cars. Area check made with negative results.

Carmel area: Yankee Point Drive resident reported someone made pry marks on the door leading to his garage. However, the marks were not in a location that would have been conducive to an attempted burglary. The purpose behind the making of the marks is unknown.

Carmel Valley: Carmel Valley Road residents called 911 to report finding their 44-year-old son unresponsive on the bedroom floor. Ambulance arrived and the subject was admitted for evaluation.

Pebble Beach: Report of golf clubs stolen from the golf rack in front of MPCC pro shop on 6/8/99. Orlimar Diamond brand, has name on clubs near the grip.

Carmel area: Carmel High School principal reported a possible embezzlement by one of their employees. Case under investigation.

Thursday, June 24

Carmel-by-the-Sea: Report of loud music coming from a vehicle parked on Scenic. Music turned down upon arrival.

Carmel area: Responded to a 911 hang-up at a Del Mesa residence. Found that a mattress had caught on fire and the resident was able to extinguish it himself. Fire personnel were unable to determine the origin or cause of the fire.

Carmel area: Night manager for a resort reported a disturbance with a guest who was upset about being charged for the cable television in his room, which did not function properly. He felt the manager was not willing to assist him.

Carmel Valley: Person reported some juveniles dressed in camouflage clothing with their faces blackened were in the area of the tennis ranch last night and damaged driveway lights and flood lights.

Carmel area: Man reported two union representatives were on a Carmel Highlands job site and refused to leave. . . .

Pebble Beach: Stevenson Drive resident reported a Rottweiler was loose in the neighborhood and in her yard. She wanted to let animal control know of the situation.

Carmel area: Schulte Road resident wanted to report that his son was threatening to run away. Arrived, counseled both parties and both agreed to a compromise.

Friday, June 25

Carmel-by-the-Sea: Removed approximately 20 garage/yard sale signs from trees, sign posts and telephone poles in the area of Lincoln and Dolores streets.

Carmel-by-the-Sea: Subject skateboarding. He was from Nevada on vacation and advised of municipal code. He walked back to his hotel.

Carmel-by-the-Sea: Woman was rummaging inside a garbage can in search of food and spilling its contents on the sidewalk. A man confronted her and told her to stop. She became agitated and cursed at him, and took a swing at him. She admitted she used obscenities but denied she tried to assault him. She had not been drinking. Information only.

Carmel-by-the-Sea: Report of a disoriented female. Additional information later revealed she was returned to the Carmel Inn for Seniors by an aide from the inn. . . .

Carmel area: Via Mar Monte resident reported things in her house are missing and that someone broke eggs in her refrigerator. She also feels she is being followed.

Carmel Valley: Princes Camp resident reported a man became upset with him for socializing with the man's ex-girlfriend. He was concerned the man may try to retaliate against him at a later date.

Carmel Valley: Via La Gitana resident reported several male juveniles were riding dirt bikes and go-carts on Via Los Tulares and Via La Estrella. She called the mother of the juveniles and was told the family rides dirt bikes and if she didn't like it, she could call the sheriff's department. The woman requested the sheriff's department not contact the mother.

Carmel Valley: Paso Hondo residents were involved in a verbal disagreement.

Saturday, June 26

Carmel-by-the-Sea: Four juveniles warned for climbing trees in Davendorf Park.

Carmel-by-the-Sea: Report of music disrupting a meditation session. No music heard—possibility the meditation had increased the person's auditory sensitivity.

Carmel-by-the-Sea: Request by CHP for a Carmel unit to block traffic at Rio Road and Highway 1. They were in pursuit of a vehicle northbound on Highway 1.

Carmel-by-the-Sea: Report of a woman inside a Lincoln business with a gun. Bartender advised she just left in a taxi. Taxi located on Dolores at Ocean. Stopped taxi at San Carlos and Fifth. Stop was a "High Risk" stop with officers' weapons drawn. The woman said she had a replica gun. It turned out to be a WWII machine gun replica she had purchased for her nephew. Released.

Pebble Beach: Man reported finding a window broken at an Ocean Pines residence where he was working. He also found a small pellet in the same room.

Carmel area: Man reported that unknown suspect(s) removed the blue 1999 license plate tab belonging to his white Toyota truck while it was parked at the Crossroads.

Carmel Valley: Woman reported that her car stereo was taken from her unlocked vehicle in the parking lot behind the Running Iron.

Carmel area: Responded to the Crystal Terrace Inn regarding a verbal domestic dispute. Contacted a guest, who stated her husband had too much to drink. Both parties counseled and agreed to stop arguing for the night.

Source: Reprinted with permission. © *The Carmel Pine Cone.*

Assignment 16

WHAT ARE YOUR CONCLUSIONS?

After reading the Carmel Police Log, what patterns do you see in the behavior of the city's residents, visitors, and police? Write an essay that describes the patterns you observe.

WRITING 100-WORD SUMMARIES

One of the best ways to learn to read carefully and to write concisely is to write 100-word summaries. Writing 100 words sounds easy, but actually it isn't. Writing 200- or 300- or 500-word summaries isn't too difficult, but condensing all the main ideas of an essay or article into 100 words is a time-consuming task—not to be undertaken in the last hour before class.

A summary presents only the main ideas of a reading, *without including any reactions to it.* A summary tests your ability to read, understand, and *rephrase* the ideas contained in an essay, article, or book.

If you work at writing summaries conscientiously, you'll improve both your reading and your writing. You'll improve your reading by learning to spot main ideas and your writing by learning to construct a concise, clear, smooth paragraph. Furthermore, your skills will carry over into your reading and writing for other courses.

SAMPLE 100-WORD SUMMARY

First, read the following excerpt from the book *Eccentrics: A Study of Sanity and Strangeness,* by Dr. David Weeks and Jamie James. It will be followed by a student's 100-word summary.

Franz Anton Mesmer

Today medicine is closely associated with chemistry, but in the past there were healers who looked to physics for the causes of illness, and for cures. Franz Anton Mesmer (1734–1815) thought he found a link between health and magnetism, and like other eccentric scientists, once he had found the connection, he devoted his lifetime to . . . his great discovery. . . .

Mesmer brought current theories of astronomy and Newton's law of gravitation into his biological model of animal magnetism. His theory assumed that there was an ethereal fluid present in all living things, similar to the *chi* of Chinese medicine. . . . Good health, he concluded, results when this inner magnetic fluid is in balance with the magnetic fluid that fills the universe. If the equilibrium got out of whack, order could be restored by pulling the fluids back into alignment with magnets.

At first Mesmer simply fitted small magnets onto various parts of his patients' bodies. . . . Soon he progressed to group healing at his lavishly appointed clinic, where patients sat around a tub filled with water and iron powder, and held tight to iron bars. . . .

Mesmer was widely criticized by the medical establishment, and he didn't help his case by the increasing theatricality of his performances. Before long, the group treatments resembled séances . . . which he presided over wearing a lilac cloak and waving an iron wand. He finally abandoned the use of magnets and began channeling the cosmic fluid through his own body and, via the iron wand, into his patients.

While Mesmer's theory of animal magnetism was, of course, without any foundation in fact, he did make a lasting contribution to science with the invention of hypnotism, which used to be known as mesmerism. . . . [H]is hypnotic technique is still in use today in legitimate medicine, with a multitude of practical applications.

Here is a student's 100-word summary of the article:

```
    Franz Anton Mesmer lived in the mid-1700s. He was an
eccentric, someone who got stuck on an idea and built his
life around it. Mesmer believed that people became sick
when their magnetic juices were unbalanced. He felt that
he could cure them by putting their juices in balance
again. At first, he treated patients with magnets but
eventually started zapping them with his magic wand.
Mesmer made quite a production out of these curing
sessions. Even though many scientists didn't take him
seriously at the time, Mesmer actually invented hypnosis.
Maybe other big ideas were considered crazy at first.
```

Assignment 17
WRITE A 100-WORD SUMMARY

Your aim in writing your summary should be to give someone who has not read the article a clear idea of it. First, read the following article by Lindsay Kallen and then follow the instructions given after it.

Men Don't Cry, Women Don't Fume

A man bursts into tears after a tough day at the office and concerned co-workers rush to support him. A woman sobs in the same situation and her distress is barely acknowledged. Why such differing reactions? It all depends on what we *don't* expect, contends Purdue University psychologist Janice Kelly, Ph.D.

Her research suggests that when men and women display emotions inconsistent with the gender stereotypes we hold, we're apt to think that those feelings are more genuine and legitimate. Men are expected to show anger and stubbornness, women to express happiness, sadness, and fear. So a crying woman is just more of the same, but a sorrowful man is such a rarity that we believe he must be on the brink of disaster. Likewise, an angry man is common, but a livid woman is so rare we think she must really be furious.

Even so, a woman's feelings still don't carry the same weight as a man's. Women typically are seen as "emotional" and their reactions viewed as overblown. "We tend to discount a large reaction in women," observes Kelly, while men are more likely to be admired for showing their true emotions. A man who panics in stressful conditions is seen as honest or vulnerable, for example, while a frightened woman might be regarded as overreacting.

The way we view men's and women's emotional expressions may have an impact on our romantic relationships. Emotions may be given more weight according to who expresses them, not how sincere they are. Thus, that heart-to-heart conversation with your partner may not be an equal trade, after all, since in the currency of emotions, a woman's feelings are worth much less.

Source: Reprinted with permission from *Psychology Today* magazine. Copyright © 1998 (Sussex Publishers, Inc.).

A good way to begin the summary of an article is to figure out the thesis statement, the main idea the author wants to get across to the reader. Write that idea down now *before reading further.*

How honest are you with yourself? Did you write that thesis statement? If you didn't, *write it now* before you read further.

You probably wrote something like this:

We judge the emotions of people differently based on whether they are male or female.

Using that main idea as your first sentence, summarize the article by choosing the most important points. *Be sure to put them in your own words.* Your rough draft may be 150 words or more.

Now cut it down by including only essential points and by getting rid of wordiness. Keep within the 100-word limit. You may have a few words less but not one word more. (And every word counts—even *a, and,* and *the.*) By forcing yourself to keep within 100 words, you'll get to the kernel of the author's thought and understand the article better.

When you have written the best summary you can, then and only then compare it with the summary on page 314. If you look at the model sooner, you'll cheat yourself of the opportunity to learn to write summaries because, once you read the model, it will be almost impossible not to make yours similar. So do your own thinking and writing, and then compare.

SUMMARY CHECKLIST

Even though your summary is different from the model, it may be just as good. If you're not sure how yours compares, answer these questions:

1. Did you include the same main ideas?

2. Did you leave out all unnecessary words and examples?

3. Did you rephrase the writer's ideas, not just recopy them?

4. Does the summary read smoothly?

5. Would someone who had not read the article get a clear idea of it from your summary?

Assignment 18

WRITE A REACTION OR A 100-WORD SUMMARY

Respond to David Gergen's article "Keeping Faith in Kids" in any of the three ways we've discussed—in a reaction paragraph, an essay, or a 100-word summary. If you plan to respond with an essay, briefly summarize Gergen's main ideas about young people in your introductory paragraph. Then write about your reactions to his ideas in your body paragraphs. Save your final thoughts for your concluding paragraph.

Keeping Faith in Kids

All across the country, people are rattled about teenagers. A national survey by Public Agenda, published early this month [May 1999], found that 74 percent of parents described kids these days as "rude," "irresponsible," and "wild." Only 40 percent said these children will grow up to make America a better place. And this survey was taken even before kids began cutting down their classmates at Littleton and Conyers.

Are we really raising a nation of hellions? What's wrong with the Y generation?

The truth is that most kids these days are not the problem we think. If anything, they will one day prove to be the answer—because this generation is much healthier than the gloomy headlines in recent weeks would suggest.

In the *New Republic* earlier this year, Gregg Easterbrook pointed out some encouraging trends. In 1980, 72 percent of high school seniors said they had been drinking alcohol recently; by 1998, that figure had dropped to 52 percent. Drug usage, especially marijuana, is down as well. Teen pregnancy rates have been falling since 1991 and most recently were at the same level as 1980. Homicides remain historically high among teens, but striking improvements have come in big cities like New York, Boston, and Los Angeles.

Creating a crusade. Meanwhile young people by the droves are signing up as volunteers in their communities. In the past five years alone, 100,000 have enlisted in AmeriCorps—more than the Peace Corps had in its first 20 years. Last week, in his annual report on "America's Promise," Gen. Colin Powell spoke glowingly about the number of teenagers as well as adults who are volunteering to work with children. He thinks the country can create not just a movement but a crusade. . . .

America does have a serious problem, but it's not the younger generation. It's the sickness that has crept into our soul. We have a culture that leaves many people feeling estranged, their dignity destroyed, and this can lead to extreme antisocial behavior by those who can't find solace in their friends or family.

Every generation, no matter how good, has had its share of loners, misfits, and plain old wackos. When many of us were growing up, these social outcasts vented their frustrations with fists or knives. Now they can break into gun arsenals their folks keep at home; their heads are filled with violent pictures they have seen on television or in movies; their hard drives are filled with pornography that floods across the Internet.

If there is a silver lining in Littleton and Conyers, maybe it will come because we change our minds about the way we should live together. Congress, at least, finally seems to understand that guns are like cars: Adults should have a right to them, but society has a right to protect itself against their dangers and to keep them strictly out of the hands of kids. With luck, we will apply the same kind of common sense to the violence and pornography that pollute our popular entertainment. . . .

It's time to see our kids for who they truly are. Most of them are not rude, wild, and irresponsible; in fact, most of them could one day make this country an immensely better place. But all of them still need a caring, compassionate adult in daily life, helping them grow up to be all they can be.

Source: Copyright *U.S. News & World Report,* 31 May 1999. Visit us at our Web site at www.usnews.com for additional information.

Answers

SPELLING

WORDS OFTEN CONFUSED, SET 1 (PP. 8–13)

EXERCISE 1

1. effects
2. course, already
3. an
4. its
5. Conscious, knew, an
6. our, desserts, all ready, clothes
7. feel
8. accept, complement, break
9. chose
10. due, a

EXERCISE 2

1. hear, know
2. an, its
3. do
4. chose, its
5. conscious
6. affect
7. advice, fill
8. an, its
9. chose, accepted
10. compliment

EXERCISE 3

1. forth, fill
2. here, affects
3. are, an
4. knew, it's
5. already
6. except
7. complement, already, know
8. have
9. fill, desserts
10. have

EXERCISE 4

1. already, do
2. clothes, choose
3. its
4. course, dessert
5. Due

6. feel, conscious
7. advice
8. have, complimented
9. course, do
10. except

EXERCISE 5

1. an, choose
2. course, it's
3. advice
4. effect
5. its, due

6. cloths, no, coarse
7. break
8. all ready, feel, it's
9. compliments
10. clothes

PROOFREADING EXERCISE

I like all of the classes I chose this semester ~~accept~~ *except* my tennis class. ~~Its~~ *It's* not what you might think. The teacher is nice, my classmates have a good attitude, and I like wearing tennis ~~cloths~~ *clothes*. ~~Its~~ *It's* just that I don't ~~no~~ *know* how to serve the ball. Everyone has given me ~~advise~~ *advice*, but I can't seem to coordinate the toss and the stroke. Or I get the toss and the stroke right, but then the ball lands in the middle of the net. At first, it wasn't too embarrassing. But now that everyone knows my weakness, I am very self-~~conscience~~ *conscious* whenever ~~its~~ *it's* my turn to serve. I ~~new~~ *knew* that I should ~~of~~ *have* taken bowling or archery instead.

WORDS OFTEN CONFUSED, SET 2 (PP. 17–22)

EXERCISE 1

1. whether, write
2. who's (who has), You're, your
3. right, through, quite
4. led, too, write, personal
5. past

6. Personnel
7. They're, past, than
8. woman, principal
9. where
10. lose, than, lose

EXERCISE 2

1. piece, through

2. their, principal, to, weather

3. than

4. their, personal

5. who's, too, where

6. quite

7. than, than

8. piece, through

9. through, their

10. two, lose

EXERCISE 3

1. lead, You're, your

2. personal, lose

3. past, too

4. quite, wear, loose

5. than, they're

6. weather

7. Then, to

8. two, there

9. whether, they're

10. who's

EXERCISE 4

1. principle, your

2. than, to

3. past, quiet

4. there

5. write

6. woman

7. through

8. women, right

9. threw

10. Whether, lose

EXERCISE 5

1. right, past

2. where, principal

3. Women

4. lose, to

5. through, quite, than

6. woman, their

7. whose

8. than, there

9. Whether, piece

10. peace, their

PROOFREADING EXERCISE

Now that the ~~whether~~ *weather* is nice, my husband and I have decided to repaint the outside of our house. We are going to paint it ourselves. But it isn't going to be an easy job since many of the shingles have come ~~lose~~ *loose* over the years. In the ~~passed~~ *past* before we moved in, the house had been repainted without the scraping and sanding necessary, so big chunks of paint have just started falling off onto the grass. We worry that ~~their~~ *there* is ~~led~~ *lead* in the old paint, but we can't decide ~~weather~~ *whether* to call in a professional. One of my husband's friends, a woman ~~who's~~ *whose* house was just remodeled, told him, "~~Your~~ *You're* going to regret doing it yourselves. After what I've been ~~threw~~ *through*, I would strongly recommend hiring a professional. That's the only way to guarantee your ~~piece~~ *peace* of mind."

CONTRACTIONS (PP. 25–29)

EXERCISE 1
1. We've
2. don't
3. isn't
4. she's, we've, it's
5. wasn't
6. There's, he's
7. she'd, couldn't
8. don't
9. can't
10. we've, weren't

EXERCISE 2
1. we'd
2. didn't, I'd
3. couldn't, hadn't
4. wasn't
5. didn't
6. weren't, they're
7. isn't, didn't, I'd
8. no contractions
9. we'd
10. we're, couldn't

EXERCISE 3
1. hasn't
2. he'd, might've
3. it's
4. wasn't
5. didn't, they're
6. hasn't, it's
7. wouldn't
8. they'd
9. What's, they've, hasn't
10. It's

EXERCISE 4
1. there's, I'm
2. I've
3. We've, haven't
4. We'll, can't
5. she's, we've
6. it's
7. aren't
8. we're, we'll
9. That's, I'll, it's
10. there's

EXERCISE 5

1. Who's

2. I've, he's, who've

3. wouldn't, would've

4. no contractions

5. wasn't

6. weren't

7. no contractions

8. it's

9. They've

10. Moore's

PROOFREADING EXERCISE

I ~~cant~~ *can't* even think of a roller coaster anymore without being afraid. I used to look forward to the warm ~~whether~~ *weather* and frequent trips to our local amusement parks. I loved everything about the rides—the speed, the dips, the turns, the loops. Then I was in a minor car accident ~~wear~~ *where* I injured my knee after crashing into the rear end of another car. It ~~was'nt~~ *wasn't* ~~to~~ *too* bad, and only my knee was hurt. I thought that a sore knee would be the only negative ~~affect~~ *effect*. I was wrong. For some reason, since the accident, I've become really frightened of going fast. I found out the hard way, by going ~~threw~~ *through* the most terrifying minutes of my life on a coaster that ~~Id~~ *I'd* been on several times in the ~~passed~~ *past*. I guess ~~its~~ *it's* time for me to find new ways of having fun.

POSSESSIVES (PP. 31–35)

EXERCISE 4

1. Picasso's

2. no possessives needing apostrophes

3. masterpiece's

4. guard's, painting's

5. woman's

6. days'

7. museum's

8. authorities', Amsterdam's, man's

9. Picasso's

10. no possessives needing apostrophes

EXERCISE 5

1. *The Simpsons'*

2. show's, "The Simpsons' House Giveaway"

3. Homer, Marge, Bart, Lisa, and Maggie's

4. house's, series'

5. contest's

6. Howard's, The Simpsons' House's

7. property's

8. Las Vegas' (or Las Vegas's)

9. Simpsons'

10. Ned Flanders', Principal Skinner's, Apu's, Chief Wiggum's

PROOFREADING EXERCISE

You might not know of Marion ~~Donovans~~ *Donovan's* claim to fame. She invented something most parents use thousands of times. When her ~~babys'~~ *baby's* crib became wet each night, Donovan used a shower curtain to create the ~~worlds~~ *world's* first plastic diaper cover. After patenting her device and calling it the "Boater," ~~Donavans'~~ *Donavan's* business sense guided her to sell the idea, which she received one million dollars for in 1951. The Boater design led to the birth of the disposable diaper, and ~~its'~~ *its* sales currently bring in nearly five billion dollars a year.

REVIEW OF CONTRACTIONS AND POSSESSIVES (PP. 36–37)

1. There's, Valentine's

2. I'm, You're

3. America's, that's

4. Necco's, they've

5. heart's (or hearts'), it's

6. company's, cookie's

7. candy's

8. country's

9. New Year's, year's, Valentine's

10. they'll

Bowling for Values

Growing up as a child, I didn't have a set of values to live by. Neither my mother nor my father gave me any specific rules, guidelines, or beliefs to lead me through the complicated journey of childhood. My parents' approach was to set me free, to allow me to experience life's difficulties and develop my own set of values.

They were like parents taking their young child bowling for the first time. They hung their values on the pins at the end of the lane. Then they put up the gutter guards and hoped that I'd hit at least a few of the values they'd lived by themselves.

If I had a son today, I'd be more involved in developing a set of standards for him to follow. I'd adopt my mom and dad's philosophy of letting him discover on his own what he's interested in and how he feels about life. But I'd let him bowl in other lanes or even in other bowling alleys. And, from the start, he'd know my thoughts on religion, politics, drugs, sex, and all the ethical questions that go along with such subjects.

Now that I'm older, I wish my parents would've shared their values with me. Being free wasn't as comfortable as it might've been if I'd had some basic values to use as a foundation when I had tough choices to make. My children's lives will be better, I hope. At least they'll have a base to build on or to remodel—whichever they choose.

RULE FOR DOUBLING THE FINAL LETTER (PP. 39–40)

EXERCISE 1
1. eating
2. cutting
3. slipping
4. talking
5. weeding
6. conferring
7. clapping
8. trimming
9. quizzing
10. mopping

EXERCISE 2
1. snapping
2. tearing
3. healing
4. flopping
5. suggesting
6. canceling
7. preferring
8. dreaming
9. dripping
10. transmitting

EXERCISE 3
1. patting
2. spanning
3. feeding
4. alarming
5. occurring
6. brushing
7. gathering
8. knotting
9. offering
10. hogging

EXERCISE 4
1. digging
2. reviewing
3. dealing
4. clogging
5. clicking
6. unhooking
7. running
8. pushing
9. aiming
10. delivering

EXERCISE 5

1. mourning
2. dressing
3. passing
4. buttoning
5. sitting

6. wishing
7. cooking
8. constructing
9. polishing
10. leading

PROGRESS TEST (P. 41)

1. A. year's
2. B. (could) have
3. A. submitted
4. A. lose
5. B. compliment
6. A. where
7. A. already
8. A. effect
9. B. principal
10. B. a (unique material)

SENTENCE STRUCTURE

FINDING SUBJECTS AND VERBS (PP. 51–53)

EXERCISE 1

1. Pleasant childhood memories are often quite vivid.
2. We remember special places, people, and things from our youth.
3. The image of our first house stays in our minds, for instance.
4. There are the neighborhood children to recall.
5. Such memories include favorite furniture and decorative objects.
6. (You) Think back to your childhood now.
7. Most likely, it brings back a flood of memories.
8. Perhaps colors and smells seemed brighter and sweeter then.
9. Such sensations strike most of us at some point in our lives.
10. At these times, we cherish the past and look forward to the future.

EXERCISE 2

1. Your brain has two halves—a right side (hemisphere) and a left side (hemisphere).

2. But one side of your brain is stronger in different ways.

3. Scientists refer to this fact as "hemispheric lateralization" and test it this way.

4. (You) Open your eyes and hold up your thumb with your arm far out.

5. Next, (you) point your thumb at something on the other side of the room.

6. (You) Keep both eyes open but cover the thing with the image of your thumb.

7. One at a time, (you) shut one eye and then the other.

8. Your thumb moves to the right or left or stays the same.

9. For most people, the thumb jumps to the right with a closed right eye.

10. Very few people experience the opposite effect and are left-eyed.

EXERCISE 3

1. Amateur talent shows celebrate the performer or "ham" in all of us.

2. Schools and charities organize these events and raise funds for their organizations.

3. There are singers, dancers, comics, and acrobats in nearly every community.

4. They are not always good singers, dancers, comics, and acrobats, however.

5. In fact, crowds often love the worst performers in talent shows.

6. A sense of humor in the audience and the performers helps enormously.

7. Otherwise, participants feel embarrassment instead of encouragement.

8. Laughing with someone is not the same as laughing at someone. (*Laughing* is not a real verb in this sentence.)

9. Amateur performers need courage and support.

10. Every celebrity started somewhere, perhaps even in a talent show.

EXERCISE 4

1. The word *toast* has a couple of different meanings.

2. We toast pieces of bread and eat them with butter and jam.

3. People also make toasts to the bride and groom at weddings.

4. There are Old French and Latin word roots for *toast*.

5. Both *toster* (Old French) and *torrere* (Latin) refer to cooking and drying.

6. *Toast* as the word for cooked bread slices arrived in the 1400s.

7. The story of *toast's* other meaning makes sense from there.

8. In the 1600s, there was a tradition in taverns.

9. Revelers placed spicy croutons in their drinks for added flavor.

10. Then they drank to the health of various ladies and invented the other meaning of *toast*.

EXERCISE 5

1. Actors in the 1997 movie *Titanic* worked under difficult conditions.

2. The script required several hundred extras besides the actors in the leading roles.

3. For nearly four months, the filmmakers shot only nighttime scenes in water.

4. At the end of each night's filming, there were hundreds of cold actors in wet costumes.

5. Earlier in production, the actors complained about another scene.

6. Jack teaches Rose the art of spitting off the ship's deck. (*Spitting* is not a real verb here or in Sentence 10.)

7. That scene took five days to film and was very unpopular at the time.

8. Later, by chance, it connected with Rose's final moment of rebellion.

9. In the original script of the lifeboat scene, Rose's character stabs her fiancé with a hairpin.

10. But Kate Winslet thought of spitting in his face instead and tied the two moments together.

PARAGRAPH EXERCISE

My aunt and uncle have an incredible cookie jar collection. At the moment, they own about eight hundred jars and get new ones every day. Some of their cookie jars date back to the late nineteenth century. But others commemorate more current cartoon or movie characters. Celebrity cookie jars bring my aunt special happiness and add to the glamour of the collection. There are Elvis, Marilyn Monroe, and James Dean jars and even ones depicting The Grateful Dead's bus or The Beatles' psychedelic car. I really appreciate my aunt and uncle's collection and hope for one of my own someday.

LOCATING PREPOSITIONAL PHRASES (PP. 56–60)

EXERCISE 1

1. My family and I live (in a house) (at the top) (of a hilly neighborhood) (in Los Angeles).

2. (On weekday mornings), nearly everyone drives (down the steep winding roads) (to their jobs) or (to school).

3. (In the evenings), they all come back (up the hill) to be (with their families).

4. (For the rest) (of the day), we see only an occasional delivery van or compact school bus.

5. But (on Saturdays and Sundays), there is a different set (of drivers) (on the road).

6. Then tourists (in minivans) and prospective home buyers (in convertibles) cram the narrow streets.

7. (On these weekend days), most (of the neighborhood residents) stay (at home).

8. Frequently, drivers unfamiliar (with the twists and turns) (of the roads) (up here) cause accidents.

9. The expression "Sunday driver" really means something (to those) (of us) (on the hill).

10. And we could add "Saturday driver" (to the list), as well.

EXERCISE 2

1. (In England), Bob Martin is a man (with a very strange claim) (to fame).

2. The seventy-year-old Martin lives (in Eastleigh), a town approximately one hundred miles south (of London).

3. (For ten years), he traveled (by train) (to London) hundreds (of times) (for one specific purpose).

4. (During these trips), Martin attended six hundred and twenty-five performances (of *Cats*), the long-running musical (by Andrew Lloyd Webber).

5. Martin's interest (in the show) started the first time he listened (to the original cast album).

6. This devoted *Cats* fan always sat (in the orchestra section), but not always (in the same seat).

7. Many (of the actors and crew members) (in the productions) befriended Bob Martin (over the years).

8. (In the eyes) (of his extended family), Martin is just a happy eccentric.

9. (Without a wife or children) to think about, Martin indulged his interest (in *Cats*).

10. (As a result), he traveled more than one hundred thousand miles (over the rails) and spent more than twenty thousand dollars (on tickets) to see the same play over and over again.

EXERCISE 3

1. (Through NASA's space-exploration projects), we learn more (about everything) (from our fellow planets) (to our sun and moon).

2. *Galileo* already discovered a layer (of ice) (on Europa), Jupiter's moon, and (in 2003) will look (for signs) (of life) (beneath the ice's surface).

3. (With the help) (of the *Hubble Space Telescope*), NASA retrieved pictures (of the planet Uranus)—its system (of rings) and its weather patterns.

4. NASA launched *Cassini* (in 1997) to study Saturn, (with an expected arrival time) (of 2004).

5. (In an effort) to put an American (on Mars) (by 2020), NASA will use information (from *Mars Surveyor 2001*).

6. NASA's *Pluto-Kuiper Express* will study Pluto, the most distant planet (in our solar system).

7. (With the *Contour Mission*) (in 2002), NASA hopes to learn (about the origin) (of comets).

8. The *Terra* satellite will look (at changes) (in Earth's weather) (as part) (of NASA's Earth Observing System).

9. The *Genesis* probe will fly (around the sun) and gather new information (about its unique properties).

10. Finally, the mission (for the *Lunar Prospector*) is to discover habitable places (on the moon).

EXERCISE 4

1. An engraved likeness (of Pocahontas), the famous Powhatan Indian princess, is the oldest portrait (on display) (at the National Portrait Gallery).

2. (In 1607), Pocahontas—still (in her early teens)—single-handedly helped the British colonists (in Virginia) to survive.

3. Later, (in 1616), Pocahontas traveled (to England) (after her marriage) (to John Rolfe) and the birth (of their son).

4. She visited the court (of King James I) and impressed the British (with her knowledge) (of English) and her conversion (to Christianity).

5. (For her new first name), she chose Rebecca.

6. (During her seven-month stay) (in England), she became extremely ill.

7. (At some point) (before or during her illness), Simon Van de Passe engraved her portrait (on copper).

8. The portrait shows Pocahontas (in a ruffled collar and ornate Anglicized clothes) but (with very strong Indian features).

9. Successful sales (of prints) (from the portrait) illustrate her fame abroad.

10. Pocahontas died (on that trip) (to England) (at the age) (of twenty-two).

EXERCISE 5

1. Gorgons have been extinct (for two hundred and fifty million years).

2. These creatures lived and died millions (of years) (before dinosaurs).

3. They perished (along with almost all life) (on the planet) (in a huge cataclysmic event).

4. (In fact), dinosaurs met a similar fate (of their own).

5. Gorgons were beasts (with both lion-like and lizard-like qualities).

6. Recently, scientists discovered a full-size fossilized skeleton (of a gorgon) (in South Africa).

7. (At seven feet long), the fossil tells a lot (about these animals).

8. They had eyes (in the sides) (of their nearly three-foot-long heads).

9. And they hunted successfully (with the help) (of their four-inch-long teeth).

10. The gorgons' extreme physical features reveal the harshness (of their prehistoric surroundings).

PARAGRAPH EXERCISE

(On November 17, 1968), (during the last seconds) (of a football game) (between the New York Jets and the Oakland Raiders), (in which) the Jets were leading (by a score) (of 32) (to 29), NBC cut the game to show the children's story *Heidi*. The switchboard was so overwhelmed (with calls) (from angry viewers) that the circuit broke down. Meanwhile, the Jets were defeated 43 (to 32). NBC was forced to show the last fifty seconds (of the game) (on the following morning's *Today* show broadcast).

UNDERSTANDING DEPENDENT CLAUSES (PP. 63–68)

EXERCISE 1

1. Jo Ann Altsman is a woman who is lucky to be alive.

2. When she had a second heart attack, no other person was there to help her.

3. Because she was in such pain, she couldn't move or easily call for help.

4. She did have two pets that she looked to as she lay on the floor of her home in what she considered her final moments.

5. She wondered if her dog might help, but he only barked at her.

6. Then Altsman's 150-pound potbellied pig LuLu took action when it became obvious that no one else could help her master.

7. The pig somehow made it through the little door that allows smaller pets to go in and out.

8. As she went through the opening, LuLu tore big scratches on her tummy, but she persisted.

9. While she whined loudly for help, LuLu walked to the nearest highway and waited for a car.

10. The man who stopped followed LuLu to Altsman's house, and he called for an ambulance.

EXERCISE 2

1. On June 8, 1924, two British men, George Mallory and Andrew Irvine, disappeared as they were climbing to the top of Mount Everest.

2. When a reporter earlier asked Mallory why he climbed Everest, his response became legendary.

3. "Because it is there," Mallory replied.

4. No living person knows whether the two men reached the summit of Everest before they died.

5. Nine years after Mallory and Irvine disappeared, English climbers found Irvine's ice ax.

6. But nothing else of Mallory's or Irvine's was found until a Chinese climber spotted their bodies in 1975.

7. He kept the news of his sighting secret for several years but finally decided to tell a fellow climber on the day before he died himself in an avalanche on Everest.

8. In May 1999, a team of mountaineers searched the area where the Chinese man had seen something, and they found George Mallory's frozen body still intact after seventy-five years.

9. After they took DNA samples for identification, the mountaineers buried the famous climber on the mountainside where he fell.

10. Mallory and Irvine were the first climbers to try to get to the top of Everest, and the question remains whether they were on their way up or on their way down when they met their fate.

EXERCISE 3

1. If you ever plan a trip to Bangkok, (you) be sure to visit the Royal Dragon restaurant.

2. Somchai T. Amornrat designed the Royal Dragon so that it would break the world's record for the largest restaurant in the world.

3. Since the previous record-holding restaurant was also in Bangkok, Amornrat did some research and made his restaurant even bigger.

4. The Royal Dragon covers twelve acres and is so sprawling that servers must wear roller skates to get around.

5. As many as ten thousand people a day eat at the Royal Dragon or Mangkorn Luang, as it is called in Thai.

6. After customers enter the huge park-like complex, they dine at tables that encircle a large reflecting pool.

7. And once every evening, a waitress entertains the diners as she flies from the top of a Pagoda that is seven stories high to a stage in the middle of the pool.

8. Before the flying waitress takes off, speakers play the theme song from *Mission: Impossible*.

9. If guests want to make their own music, they can visit one of the Royal Dragon's fifty karaoke bars.

10. The one thousand people who cook and serve the food and who do the dishes afterward never worry about being late to work since most of them live in the restaurant complex.

EXERCISE 4

1. I just read an article that described the history of all the presidents' dogs.

2. Our first president, George Washington, cared so much about dogs that he bred them; Washington even interrupted a battle to return a dog that belonged to a British general.

3. Abraham Lincoln, whose dog was actually named Fido, left his loyal pet in Illinois after the Lincolns moved to the White House.

4. Teddy Roosevelt had lots of dogs but met and adopted Skip, the one that he loved best, as the little terrier held a bear at bay in the Grand Canyon.

5. FDR's pooch was always with him; he was a black Scottie named Fala, and they say that Roosevelt was so devoted to this pet that he made a U.S. Navy ship return to the Aleutians to pick Fala up after the diplomatic party accidentally left the dog behind.

6. Warren G. Harding's Laddie Boy was the most pampered of the presidential dogs since the Hardings gave him birthday parties and ordered a specially made chair for Laddie Boy to sit in during presidential meetings.

7. Soviet leader Nikita Khrushchev brought with him Pushinka, a dog that he gave to John F. Kennedy's daughter Caroline.

8. At a filling station in Texas, Lyndon Johnson's daughter Luci found a little white dog, Yuki, whom President Johnson loved to have howling contests with in the Oval Office.

9. Of course, Nixon had his famous Checkers, and George Bush had a spaniel named Millie, who wrote her own best-selling book with the help of Barbara Bush.

10. And just when it seemed that all presidents prefer dogs, Bill Clinton arrived with Socks, a distinctively marked black-and-white cat.

EXERCISE 5

1. When Susan Lucci won a Daytime Emmy award in 1999, everyone was happy and surprised.

2. For Lucci, the award ended a losing streak that lasted nineteen years.

3. Since she has played the part of Erika Cane on *All My Children* for nearly thirty years, Lucci naturally wanted to win.

4. And whenever she didn't win, Lucci's family and friends gave her extra support.

5. Her children decorated the house while she attended the award ceremonies so that she felt appreciated even if she lost again.

6. As her string of losses got longer, Lucci revealed a good sense of humor when she did commercials that alluded to her infamous losing streak.

7. For a long time, nothing that Lucci did seemed to help her chances, however, and many thought that she might never win.

8. Some believe that she won the Emmy in 1999 because the scenes that Lucci submitted to the award board showed her as Erika the mom, dealing with a daughter who suffered from anorexia.

9. Since Lucci has a daughter herself, the scenes had the power of true emotions behind them.

10. Lucci's own daughter Liza is now a soap opera actress too, and everyone hopes that, as far as awards go, she will have better luck than her mother did.

PARAGRAPH EXERCISE

If the moon is full and the night skies are alive with the calls of bird migrants, then the way is open for [an] adventure with your child, if he [or she] is old enough to use a telescope or a good pair of binoculars. The sport of watching migrating birds pass across the face of the moon has become popular and even scientifically important in recent years, and it is as good a way as I know to give an older child a sense of the mystery of migration.

(You) Seat yourself comfortably and focus your glass on the moon. You must learn patience, for unless you are on a well-traveled highway of migration you may have to wait many minutes before you are rewarded. In the waiting periods you can study the topography of the moon, for even a glass of moderate power reveals enough detail to fascinate a space-conscious child. But sooner or later you should begin to see the birds, lonely travelers in space glimpsed as they pass from darkness into darkness.

CORRECTING FRAGMENTS (PP. 71–75)

EXERCISE 1
Answers may vary, but here are some possible revisions.

1. Sarah Winchester was a rich, eccentric woman.
2. Her husband *was* William Winchester.
3. William inherited the Winchester rifle fortune.
4. The weapon *was* responsible for the deaths of more people and animals than any gun before it.
5. After William's death, the Winchester millions *passed* down to Sarah.
6. But bad luck and other deaths in her family made her superstitious.
7. A psychic *called* it revenge by all those spirits killed by Winchester rifles.
8. To avoid more trouble, the psychic told Sarah to buy a house out west and use her money to constantly rebuild it.
9. The spirits *would guide* the renovation along the way to give them a nice place to visit and keep them happy.
10. That way Sarah *could avoid* the curse of the Winchester ghosts.

EXERCISE 2
Answers may vary, but here are some possible revisions.

1. The Winchester Mystery House, located in San Jose, California, *was* built by Sarah Winchester.
2. *The house grew* from its original form—a small field house with fewer than ten rooms—to a sprawling mansion with more than one hundred rooms.
3. *It has* thousands of windows and doors, some without openings on the other side.
4. One Sarah-sized door *stands* just five feet high right next to one of normal size.
5. *There are* nearly fifty bedrooms and as many staircases, several leading to a dead end at the ceiling.

6. Thirteen was Sarah's lucky number.

7. So she set twelve other table settings at dinner for her ghost guests.

8. *She even signed* her will (with thirteen sections) thirteen times.

9. Sarah died in 1922 and left the Winchester Mystery House behind as a museum.

10. Many people *visit* Sarah's strange house and *explore* its odd interiors every year.

EXERCISE 3
Answers may vary, but here are some possible revisions.

1. Finding a parking space on the first day of classes seems impossible. *I drive* endlessly around campus looking for an empty spot.

2. With hope that the situation will improve, I always spend the sixty dollars for a parking permit.

3. My old car's engine doesn't like the long periods of idling. *It stalls* a lot and won't start up again easily.

4. In order to get a space close to my first class, I always follow anyone walking through the parking lot closest to the science building.

5. I am usually disappointed by this method, however. Most people *are* just walking through the parking lot to get to farther lots or to the bus stop.

6. I was really lucky on the first day of the semester two semesters ago. *I drove* right into a spot vacated by a student from an earlier class.

7. Maybe I should get up before dawn myself, *for that's* a fool-proof way to secure a perfect parking place.

8. Every morning, I see these early birds in their cars with their seats back. *They sleep* there for hours before class but in a great spot.

9. I don't think I can solve the problem this way. *I find* it hard to get out of bed in the dark.

10. Due to the rise in college populations, campus parking problems will most likely only get worse.

EXERCISE 4
Answers may vary, but here are some possible revisions.

1. We were writing in our journals when suddenly the fire alarm rang.

2. Everyone in the class looked at each other first and then at the teacher. *He told* us to gather up our things and follow him outside.

3. The series of short bells continued as we left the room and noisily walked out into the parking lot beside the main building.

4. The sunlight was very warm and bright compared to the classroom's florescent lights, which make everything look more clinical than natural.

5. As we stood in a large group with students and teachers from other classes, we wondered about the reason for the alarm.

6. I have never been roused by a fire alarm that was anything but a planned drill.

7. Without the danger of injury, a party atmosphere quickly develops since we all get a break from our responsibilities.

8. I've noticed that the teachers seem the most at ease because they don't have to be in control during these situations.

9. After we students and the teachers chatted for ten minutes or so, the final bell rang to signal the end of the drill.

10. When we sat down at our desks again, the teacher asked us to continue writing in our journals until the end of the hour.

EXERCISE 5

Answers may vary, but here are some possible revisions. (Added independent clauses are in italics.)

1. *I am surprised* that you know so much about the politics of South American countries.

2. While the jury deliberated, *everyone else waited.*

3. But that story sounds unbelievable.

4. Be sure to send me a postcard.

5. Harry Houdini promised to visit his wife after his death.

6. Taking artistic photographs requires skill and patience.

7. *We returned* to the restaurant where we first met.

8. Until he noticed the price tag hanging from the side of the couch, *he liked it.*

9. *She was* a woman who traveled extensively during her childhood.

10. If the rain stops, *the game will go on.*

PROOFREADING PARAGRAPH
Answers may vary, but here are some possible revisions. (Corrections are in italics.)

When a ten-year-old girl named Stephanie Taylor heard about the shooting death of a police dog in New Jersey. S *, she* decided to do something to protect the dogs. W *who* work for the police in Oceanside, California. *That's where* Stephanie lives with her family. Raising *She raised* enough money to buy bullet-proof vests for all of Oceanside PD's K-9 (canine) officers. Stephanie is glad now. Knowing that *she knows that* the dogs who serve and protect her neighborhood will be protected themselves.

CORRECTING RUN-ON SENTENCES (PP. 78–82)

EXERCISE 1
Your answers may differ depending on how you chose to separate the two clauses.

1. Frank Epperson invented something delicious and refreshing, and it comes on a stick.

2. In 1905, Epperson was an eleven-year-old boy. He lived in San Francisco.

3. The sentence is correct.

4. The sentence is correct.

5. There was a record-breaking cold snap that evening, and the drink froze.

6. In the morning, Frank Epperson ate his frozen juice creation; it made a big impression.

7. Epperson grew up and kept making his frozen "Epsicles"; they came in seven varieties.

8. The sentence is correct.

9. Epperson's kids loved their dad's treat, and they always called them "pop's sicles."

10. So Popsicles were born, and people have loved them ever since.

EXERCISE 2
Your answers may differ depending on how you chose to separate the two clauses.

1. Last week I decided to adopt a pet from an animal shelter, so I visited the SPCA near my house.

2. There were lots of great potential pets there. At first I couldn't choose between the dogs or the cats.

3. The sentence is correct.

4. My house doesn't have a fenced yard, so a dog would need to be walked in the mornings and evenings.

5. The sentence is correct.

6. But I am at work for most of the day; it might bark and disturb the neighbors.

7. The sentence is correct.

8. Cats are also independent; therefore, a cat wouldn't miss me during the day.

9. By coincidence, the shelter had just received a litter of gray and white kittens. I was lucky enough to have first choice and picked the best one.

10. I named her Dizzy, for she loved to chase the white tip of her tail around.

EXERCISE 3

Your answers may differ since various words can be used to begin dependent clauses.

1. Now that I've been learning about sleep in my psychology class, I know a lot more about it.

2. Sleep has five stages, which we usually go through many times during the night.

3. As the first stage of sleep begins, our muscles relax and mental activity slows down.

4. The sentence is correct.

5. Because stage two takes us deeper than stage one, we are no longer aware of our surroundings.

6. The sentence is correct.

7. Next is stage three, in which we become more and more relaxed and are very hard to awaken.

8. Stage four is so deep that we don't even hear loud noises.

9. The fifth stage of sleep is called REM (rapid-eye-movement) sleep because our eyes move back and forth quickly behind our eyelids.

10. Although REM sleep is only about as deep as stage two, we do all our dreaming during the REM stage.

EXERCISE 4

Your answers may differ since various words can be used to begin dependent clauses.

1. The sentence is correct.

2. The New York police had to break up the crowds who got out of control after seeing and *smelling* the amazing plant.

3. The Titan Arum, which is native to Sumatra, is known for its size and its odor.

4. Because the blooming plant smells like dirty feet or dead animals, some people call it the "corpse flower."

5. The sentence is correct.

6. Since no Titan had ever bloomed in California, thousands of people visited the Huntington to experience the spectacle.

7. Visitors came in such large numbers that the Huntington extended its hours and even stayed open on Monday when it's normally closed.

8. Within a couple of days, the Huntington gift shop ran out of Titan Arum souvenirs, which depicted the tall plant in full bloom.

9. When the blossom finished growing, it measured six feet tall and nearly four feet across.

10. Although the Huntington Gardens usually close at 4:30, the Huntington's Titan Arum bloomed at 5:00 on August 1, 1999, to the "delight" of everyone.

EXERCISE 5

Your answers may differ depending on how you chose to separate the clauses.

1. In 1999, the BBC released its documentary series called *The Life of Birds.* Sir David Attenborough was the host.

2. The series took nearly three years to complete as the crew filmed in more than forty countries and shot about two hundred miles of film.

3. The BBC spent fifteen million dollars making *The Life of Birds,* a cost that included Attenborough's traveling the equivalent of ten times around the world.

4. The BBC takes such shows very seriously; this one about birds comes after the BBC's amazing documentary called *The Private Life of Plants.*

5. For the plant series, BBC filmmakers even invented new ways to film plants and record the sounds they make, and a lot of the filming had to take place under artificial conditions. However, for the bird series, the BBC wanted a more realistic feeling.

6. All of the filming was done in the birds' own habitats so that it showed their natural behavior, some of which had never been seen or filmed before.

7. To capture these rare moments, filmmakers had to live with birds in the wild, but it was not a very safe environment at times.

8. A tree full of BBC filmmakers was struck by lightning in an Amazon rain forest; they were covered with insects in Jamaica, and Attenborough had to speak to the camera in total darkness in a cave in Venezuela.

9. Makers of the series were especially proud of their bird of paradise footage, which they shot in New Guinea.

10. It turned out to be one of their biggest disappointments because the priceless film was erased by an especially powerful x-ray machine at the airport.

REVIEW OF FRAGMENTS AND RUN-ON SENTENCES (P. 83)

Your revisions may differ depending on how you chose to correct the errors.

Most people would not recognize the name Joseph Ignace Guillotin, but they probably have heard of the machine named after him, the guillotine. It's the device used when many a king or queen said, "Off with his—or her—head!" The guillotine consists of a slanted blade that falls down a window-frame-shaped tower and can be reset after it does its job. Guillotin was a doctor in France during the French Revolution. Even though he was not the inventor of the machine, he did suggest that it be used to behead people quickly and easily. Guillotin's name was first associated with the device in 1793. Now doctors everywhere also use the word *guillotine* to describe cutting procedures that they perform during tonsillectomies and other surgeries.

IDENTIFYING VERB PHRASES (PP. 85–89)

EXERCISE 1

1. I have always wondered how an Etch-A-Sketch works.

2. This flat TV-shaped toy has been popular since it first came out (in the 1960s).

3. Now I have discovered a Web site that answers questions (like the following): "How does an Etch-A-Sketch work?"

4. An Etch-A-Sketch is filled (with a combination) (of metal powder and tiny plastic particles).

5. This mixture clings (to the inside) (of the Etch-A-Sketch screen).

6. When the pointer that is connected (to the two knobs) moves, the tip (of it) "draws" lines (in the powder) (on the back) (of the screen).

7. The powder (at the bottom) (of the Etch-A-Sketch) does not fill in these lines because it is too far away.

8. But if the Etch-A-Sketch is turned upside down, the powder clings (to the whole underside surface) (of the screen) and "erases" the image again.

9. Although the basic Etch-A-Sketch has not changed since I was a kid, it now comes (in several different sizes).

10. Best (of all), these great drawing devices have never needed batteries, and I hope that they never will [need batteries].

EXERCISE 2

1. Most people would not think (of bar codes and cockroaches) together.

2. We would expect bar codes (on products) (in supermarkets and shopping malls).

3. And we might not be surprised if a cockroach showed up (by a trash can) (behind the supermarket or shopping mall).

4. But we would definitely look twice if we saw a cockroach (with a bar code) (on its back).

5. That is just what exterminator Bruce Tennenbaum wanted everyone to do (in 1999), however.

6. He attached bar codes (to one hundred) (of these insects) and released them (in Tucson, Arizona) (as a public-awareness campaign).

7. When people found a bar-coded bug, they could return it (for a hundred-dollar prize).

8. (In an effort) to increase public participation, one (of the roaches) was tagged (with a unique bar code) that would earn its finder fifty thousand dollars.

9. Many (of the citizens) (of Tucson) searched (for these "prizes,") and some of the tagged roaches were found.

10. But Tennenbaum should have put a tracking device (on the fifty-thousand-dollar bug) because it was never seen again.

EXERCISE 3

1. When we think (of ancient structures), Stonehenge (in England) and the Great Pyramids (of Egypt) come (to mind).

2. Fairly recently, Fred Wendorf discovered an arrangement (of stones) possibly a thousand years older (than Stonehenge).

3. Wendorf uncovered the stone structures (of Nabta Playa) while he was researching nomadic people (in Egypt).

4. Wendorf dug down (to the level) where eight huge stone tablets formed a circle.

5. He and other anthropologists believe that nomads must have created the site (for astronomical purposes).

6. The slabs and their arrangement date back seven thousand years.

7. They were placed (in groups) (of two) and were aligned (with different points) (of the compass).

8. (Near the circle) (of stones) was a tomb that had not been found before.

9. It had been used not (for a dead king) but (for the nomads' cattle).

10. These nomadic people may have been the first citizens (of the Nile Valley) so many thousands (of years) ago.

EXERCISE 4

1. (During the last semester) (of high school), my English teacher assigned a special paper.

2. He said that he was becoming depressed (by all the bad news) (out there), so each (of us) was assigned to find a piece (of good news) and write a short research paper (about it).

3. I must admit that I had no idea how hard that assignment would be.

4. Finally, I found an article while I was reading my favorite magazine.

5. The title (of the article) was a pun; it was called "Grin Reaper."

6. I knew instantly that it must be just the kind (of news) my teacher was searching for.

7. The article explained that one woman, Pam Johnson, had started a club that she named The Secret Society (of Happy People).

8. She had even chosen August 8 (as "(You) Admit You're Happy Day") and had already convinced more than fifteen state governors to recognize the holiday.

9. The club and the holiday were created to support people who are happy so that the unhappy, negative people (around them) will not bring the happy people down.

10. As I was writing my essay, I visited the Happy People Web site and, (for extra credit), signed my teacher up (for their newsletter).

EXERCISE 5

1. Last night I took my daughter (to a performance) (by her favorite group).

2. The tickets were not too expensive, and I remembered how much fun I had had at concerts (in my younger days).

3. I had not been (to an open-air event) (for several years), however, and I was expecting the same kind (of experience).

4. I should have considered the changes that have occurred (since then).

5. The first difference was that, when we arrived, people were waiting (in a long line) (in the hot sunshine) to get (into the stadium) even though everyone had assigned seats.

6. I asked a staff member why they weren't spending time (in their cars) or (in the cool shade).

7. He told me that they were hoping to get in first so that they could buy the best souvenirs.

8. Once we were (inside the place), I saw what he meant; T-shirts were hanging (with thirty-five-dollar price tags), and every other kind (of object) (with the group's name or picture) (on it) was being bought (by frantic fans).

9. I understood then why the tickets had been so inexpensive; as long as they brought the customers (to the merchandise), they had done their job.

10. (After three opening acts), my daughter's favorite group finally arrived (on stage), overwhelmed the crowd (with special effects), and left everyone (with lots) (of souvenirs) (as memories).

REVIEW EXERCISE

(For business wear) bow ties give off several negative effects. You will not be taken seriously when [you are] wearing one. The only positive use comes if you are too powerful a personality, (in which case) they can soften your image. But otherwise you will not be thought responsible if you wear a bow tie. Most people will not trust you (with anything important). It is a death knell (for anyone) selling his services (as a consultant or lawyer, etc.) The number (of people) who will trust you (at all), (with anything), will be cut (in half).

(In general), I have found that people believe that a man (in a bow tie) will steal. It creates the impression (of being unpredictable), thus some experienced trial lawyers who believe [that] they have a good case will try to keep a man wearing a bow tie (off a jury).

Bow ties are acceptable (as sports attire), and if you do wear them (for such occasions), [you] stick (to the same patterns) recommended (for all other ties).

USING STANDARD ENGLISH VERBS (PP. 92–95)

EXERCISE 1

1. prepares, prepared
2. help, helped
3. are, were
4. have, had
5. does, did

6. needs, needed
7. has, had
8. is, was
9. works, worked
10. am, was

EXERCISE 2

1. are, were
2. does, did
3. has, had
4. opens, opened
5. have, had

6. counts, counted
7. are, were
8. do, did
9. look, looked
10. is, was

EXERCISE 3

1. changed, want
2. had
3. signed, turned
4. was, were
5. did, were, does
6. observed, had
7. watched, helped
8. had
9. imagined, had
10. needs, are, am

EXERCISE 4

1. watch
2. watches, watch
3. am, is
4. are
5. decides
6. wager
7. add, calls, is
8. love, have
9. plan
10. likes

EXERCISE 5

1. Yesterday my English teacher *assigned* a narration essay.
2. The sentence is correct.
3. The sentence is correct.
4. They *were* about holiday traditions in different families.
5. In one essay, the writer *explained* the tradition of Thanksgiving at her house.
6. I *liked* the part about making pies for the adults and candy for the kids.
7. The second essay *outlined* the steps another family goes through to prepare for Chinese New Year.
8. That one *had* even more details about food and gifts for the children.
9. The sentence is correct.
10. I *started* my rough draft last night; it's about my dad's obsession with Halloween.

PROOFREADING EXERCISE

I have a new piano teacher, Mr. Stevensen, who *talks* very softly and *plays* the piano beautifully. When he wants to teach me a new song, he *starts* by showing me the sheet music. Then he *asks* me to look it over. I am always nervous if it *shows* a new hand position or a new dynamic sign. But then he *calms* me down with his soothing voice and patient manner. Once I figure the piece out by looking at it, I *play* it through slowly. Mr. Stevensen *doesn't* do any of the annoying things my other piano teachers did. I like him a lot.

USING REGULAR AND IRREGULAR VERBS (PP. 100–104)

EXERCISE 1
1. practice
2. practiced
3. practicing
4. practice
5. practiced
6. practices
7. practice
8. practicing
9. practicing
10. practice

EXERCISE 2
1. try, tries
2. bought, buys
3. was, am
4. thought, think
5. grown, grown
6. leave, left
7. watches, watching
8. hears, hear
9. speaks, spoken
10. was, is

EXERCISE 3
1. took, supposed
2. did, earned
3. called, told, feel
4. thought, was
5. leaving, drove, saw
6. felt, knew, tell
7. tried, went (or got)
8. been, undo
9. wishes, take
10. used, called, does

EXERCISE 4
1. use, puts
2. does, do
3. transfers, spend
4. is, like, choose
5. does, wants
6. trusts, is
7. imagine, made
8. talking, asked, worries
9. looked, said, understand
10. trust, been

EXERCISE 5

1. lying, fell
2. was, done
3. wearing, shielded
4. lain, woke, realized, happened
5. felt, started

6. passed, turned, began
7. describe, experienced
8. was, felt, saw
9. looked, taped, was, protected, wearing
10. had, felt

PROGRESS TEST (P. 105)

1. A. fragment (*I took* a nap for several hours in the afternoon.)
2. B. incorrect verb form (Last semester we *enrolled* in the same math class.)
3. B. fragment (Attach the dependent clause to the previous sentence.)
4. A. incorrect verb form (Karen *used* to take the bus . . .)
5. B. missing comma to prevent misreading (Because Tim was driving, his mother . . .)
6. B. unnecessary comma (I will write in my journal every day and will turn . . .)
7. A. incorrect verb form (were *supposed*)
8. A. incorrect verb form (had already *finished*)
9. B. incorrect verb form (were *lying*)
10. B. fragment (*Packing is especially difficult when the weather is uncertain.*)

MAINTAINING SUBJECT/VERB AGREEMENT (PP. 108–112)

EXERCISE 1

1. collects
2. has, is
3. is
4. includes
5. has

6. was
7. stems
8. stays
9. are
10. was

EXERCISE 2

1. are, involve

2. suffer

3. are

4. come, lead

5. start, works, plays

6. starts

7. are

8. cause

9. is

10. warn

EXERCISE 3

1. were

2. was

3. have, have

4. is

5. contains

6. supports, has, are

7. says, was

8. believes, have, dries, finds

9. has, dates

10. agree, is

EXERCISE 4

1. is

2. has

3. starts

4. puts, wants

5. likes

6. have, looks

7. let, wants

8. have

9. helps, turn

10. am, is

EXERCISE 5

1. pictures, does

2. are, visit

3. is

4. are, have

5. were

6. have

7. have

8. create

9. are

10. are

PROOFREADING EXERCISE

All of the students in my drama club *have* chosen the play *Cyrano de Bergerac* for our next production. There *are* actually two famous Cyrano de Bergeracs. One of them is the title character of the play, and the other is the real person who had that name. Both of these men *are* famous for their large noses and for their writing. But only the fictional Cyrano loves Roxane. The tragic story of Cyrano and Roxane *was* written by Edmond Rostand. In it, Cyrano *believes* that Roxane could never love an ugly man. She thinks that she *loves* Christian, Cyrano's fellow soldier who is extremely handsome. But she really *loves* Cyrano, who writes all of the love letters that Christian gives Roxane. In those letters *is* the soul that Roxane *admires*, but she finds out too late. It's a very sad and dramatic story, and I hope that either my friend Lisa or I *get* the part of Roxane.

AVOIDING SHIFTS IN TIME (PP. 114–115)

1. Melinda French majored in computer science at Duke University and later earned an MBA. Then she got a job at Microsoft and started making a good living of her own. But when Melinda French married Bill Gates in 1994, she no longer had to think about money. Bill and Melinda Gates bought a mansion worth seventy-five million dollars. In 1996, their daughter Jennifer was born, and in 1999 they had a son. They named him Rory. Together, the couple created the Bill and Melinda Gates Foundation, a fund of nearly twenty billion dollars to give to charities.

2. The paragraph is correct.

3. I really enjoyed my summer vacation this year. It wasn't long enough, of course, but I made the most of the time I had. My geology club took a trip to Baja. We didn't pack enough to eat, but the beautiful scenery took my breath away. Once I was back home, I played a lot of tennis with my roommates. One night we stayed at the tennis court until after it closed. We were just hitting volleys in the dark with only the moon for lighting. It was an unplanned thing, and we could barely see the ball. It was fun to goof off with my friends on a summer evening. Overall, the trip to Baja and the after-hours tennis match were the highlights of my summer vacation.

RECOGNIZING VERBAL PHRASES (PP. 117–122)

EXERCISE 1

1. The idea of [home schooling children] has become more popular recently.

2. Many parents have decided [to teach kids themselves] instead of [sending them off to public or private school classrooms].

3. There are many different reasons [to choose home schooling].

4. In Hollywood, for instance, child actors often are forced [to drop out of traditional schools due to their schedules].

5. The [home schooling] option allows for one of their parents, or a special teacher, [to continue] [to instruct them on the set].

6. Other parents simply want [to be directly involved in their child's [learning]].

7. Many school districts <u>have</u> special independent study "schools," [offering parents the structure and materials] that they <u>need</u> [to provide an appropriate curriculum on their own].

8. Children <u>do</u> all of their [reading] and [writing] at home with their parents [guiding them along the way].

9. The family <u>meets</u> with the independent study school's teacher regularly [to go over the child's work] and [to clarify any points of confusion].

10. Many parents <u>would like</u> [to have the time] [to home school their children].

EXERCISE 2

1. By 2003, a Japanese company [called Matsushita] <u>expects</u> [to offer fully interactive houses] [operated by computer network].

2. [Getting ready for work in the morning] <u>will be</u> very different.

3. The electronic toilet-of-the-future <u>is designed</u> [to take care of everything]— [weighing you], [checking your health through various tests], and even [sending the data to your doctor if necessary].

4. [Talking into your television's remote control] <u>will turn</u> on the space-age TV screens of the future [positioned in almost every room of the house].

5. [Using a cell phone with its own video screen from your desk at work], you'<u>ll</u> <u>be</u> able [to check the contents of your refrigerator] before [shopping for groceries].

6. And once you <u>return</u> home with the food, you <u>can update</u> the fridge's contents [using voice commands].

7. [Glancing at monitors] [set up in key areas], you <u>can check</u> the status of your laundry room, [living] room, and kitchen simultaneously.

8. The rooms themselves <u>will respond</u> to your movements through the use of infrared sensors—[lighting up], [cooling off], or [heating up] as necessary.

9. A security system <u>will be used</u> [to take the picture] of anyone [approaching the front door] and [to store the snapshot for twelve months].

10. Needless [to say], the fully [wired] Japanese house of the new millennium <u>will</u> <u>be</u> expensive, [costing nearly five percent more than an ordinary, [old-fashioned] one].

EXERCISE 3

1. Binney & Smith is a company [headquartered in Easton, Pennsylvania].

2. The company is responsible for [making one of the most [treasured] memories of many people's childhoods]—Crayola crayons.

3. Company officials took a controversial step in 1990 by [retiring eight old colors of crayons] and [replacing them with new, more modern hues].

4. Before Binney & Smith canceled the eight colors, they asked children [to help them make the decision].

5. Grownups were very upset with the choices, [forming groups] with names like RUMPS (Raw Umber and Maize Preservation Society) and CRAYON (Committee to Reestablish All Your Old Norms).

6. These angry adults continued [to write and call the company] until a solution was found.

7. Binney & Smith opened a Crayola Hall of Fame at company headquarters, briefly [re-issuing crayon sets with the original colors intact].

8. Crayola Hall of Fame visitors now get [to walk past five-foot-high statues of Crayolas in the eight [retired] colors].

9. [Pushing a button by one of the statues] activates a [recording] of children and adults' fond memories of the color.

10. For instance, a little girl's voice tells how important raw umber was to her; she explains that she used it [to color her skin] in the pictures she drew of herself.

EXERCISE 4

1. It is very easy [to give someone the bubonic plague these days]—in tie form, that is.

2. A microscopic picture of the plague is just one of the "decorations" [adorning the Infectious Awareables collection of ties] [sold by Roger Freeman].

3. Freeman was a dentist before [becoming a tie salesman].

4. The diseased ties are just starting [to become popular].

5. There are ties [showing cholera, staph, ebola, and malaria], [to name just a few].

6. Inventors decided [to label the ties with information about the conditions] [pictured on their surfaces].

7. Freeman took over [selling the stock of ties] after [being given a herpes tie as a present].

8. Freeman loves the disease patterns [seen through a microscope].

9. Their vivid colors and abstract shapes make them perfect [to use as tie designs].

10. The Infectious Awareables ties are priced reasonably, [selling for around forty dollars a piece].

EXERCISE 5

1. John Steinbeck, author of *The Grapes of Wrath,* was the first native of California [to receive the Nobel Prize for literature].

2. [Calling his hometown of Salinas "Lettuceberg,"] Steinbeck's [writing] made the area famous.

3. At the time, not everyone liked the attention [brought by his portrayals of life in *Cannery Row* and other works].

4. Steinbeck's father was the treasurer of Monterey County for ten years, [working also for the Spreckels company].

5. John Steinbeck tried [to find satisfaction in his birthplace], [enrolling in and quitting his studies at Stanford University many times].

6. Finally, Steinbeck moved to New York, [distancing himself from his California roots].

7. Steinbeck won the Nobel Prize in 1962, [revealing the literary world's esteem for his work.]

8. Not [writing anything of the caliber of the Salinas stories] while [living in New York], Steinbeck did return to California before he died in 1968.

9. In 1972, the Salinas library changed its name, [to be known thereafter as the John Steinbeck Library].

10. And the house Steinbeck was born in became a restaurant and then a full-[fledged] museum [chronicling the life of Salinas' most [celebrated] citizen].

PARAGRAPH EXERCISE

Simon Rodia (Sam Rodia, 1879–1965). The southeastern L.A. neighborhood of Watts is known for two things, the 1965 epidemic of destruction [called the Watts Riots] and the unique act of creative construction [known as the Watts

Towers]. Rodia was a loner, an Italian-born tile setter and all-around handyman who lived in the [mixed] Chicano and black neighborhood. . . . What is known is that he spent 30 years [constructing an elaborate structure out of . . . scrap iron and metal, [broken] glass and crockery]. [Considered "highly significant" in the words of art history]—"possibly the most significant structure ever [created by one man alone]"—the Watts Towers look something like an ornate oil derrick, a Gothic cathedral, and a jungle gym all in one. Rodia, a man whose acts spoke for themselves, deeded his property to a neighbor in 1954 and left. Five years later, the City of Los Angeles tried [to demolish the towers as a public hazard]. Then [living in the Suisun Bay town of Martinez], Rodia remained silent. The towers survived a stress test [to become a remote outpost on the Los Angeles tourist circuit]. Rodia died a month before the riots which spared his corner of the old neighborhood.

SENTENCE WRITING
Your sentences may vary, but make sure that your verbals are not actually the main verbs of your clauses. You should be able to double underline your real verbs, as we have done here.

1. [Owning property] brings many responsibilities.

2. I love [taking pictures of Yosemite].

3. My mother enjoys [bowling in a league with her friends from work].

4. I watched my son [cutting out the shape of a heart for Valentine's Day].

5. [To get a degree in architecture], she must be serious from the start.

6. I am attempting [to be a better listener].

7. He tried [to cut a hole in the center of the heart].

8. Students and teachers need [to respect each other].

9. [Shaped more like a peach than a heart], my Valentine's Day card was adorable.

10. [Driven to the prom in a limousine], the young couple felt very special.

CORRECTING MISPLACED OR DANGLING MODIFIERS (PP. 123–126)

EXERCISE 1
1. After *I checked* the time, my watch dropped on the floor.

2. I located my car *by* walking around the parking lot several times.

3. The sentence is correct. [or *With special glasses,* we watched the 3-D movie.]

4. A day after *I took* the midterm, my instructor was absent.

5. The sentence is correct.

6. The sentence is correct.

7. We read an essay *in our textbook* about George Orwell's definition of *imperialism.*

8. The sentence is correct.

9. *When I purchased my first car, it had a sunroof, but I'll never buy a car with a sunroof again.*

10. My cousin sent me a picture *in a large envelope; the picture was from our family reunion.*

EXERCISE 2

1. The sentence is correct.

2. I drank a cup of tea *while I read the newspaper.*

3. The sentence is correct.

4. The sentence is correct.

5. We arrived at the zoo, *but we didn't have* any money.

6. The sentence is correct.

7. I finally finished the reading assignment *that was lying on my desk for two weeks.*

8. The sentence is correct.

9. *While waiting in the lobby,* my friends and I ate a whole bucket of popcorn.

10. *Before I called* the dentist, my tooth started to feel better.

EXERCISE 3

1. Travelers *flying from Los Angeles to New York* encountered delays.

2. The sentence is correct.

3. We *used binoculars to watch* the ballet dancers.

4. He *accidentally kicked his classmate.*

5. *Looking over her essay,* she found a few mistakes.

6. The valet parking attendant *winked as he handed* my mother the keys.

7. *Since my brother loves the smell of fresh coffee,* Starbucks is the perfect place *for him* to work.

8. They sent us *a wedding invitation in a fancy envelope.*

9. *When I was ten,* we moved to Michigan.

10. *Before we take the final exam,* the teacher will return our essays on smoking.

EXERCISE 4

1. *We finally made it to our destination after we got a headache from the fumes of our small plane.*

2. *That carnival sold cotton candy full of empty calories, but it was the best I'd ever tasted.*

3. *Two months after we moved out,* our old apartment is still empty.

4. *In her e-mail message,* she promised to return the library books.

5. *Sitting in small groups,* the students took the notes.

6. *Before we said goodnight,* the porch light burned out.

7. *Our hostess showed us her favorite room; it was decorated beautifully.*

8. *I saw a tiny gray mouse* scampering along the baseboards of the cabin.

9. The sentence is correct.

10. All along the highway, volunteers *wearing special T-shirts* planted trees.

EXERCISE 5

1. Feeling the excitement of the first day of school, *I left my backpack behind.*

2. We saw the new movie that everyone is talking about; *it was full of surprises.*

3. My cousins and I, *wearing our pajamas,* always wrapped our gifts on the night before the holiday.

4. *Now that he practices for an hour a day,* his tennis has improved.

5. *Rising and falling several times a year,* the price of gasoline fluctuates.

6. The sentence is correct.

7. *Hiking in the nearby mountains,* they discovered a new trail.

8. She felt pressure *from her parents to get good grades.*

9. The sentence is correct.

10. The sentence is correct.

PROOFREADING EXERCISE
Corrections are italicized. Yours may differ slightly.

Hoping to become famous and wealthy, a man in Edinburgh, Scotland, has invented a device. *Located just above the trunk and visible from behind*, the device is a variation on the center-mounted brake light used in the design of many new cars. Instead of just a solid red brake light, however, this invention displays to other drivers *words* written in bold, red-lighted letters.

With simplicity in mind, the inventor limited the machine's vocabulary to three words: "Sorry," "Thanks," and "Help." After making an aggressive lane change, *we could use the machine* to apologize. Or after being allowed to go ahead of someone, we could thank the considerate person responsible. Of course, *with the use* of the "Help" display, we could summon fellow citizens for assistance.

And there is no need to worry about operating the device while driving. With three easy-to-reach buttons, *we could activate the messages* without taking our eyes off the road.

FOLLOWING SENTENCE PATTERNS (PP. 130–133)

EXERCISE 1

1. My sister Belinda is allergic (to many things).
   S — LV DESC.

2. She gets hives (from mold and pollen).
   S AV OBJ.

3. (Of course), milk upsets her stomach.
   S AV OBJ.

4. Strawberries and raspberries are many people's favorite fruits.
   S S LV DESC.

5. But they give Belinda a rash (on her face and arms).
   S AV OBJ.

6. The doctor has made a list (of Belinda's allergies).
   S AV OBJ.

7. Soon she'll be receiving allergy shots.
   S AV OBJ.

8. The shots should reduce Belinda's sensitivity (to these substances).
   S AV OBJ.

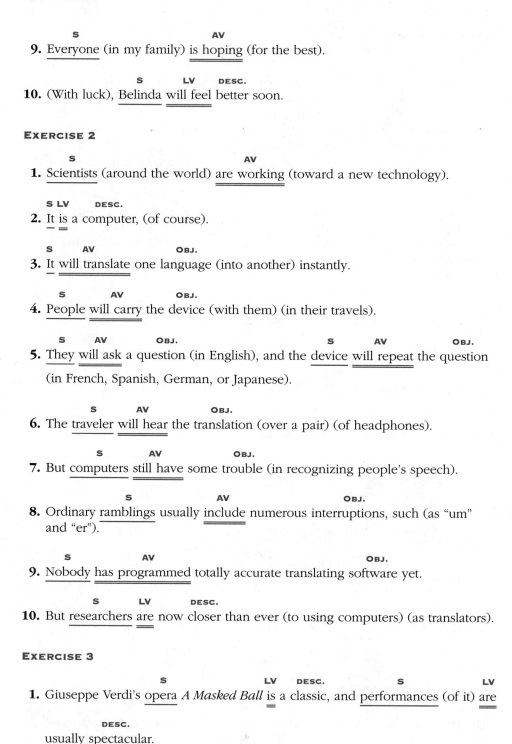

       S   AV

9. Everyone (in my family) is hoping (for the best).

                              S   LV   DESC.

10. (With luck), Belinda will feel better soon.

EXERCISE 2

         S   AV

1. Scientists (around the world) are working (toward a new technology).

     S LV   DESC.

2. It is a computer, (of course).

      S   AV   OBJ.

3. It will translate one language (into another) instantly.

      S   AV   OBJ.

4. People will carry the device (with them) (in their travels).

      S   AV   OBJ.   S   AV   OBJ.

5. They will ask a question (in English), and the device will repeat the question

(in French, Spanish, German, or Japanese).

        S   AV   OBJ.

6. The traveler will hear the translation (over a pair) (of headphones).

        S   AV   OBJ.

7. But computers still have some trouble (in recognizing people's speech).

        S   AV   OBJ.

8. Ordinary ramblings usually include numerous interruptions, such (as "um"
and "er").

        S   AV   OBJ.

9. Nobody has programmed totally accurate translating software yet.

         S   LV   DESC.

10. But researchers are now closer than ever (to using computers) (as translators).

EXERCISE 3

                         S   LV   DESC.   S   LV

1. Giuseppe Verdi's opera *A Masked Ball* is a classic, and performances (of it) are

           DESC.

usually spectacular.

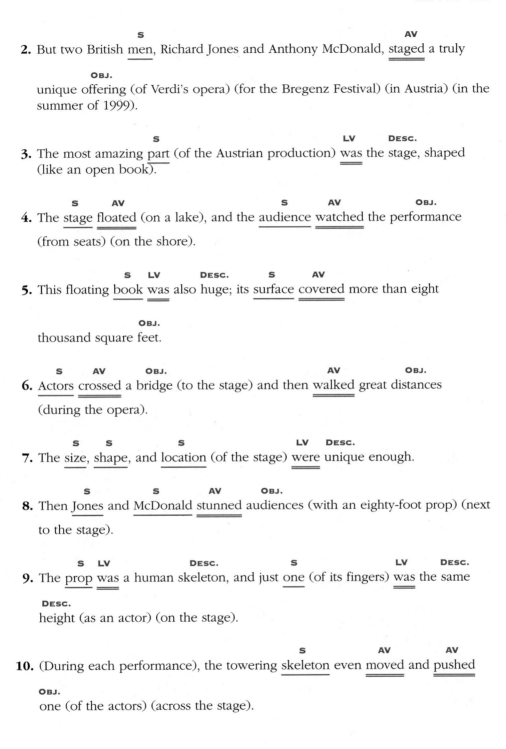

2. But two British <u>men</u>, Richard Jones and Anthony McDonald, staged a truly
          S   **AV**

unique **offering** (of Verdi's opera) (for the Bregenz Festival) (in Austria) (in the
OBJ.
summer of 1999).

3. The most amazing <u>part</u> (of the Austrian production) <u>was</u> the stage, shaped
                     S   **LV**   **DESC.**
(like an open book).

4. The <u>stage</u> <u>floated</u> (on a lake), and the <u>audience</u> <u>watched</u> the performance
       S   **AV**   **S**   **AV**   **OBJ.**

(from seats) (on the shore).

5. This floating <u>book</u> <u>was</u> also huge; its <u>surface</u> <u>covered</u> more than eight
              S   **LV**   **DESC.**   **S**   **AV**

thousand square feet.
     OBJ.

6. <u>Actors</u> <u>crossed</u> a bridge (to the stage) and then <u>walked</u> great distances
     S   **AV**   **OBJ.**   **AV**   **OBJ.**

(during the opera).

7. The <u>size</u>, <u>shape</u>, and <u>location</u> (of the stage) <u>were</u> unique enough.
       S   **S**   **S**   **LV**   **DESC.**

8. Then <u>Jones</u> and <u>McDonald</u> <u>stunned</u> audiences (with an eighty-foot prop) (next
        S   **S**   **AV**   **OBJ.**

to the stage).

9. The <u>prop</u> <u>was</u> a human skeleton, and just <u>one</u> (of its fingers) <u>was</u> the same
       S   **LV**   **DESC.**   **S**   **LV**   **DESC.**

height (as an actor) (on the stage).
DESC.

10. (During each performance), the towering <u>skeleton</u> even <u>moved</u> and <u>pushed</u>
                                        S   **AV**   **AV**

one (of the actors) (across the stage).
OBJ.

EXERCISE 4

$$\overset{S}{}\ \overset{AV}{}\ \overset{OBJ.}{}$$

1. (In America), we love our pets.

$$\overset{S}{}\ \overset{AV}{}\qquad\qquad \overset{OBJ.}{}$$

2. We own more than one hundred million (of them).

$$\overset{S}{}\qquad\qquad\qquad\qquad \overset{AV}{}$$

3. Almost sixty percent (of the people) (in the United States) live (with pets).

$$\overset{S}{}\ \overset{AV}{}\ \overset{OBJ.}{}$$

4. (Of these pet owners), thirty percent have chosen dogs (as their favorites).

$$\overset{S}{}\ \overset{AV}{}\ \overset{OBJ.}{}$$

5. Twenty-seven percent prefer cats.

$$\overset{S}{}\qquad\qquad \overset{AV}{}$$

6. Pet food and supply companies are prospering (at the moment).

$$\overset{S}{}\qquad \overset{AV}{}\qquad \overset{OBJ.}{}$$

7. Americans are even buying health insurance (for their pets).

$$\overset{S}{}\qquad\qquad\qquad \overset{LV}{}$$

8. (In the 1980s), the average cost (for pet medical treatment) was slightly more

DESC.

than two hundred dollars.

$$\overset{S}{}\ \overset{AV}{}\ \overset{OBJ.}{}$$

9. Now people will spend thousands (for pet-care measures).

$$\overset{S}{}\ \overset{AV}{}\qquad\qquad \overset{OBJ.}{}$$

10. The pet-care industry makes more than eleven billion dollars a year.

EXERCISE 5

$$\overset{S}{}\qquad\qquad \overset{AV}{}\qquad\qquad \overset{OBJ.}{}$$

1. One pet owner (in Vermont) demonstrates some people's devotion (to their animals).

$$\overset{S}{}\ \overset{AV}{}\ \overset{OBJ.}{}$$

2. Richard Durgin had a schnauzer named Ben.

    S   AV   OBJ.   S   AV   OBJ.

3. Ben developed kidney disease, and Durgin paid six thousand dollars (in vet

bills).

         S   AV   S   AV

4. Then Ben suffered (from injuries) (in a car accident), and Durgin spent even

  OBJ.

more (on a new hip and a reconstructed paw) (for Ben).

         S   AV   OBJ.

5. When a vet suggested a five-thousand-dollar kidney transplant (for the pet

                  S   AV

schnauzer), Durgin declined.

              S   AV   OBJ.

6. Ben's kidney problems finally took their toll.

   S   AV   S   AV

7. Ben no longer runs (around Durgin's house), but his memory lives on.

     S   AV   OBJ.

8. Durgin drinks his morning coffee (from a specially made set) (of mugs).

    S   LV   DESC.

9. One (of the ingredients) (in the clay) was Ben's ashes.

     S LV   DESC.

10. Ben was one beloved dog.

PARAGRAPH EXERCISE

       S   LV   DESC.   S   AV

    Color is perhaps the most powerful tool (at an artist's disposal). It affects our

  OBJ.   AV   OBJ.

emotions (beyond thought) and can convey any mood, (from delight) (to

       S LV   DESC.   AV   OBJ.   AV   OBJ.

despair). It can be subtle or dramatic, capture attention or stimulate desire. [Used

                                            S   AV   OBJ.

more boldly and freely today than ever before], color bathes our vision (with an

infinite variety) (of sensations), (from clear, brilliant hues) (to subtle, elusive mix-

```
     S   LV      DESC.
```
tures). <u>Color</u> <u>is</u> the province (of all artists), (from painters and potters) (to product

designers and computer artists).

AVOIDING CLICHÉS, AWKWARD PHRASING, AND WORDINESS (PP. 137–141)

Your answers may differ from these possible revisions.

EXERCISE 1

1. I should practice my piano, but I can't.

2. I've been studying it for about two years.

3. At first, I wanted to learn the notes and hand positions, but now they seem old-fashioned.

4. Keyboards today play music themselves.

5. Sentence 5 may be omitted if combined with Sentence 6.

6. I bought a keyboard because I couldn't afford a piano.

7. My upright digital keyboard feels and sounds like a real piano.

8. But my music teacher doesn't know that, instead of practicing for hours, I listen to the demo songs.

9. I just push a button to hear the theme from *Star Wars*.

10. I'll probably never learn to play the piano.

EXERCISE 2

1. My family reunited recently to celebrate my grandmother's birthday.

2. We wanted to surprise Grandma and see her happy face when she found us all there.

3. Each of us had to travel to reach the reunion since we live in different parts of the country.

4. Luckily, we all arrived before Grandma.

5. We had chosen my cousin Jeff to distract Grandma before the reunion.

6. He asked her to help him buy a new coat at the mall.

7. She was flattered and agreed to help.

8. While at the mall, Jeff pretended to remember a date with a friend, and he drove Grandma to the campground.

9. When they arrived, we hid behind trees and tables then jumped out and yelled "Surprise!"

10. We sat Grandma down in a big chair and treated her like a queen.

EXERCISE 3

1. An article in *Discover* (Sept. 1999) explains that ancient Egyptians used makeup in many different ways.

2. First, they painted their faces to make themselves attractive.

3. Egyptians seemed to be as vain as we are.

4. Surprisingly, Egyptian men also wore makeup.

5. French scientists and beauty experts have studied the contents of vessels found inside the tombs of kings and queens of the Nile from as early as 2700 B.C.

6. From these remains, scientists have identified the ingredients that Egyptians used in their makeup.

7. The ingredients include goose fat, lettuce, animal blood, crushed beetles, cinnamon, and a few artificial ingredients.

8. Like us, the Egyptians knew enough about chemistry to create these artificial substances.

9. Finally, the Egyptians may have used makeup as medicine.

10. Two of their makeup's artificial ingredients, laurionite and phosgenite, may have helped cure eye problems that resulted when the Nile flooded the valley and contained bacteria that infected people's eyes.

EXERCISE 4

1. This year I'll get an eight-hundred-dollar tax return.

2. I used to do my own taxes.

3. I would wait for my W-2 forms, fill out the short form, and receive a small refund.

4. Then my mom convinced me to be serious about my taxes.

5. Sentence 5 may be omitted if combined with Sentence 4.

6. I asked my friends at work for any recommendations, and Jason gave me a phone number.

7. I called Helen, Jason's tax preparer.

8. Helen explained that I could control the amount of taxes withheld from my paycheck.

9. Before speaking with Helen, I was ignorant about taxes.

10. And I there may be more that I don't understand.

EXERCISE 5

1. Americans eat nearly four hundred slices of pizza every second.

2. Sentence 2 may be omitted if combined with Sentence 1.

3. The name of one of the biggest pizza companies in America has an interesting story behind it.

4. In the late 1950s, two brothers, Frank and Dan Carney, lived in Kansas and went to a nearby State University.

5. They decided to start their own business with about five hundred dollars that they borrowed from their mom.

6. They bought some used restaurant equipment and opened their own little pizza place.

7. They ordered a sign for their restaurant, but it had only a small space after the word *Pizza*.

8. They had room for three more letters, so they chose *hut,* and "Pizza Hut" was born.

9. Frank and Dan have been very successful.

10. Ten thousand Pizza Huts serve pizza around the world.

PROOFREADING EXERCISE

Nobody in my family is "normal." The oddest of all is my Uncle Crank. His real name is Frank, but ever since I was young, Uncle Frank has been called Uncle "Crank" because his arm doesn't bend the right way at the elbow. It turns like the crank of an old car in silent films. My uncle is proud of his unique arm, but I wish the doctors had fixed it so that Uncle "Crank" could have just been normal Uncle Frank.

CORRECTING FOR PARALLEL STRUCTURE (PP. 144–148)

Your revisions may vary.

EXERCISE 1

1. Nearly anyone who has grown up in America during the last century remembers putting a baby tooth under a pillow and finding a quarter or two in its place in the morning.

2. The tradition and significance of leaving a tooth for the Tooth Fairy are hard to trace.

3. One person who is trying to understanding the myth and who collects everything to do with it is Dr. Rosemary Wells.

4. Dr. Wells runs the Tooth Fairy Museum in Deerfield, Illinois, and she knows as much as anyone else about the elusive tooth taker.

5. The sentence is correct.

6. Since then Wells has gathered books, written essays, assembled an art collection, and received gifts about the Tooth Fairy.

7. One of the most intriguing things about the story is that, unlike Santa Claus, the Tooth Fairy does not have any specific "look" or even a particular gender.

8. Wells has discovered a few ancient rituals having to do with lost teeth, such as tossing the tooth into the air or pitching it at a rat.

9. Both European and Mexican children have the story of the "Tooth Mouse" that comes to take away discarded baby teeth.

10. The sentence is correct.

EXERCISE 2

1. The use of bar codes has a clear past but an uncertain future.

2. The bar code scanner was first used on June 26, 1974, and the product first scanned was a pack of chewing gum.

3. The sentence is correct.

4. The bar codes themselves had been used on products all the way back to the 1960s but not to add up a customer's bill at the checkout counter until that day in 1974.

5. The sentence is correct.

6. Prisons track inmates, shipping companies scan railroad cars, hospitals verify blood samples, and cattle ranchers identify cows.

7. Some people worry about the future use and possible misuse of bar codes.

8. Several years ago, there was a rumor that the government would bar-code people and keep track of them for the rest of their lives.

9. Such paranoid and far-fetched ideas are usually not true.

10. But the possibilities of bar codes do make people wonder about how, where, and why they will be used in the years to come.

EXERCISE 3

1. I was washing my car two weeks ago and noticed a few bees buzzing around the roof of my garage.

2. I didn't worry about it at the time, but I should have.

3. The sentence is correct.

4. The sentence is correct.

5. They flew in a pattern as if they were riding on a roller coaster or over waves.

6. The sentence is correct.

7. There was nothing I could do but wait in my car until they went away.

8. Finally, the bees flew straight up into the air and disappeared.

9. Once inside my house, I opened the phone book and called a bee expert.

10. The sentence is correct.

EXERCISE 4

1. The Smithsonian's National Museum of Natural History is older and more popular than many other Smithsonian branches.

2. The museum began serving the country in 1910 and has continued to add objects of interest to its collections.

3. Visitors to the Natural History museum can view and learn more about its huge assortment of gemstones, minerals, and cultural artifacts.

4. According to Smithsonian officials, the National Museum of Natural History hopes to achieve three different goals simultaneously.

5. The museum's primary goal is to increase its already gigantic collection of natural history objects; these items are of global significance and allow scientists to study historical evidence from hundreds of millions of years ago.

6. The second goal is to teach young people the importance and the benefits of studying natural history.

7. The museum is especially proud of its plans for interactive children's exhibits, such as an Insect Zoo, Africa Hall, and Discovery Room.

8. The final goal for the museum is to satisfy the needs of researchers and prepare them to solve the problems of the future.

9. The sentence is correct.

10. The sentence is correct.

EXERCISE 5

1. To cut down on fuel bills while cooking, consider the following energy-saving hints.

2. Avoid preheating your oven unless it is electric.

3. Cover all pots when cooking.

4. Don't open the oven door to check on food.

5. Use the oven light instead.

6. Don't use a flame that extends past the bottom of the pan.

7. Follow the time and temperature directions given in a recipe.

8. Prepare your whole meal in the oven or on top of the stove, not both.

9. Check all the burners and be sure they are off after use.

10. If you follow these suggestions, you will save money on your energy bills and cook better meals.

PROOFREADING EXERCISE

Your revisions may differ.

Shirley Temple was born in 1928 and discovered in 1931 when she was just three years old. Someone recognized her natural talent at a dance lesson and asked her to be in movies. She starred in many films that are still popular today. Among them are *Heidi, Rebecca of Sunnybrook Farm,* and *Curly Top.* Directors loved Shirley's acting style and her ability to do a scene in only one take, but not everyone trusted Shirley Temple. Graham Greene was sued when he claimed that Shirley was really about thirty years old and a dwarf. Little Shirley's parents helped with her career and earned money for their efforts. In the early days, the studios paid her mother several hundred dollars a week to put fifty-six curlers in Shirley's hair each night. That way, her famous ringlets would always be perfect and consistent. Shirley's father managed her money, so much money that at one point Shirley Temple was among the ten highest paid people in America. It was 1938, and she was only ten years old.

USING PRONOUNS (PP. 154–157)

EXERCISE 1

1. I

2. she

3. she and I

4. I

5. she and I

6. she

7. I

8. you and me

9. her and me

10. her

EXERCISE 2

1. its

2. its

3. its

4. their

5. One day last week, the *passengers* had to gather *their* belongings and leave the bus, even though it had not reached a scheduled stop.

6. their

7. their

8. The passengers did *their* best to hide *their* annoyance from the driver because he had been so nice.

9. As *the passengers* stepped off the bus at the end of the line, the driver thanked *them* for *their* patience and understanding.

10. it

EXERCISE 3

1. its

2. she

3. Each of the new employees *receives a* locker in the employee lounge.

4. their

5. Every member of the audience had *an* opinion of the play and expressed it in the volume of *the* applause.

6. he

7. me

8. You and he

9. she

10. their

EXERCISE 4

1. Mr. Martin told his student, *"I don't understand you."* or Mr. Martin told his student, *"You don't understand me."*

2. As we were arranging the sign on the easel, *the sign* (or *the easel*) fell over.

3. Our hamster escapes from its cage at least once a year *and makes us all frustrated.*

4. Tracy asked her old roommate, *"Why wasn't I invited to the reunion?"* or Tracy asked her old roommate, *"Why weren't you invited to the reunion?"*

5. The sentence is correct.

6. I finished washing my car, turned off the hose, and drove *my car* into the garage.

7. Janice told her sister, *"There is a kite on top of your roof."* or Janice told her sister, *"There is a kite on top of my roof."*

8. We arrived early at the theater, *so we were able to relax a little.*

9. Ken *borrowed his boss's laptop computer and used it at night school.*

10. When I cooked a potato in the microwave, *the potato* blew up.

EXERCISE 5

1. The Howells purchased new lawn chairs, but *the chairs* were too fancy for them.

2. The sentence is correct.

3. I initialed the changes on the contract, put the top back on my pen, and handed *the contract* to the real estate agent.

4. *Study groups help students* a lot.

5. As we placed the jars in pans of boiling water, *the jars* shattered.

6. I *always enjoy receiving good news.*

7. The sentence is correct.

8. Dan's tutor *advised Dan to rewrite his essay.*

9. Many people visit amusement parks *to experience the* thrilling rides.

10. The committee members interviewed the applicants in *the members'* offices.

PROOFREADING EXERCISE (CORRECTIONS ARE ITALICIZED)

My friend Kevin and *I* went out the other day. We saw a movie at the new theater complex down the block. After the cashier handed Kevin and *me* our tickets, we went into the lobby and were impressed with *its* decorations. Old movie posters *in really fancy gold frames* lined the hallways to the theaters. After the movie, I asked Kevin if he liked *the new theater complex*. He said that it was the worst one he had ever been to. He told me that the parking was impossible, the screen was too small, and the seats were uncomfortable. He said that he would rather go to the place where we saw our last movie. At least *that theater* had a full-size screen and good sound, even if *the theater itself* wasn't as pretty as the new one.

AVOIDING SHIFTS IN PERSON (PP. 158–160)

1. The paragraph is correct.

2. Communicating through e-mail has made people lose their manners. A letter used to begin with a polite salutation at the top, such as "Dear Sirs" or even "To whom it may concern," and end with a signature or printed name at the bottom to identify who sent it. And an old-fashioned letter had not only the sender's address but also the receiver's address on it too. Then there was the postmark to tell what town the letter was mailed from. Now, with different people using the same e-mail accounts and sending them from all over the world, it is never clear where electronic mail comes from unless the person follows the old rules of correspondence. But many people writing e-mail don't include salutations or signatures. In the old days, people took more time on their correspondence.

3. Christopher Wolfe will always have a reason to be proud. When he was seven years old, Christopher discovered a new dinosaur, and scientists named it after him. They called it *Zuniceratops christopheri.* This unknown species of dinosaur had two horns, one over each eye. There have been other discoveries of dinosaurs with horns, but the one whose bones Christopher found lived twenty million years earlier than any others. Christopher's father, Douglas Wolfe, was with him when he spotted the fossil in the Arizona/New Mexico desert. Douglas, a paleontologist, knew right away that his son's find was genuine. However, the kids at school had a hard time believing Christopher when he came in the next school day and told his classmates that he had discovered a new dinosaur species.

REVIEW OF SENTENCE STRUCTURE ERRORS (PP. 160–162)

Your corrections may differ.

1. A. cliché (I *dislike* news programs that report only gossip.)

2. A. subject/verb agreement error (Each . . . *was* the same size.)

3. B. dangling modifier (After *I made* a quick phone call, the dog next door was quiet.)

4. B. dangling modifier (One of my ankles was sore after *I played* tennis all afternoon.)

5. A. run-on sentence (The customers filled out suggestion cards; they contained some good ideas.)

6. A. cliché (I never wanted to choose a major.)

7. B. pronoun agreement (Everyone at the party brought *a* swimsuit.)

8. A. shift in person (I enjoy watching videos . . . because *I* can stop . . . whenever *I* want.)

9. B. misplaced modifier (*Waiting for a table at the new restaurant,* we stared at a tank of goldfish.)

10. B. cliché (I *will never take that class*).

11. A. not parallel (We applied for *a scholarship, a loan, and the honors program.*)

12. A. fragment and wordy (Many people *wonder* about the shape of a face found on Mars.)

13. B. subject/verb agreement error (These studies of children's behavior *have* to be done carefully.)

14. B. wordy (Knowing what is valuable is difficult, however.)

15. B. subject/verb agreement error (Either the *tutor or the students* are correct.)

Mother Tells All

I have learned the most memorable lessons about myself from my children. A mother is always on display; she has nowhere to hide. And children are like parrots; they repeat whatever they hear. If I change my mind about something, they will remind me of every word I said.

For example, last summer I told my kids that I planned to take an exercise class and lose about forty pounds. I did lose some weight, and I attended an exercise class. But I started to feel like a balloon losing air. I decided that I did not want to lose any more weight or exercise anymore. I expected my children to accept my decision.

When I stopped, one of my sons said, "Mom, you need to go back to exercise class." Then they all started telling me what to eat, and I felt horrible. I had given up these things because I wanted to, but my words were still being repeated like a nonstop alarm clock. Finally, my kids got bored with the idea of my losing weight. Sometimes, when one of them makes a joke about my "attempt" to lose weight, it hurts me that they don't understand.

From this experience, I have learned not to tell my children about a plan unless I am going to finish it. Otherwise, they will never let me forget.

PUNCTUATION AND CAPITAL LETTERS

PERIOD, QUESTION MARK, EXCLAMATION POINT, SEMICOLON, COLON, DASH (PP. 164–169)

EXERCISE 1

1. Wasn't the weather beautiful today?

2. I wonder when the autumn breezes will start to blow.

3. It still felt like summer—at least while the sun was shining.

4. At sunset the white, wispy clouds turned pink; then the blue sky behind them started to turn gold.

5. It was breathtaking!

6. The only hint of fall came after the sun went down: (or ;) the temperature dropped about twenty degrees in an hour.

7. I have always thought of summer as my favorite season; however, today may have convinced me to switch to fall.

8. I never noticed that the leaves are so beautiful even after they have dropped from the trees.

9. I walked through the park and collected a bouquet of huge autumn leaves; it was fun. (or !)

10. I hope tomorrow will be as pretty as today.

EXERCISE 2

1. Nancy Cartwright is a well-known actress on television; however, we never see her when she is acting.

2. Cartwright is famous for playing one part: the voice of Bart Simpson.

3. Besides her career as the most mischievous Simpson, Cartwright is married and has children of her own—a boy and a girl.

4. Wouldn't it be strange if your mother had Bart Simpson's voice?

5. Cartwright admits that she made her own share of trouble in school.

6. But the similarities between her and her famous character end there.

7. Bart is perpetually ten years old; Cartwright is in her forties.

8. Bart is a boy; Cartwright is obviously a woman.

9. It's no surprise that Cartwright is very popular with her children's friends.

10. When they yell for her to "Do Bart! Do Bart!" she declines with Bart's favorite saying: "No way, man!"

EXERCISE 3

1. I have just discovered the fun of fondue!

2. The story of the invention of fondue goes this way: a farmer's wife accidentally dropped a chunk of cheese on the warming pan near the fire, and after

mopping up the liquefied cheese with a piece of bread, she popped the morsel in her mouth and decided to make a meal of it.

3. Since its discovery, fondue has always been a process rather than a product; there are special pans to melt the cheese, fuel to keep it warm, and forks to hold the bread or meat to dip in it.

4. I now understand why fondue was especially popular in the 1960s and 1970s.

5. People then probably enjoyed the ritual of sitting down together and participating in a meal eaten from one pot.

6. And the ingredients of bread and cheese couldn't be simpler, could they?

7. There is also a rule that we might find distasteful now but thirty years ago must have seemed like fun; according to the book *Fabulous Fondues,* the person who lost a piece of bread in the fondue pot had to pay a forfeit.

8. The forfeits were listed as follows: if a man lost the cube of bread, he owed the hostess a bottle of wine; however, if a woman lost the cube of bread, she had to give one of the men at the table a kiss.

9. Of course, other foods can be substituted for the traditional chunks of bread: boiled potatoes, celery sticks, pretzels, crackers, mushrooms, and even nuts.

10. I plan to have a fondue party as soon as I possibly can!

EXERCISE 4

1. Other nations have given America gifts that have become part of our national landscape; for example, France gave us the Statue of Liberty.

2. In 1912, Japan sent the United States three thousand cherry trees as a goodwill gesture.

3. The Japanese wanted to share their own tradition of Sakura Matsuri; that is the spring celebration of the beauty of the cherry blossoms.

4. During cherry blossom time, there are picnics and field trips wherever the cherry trees are blooming in Japan.

5. Of the three thousand cherry trees that Japan sent to America, only 125 remain; they bloom in Washington, D.C., every spring.

6. Thanks to the National Park Service, the lost Japanese trees have been replaced with ones grown in America; however, the original gift trees are the most prized of all.

7. New technology has allowed scientists to take clippings from the original Japanese cherry trees and grow new ones; consequently, the gift will live on.

8. Every spring in Washington, D.C., thousands of people come to join in the Japanese enjoyment of cherry blossom time; in America it's called the Cherry Blossom Festival.

9. And beginning in 2001, the first five hundred offspring of the gift trees will be planted; they will continue to grow next to the originals.

10. The Statue of Liberty stands in New York Harbor; the cherry trees bloom in the capital; both were gifts from other nations that add to the beauty of our own.

EXERCISE 5

1. In 1999 Nancy Mace did something no woman had ever done before: (or ;) she graduated from the Citadel.

2. The South Carolina military academy had been in the news before; however, the news had not been good.

3. Six years before Mace graduated from there, the Citadel admitted its first female cadet: Shannon Faulkner.

4. But Faulkner met with unrelenting resistance and hostility from her classmates.

5. Faulkner left the Citadel without finishing a term; nevertheless, other women enrolled there, including Nancy Mace.

6. Mace took an extra heavy load of classes to finish her studies in just three years.

7. She received some of the same treatment as Faulkner; however, Mace was prepared for it.

8. She also had a Brigadier General in her family; in fact, he handed her the diploma at the Citadel's graduation ceremony.

9. Mace was the first woman to graduate from the last class of the twentieth century at the Citadel.

10. There are currently dozens of female cadets at the Citadel; many more will probably follow.

PROOFREADING EXERCISE

The ingredients you will need for a lemon meringue pie are lemon juice, eggs, sugar, cornstarch, flour, butter, water, and salt. First you combine flour, salt, butter, and water for the crust and bake until lightly brown; then you mix and cook the lemon juice, egg yolks, sugar, cornstarch, butter, and water for the filling. Once the filling is poured in the cooked crust, you whip the meringue. Meringue is made of egg whites and sugar. Pile the meringue on top of the lemon filling;

place the pie in the hot oven for a few minutes, and you'll have the best lemon meringue pie you've ever tasted!

COMMA RULES 1, 2, AND 3 (PP. 171–175)

EXERCISE 1

1. For the first time in my life, I feel like an adult.

2. I am taking general education classes in college, and I am getting good grades.

3. Even though I receive some financial aid, I mostly support myself.

4. I have a job, a car, and an apartment of my own.

5. When I am ready, I plan to transfer to a university.

6. After I complete the course work at community college, my parents will be proud of me, but they will be even prouder when I get my degree.

7. I know that my father wants me to major in business, yet my mother wants me to be a teacher.

8. Eventually, it will be my decision.

9. Although I don't see myself in front of a class full of students, I have always loved the school environment.

10. The sentence is correct.

EXERCISE 2

1. When the government issued the Susan B. Anthony dollar coin, it met with some disapproval.

2. The sentence is correct.

3. It was nearly the same size as a quarter, had a rough edge like a quarter's, and was the same color as a quarter.

4. It differed from a quarter in that it was faceted around the face, was lighter in weight, and was worth four times as much.

5. Due to these problems, the Susan B. Anthony dollar has been replaced by a new dollar coin.

6. Like the Anthony dollar, the new coin holds the image of a famous American woman.

7. She was the young Native American guide and interpreter for the Lewis and Clark expedition, and her name was Sacagawea.

8. The story of Sacagawea's life tells of hardship, suffering, and illness, but it also tells of incredible knowledge, courage, and strength.

9. While the men on the famous expedition had only themselves to worry about, Sacagawea assisted the men and made the treacherous journey from North Dakota to the Pacific with her baby strapped to her back.

10. Although the same size as the previous dollar coin, the Sacagawea dollar has a smooth, wide edge, and it is gold.

EXERCISE 3

1. There are more than 3,700 colleges and universities in the country, and they have all chosen names for their mascots.

2. The sentence is correct.

3. You have your traditional Knights, Lancers, Spartans, and Raiders.

4. Then there are the Rams, Bulls, Mustangs, Gators, and Razorbacks.

5. In the animal category, a few odd choices are the Gila Monsters of Eastern Arizona College, the Horned Frogs of Texas Christian University, and the Slugs of the University of California at Santa Cruz.

6. The sentence is correct.

7. In an effort to include female mascot names with their previously male-only counterparts, some schools have added the Women of Troy to the Trojans, Yeowomen to the Yeomen, and Ladybraves to the Scalping Braves.

8. In the polite category, there are the Gentlemen and Ladies of Centenary College in Louisiana and the Lords and Ladies of Kenyon College in Ohio.

9. At the extreme end of this inclusive trend are the Lumberjacks and Lumberjills, the Vikings and Vi Queens, and the Wildcat and Kittens.

10. The most esoteric are the Lights and Skylights of Montana State University-Northern in Havre, Montana, and the most edible are the Artichokes of Scottsdale Community College.

EXERCISE 4

1. The sentence is correct.

2. They were supposed to cure disease, lengthen life, and protect innocence.

3. Part of their appeal was how rare they are, for emeralds are even rarer than diamonds.

4. Geologists have been mystified by emeralds because they are produced through a unique process—the blending of chromium, vanadium, and beryllium.

5. These are substances that almost never meet, nor do they often combine—except in emeralds.

6. In South Africa, Pakistan, and Brazil, emeralds were created by intrusions of granite millions to billions of years ago.

7. These areas are known for their beautiful gems, but emeralds from Columbia are larger, greener, and more sparkling.

8. The sentence is correct.

9. Instead of the granite found in other emerald-rich countries, the predominant substance in Columbia is black shale.

10. Even though these lustrous green gems can now be synthesized, a real emerald always contains a trapped bubble of fluid, and this minuscule natural imperfection is known in the gem business as a "garden."

EXERCISE 5

1. If you're ever in Palo Alto, California, you must visit the Barbie Hall of Fame there.

2. The sentence is correct.

3. Barbie was born in the late 1950s, but she remains ageless at the Barbie Hall of Fame.

4. The Barbie museum's founder and curator is Evelyn Burkhalter, and she knows everything about Barbie.

5. The sentence is correct.

6. Barbie has served in the army, the air force, and the marines.

7. She has worked as a doctor, a ballerina, and an astronaut.

8. She has driven a Volkswagen, a Mercedes, and a limo.

9. She has figure-skated for Olympic medals, has managed a fast-food restaurant, and has run her own beauty salon.

10. Evelyn Burkhalter's Barbie collection is worth close to a million dollars, and it includes every Barbie product with the exception of half a dozen outfits that have eluded her so far.

PROOFREADING EXERCISE

When Niels Rattenborg studied the brains of mallard ducks, he made an interesting discovery. Rattenborg wondered how ducks protected themselves as they slept. The ducks slept in rows, and these rows were the secret to their defense. To his surprise, Rattenborg found that the two ducks on the ends of the row did something special with the sides of their heads facing away from the row. Instinctively, the ducks on the edge kept one eye open and one half of their brains awake as they slept. The rest of the ducks slept with both eyes closed and both sides of their brains inactive. The two guard ducks were able to frame the ducks in the middle, watch for danger, and sleep almost as soundly as their neighbors.

SENTENCE WRITING
Here are some possible revisions. Yours may differ.

> I am taking an archery class, and it's more fun than I expected it to be.

> When I get home from school, I do my homework, eat dinner, watch a little television, and go to sleep.

> Grant and Gretchen don't know what to do now that they are getting married, for Grant's last name is Ketchem, and Gretchen doesn't want to be known as Gretchen Ketchem, so she might keep her maiden name instead.

COMMA RULES 4, 5, AND 6 (PP. 178–181)

EXERCISE 1
1. This year's Thanksgiving dinner, I think, was better than last year's.

2. The sentence is correct.

3. The sentence is correct.

4. Certainly, it was more entertaining this year.

5. The sentence is correct.

6. My sister's new boyfriend, who brought the apple pie, sang karaoke with our mom after dinner.

7. The person responsible for basting the turkey, Uncle Ken, did a great job; it was moist and delicious.

8. The sentence is correct.

9. The gravy, however, was better last year.

10. You may leave the sentence alone , or you may use a comma after *However*.

EXERCISE 2
1. We trust, of course, that people who get their driver's licenses know how to drive.

2. The sentence is correct.

3. The sentence is correct.

4. Mr. Kraft, who tests drivers for their licenses, makes the streets safer for all of us.

5. The sentence is correct.

6. Therefore, we may understand when we fail the driving test ourselves.

7. The driver's seat, we know, is a place of tremendous responsibility.

8. The sentence is correct.

9. The sentence is correct.

10. No one, we believe, should take that responsibility lightly.

EXERCISE 3

1. The sentence is correct.

2. The sentence is correct..

3. My daughter's friend Harry doesn't get along with her best friend, Jenny.

4. My daughter's best friend, Jenny, doesn't get along with one of her other friends, Harry.

5. The tiger, which is a beautiful and powerful animal, symbolizes freedom.

6. The sentence is correct.

7. The sentence is correct.

8. Kim and Teresa, who helped set up the chairs, were allowed to sit in the front row.

9. My car, which had a tracking device, was easy to find when it was stolen.

10. The sentence is correct.

EXERCISE 4

1. Frozen "TV" dinners, which were first sold by Swanson & Sons in 1954, had only one original variety—turkey on cornbread with sweet potatoes, peas, and gravy.

2. The sentence is correct.

3. Campbell Soup Company, seeing the success of the TV dinner concept, bought the Swanson brand in 1955.

4. The sentence is correct.

5. These women's families, who had been used to complete home-cooked meals, needed a fast alternative.

6. Clarke Swanson, who inherited his father's business, brought the TV dinner concept to life.

7. The sentence is correct.

8. The sentence is correct.

9. The sentence is correct.

10. The frozen TV dinner, which was born in the 1950s, lives on as a billion-dollar industry today.

EXERCISE 5

1. Zippo lighters, the only domestic lighters that can still be refilled, are highly useful tools and highly prized collectibles.

2. The sentence is correct.

3. The value of Zippo lighters is well known in Guthrie, Oklahoma, home of the National Lighter Museum.

4. Zippos have always been special to soldiers, who often had to rely on the flame from their Zippo to warm food or light a fire.

5. The sentence is correct.

6. There have been many special edition Zippos made to celebrate an event, the first moon landing, for example.

7. Eric Clapton, famed guitarist and songwriter, used a clicking Zippo as an instrument in a song he wrote for the movie *Lethal Weapon 2*.

8. George G. Blaisdell, the man responsible for distributing, naming, and refining the Zippo as we know it, died in the late 1970s, but he cared about his customers.

9. All Zippo lighters come with a lifetime guarantee, which covers the lighters' inner workings but not the outer finish.

10. The Zippo Repair Clinic, which fixes around a thousand lighters a day, refunds any money sent by the customer.

PROOFREADING EXERCISE

There are many NASA facilities spread throughout the United States. The most well known of the centers in California is the Jet Propulsion Laboratory, located in Pasadena, home of the annual Tournament of Roses Parade. The parade itself is not a NASA project, however. Another of California's facilities is the Ames Research Center, where NASA scientists use massive wind tunnels in their research. There are also NASA facilities in Texas, Virginia, Alabama, New York, New Mexico, and Maryland, to name a few. The most famous center of all, of course, has to be the John F. Kennedy Space Center. No doubt everyone has seen the live image of a spacecraft lifting off the launching pad at Cape Canaveral. It is a sight, I believe, that a person never forgets.

SENTENCE WRITING
Here are some possible combinations. Yours may differ.

Las Vegas, a city famous for its casinos, also has lots of little chapels, where some people choose to get married.

I think she has a black belt in Karate. (or) She has a black belt in Karate, I think.

Barbara, my roommate, received scholarship money, which she thought she had to pay back.

REVIEW OF THE COMMA
I'm writing you this reminder, Tracy, to be sure that you don't forget our plans to visit the zoo this Saturday. [4] I know we're good friends, but lately you have let our plans slip your mind. [1] When we were supposed to go to the flea market last week, you forgot all about it. [3] I'm taking this opportunity therefore to refresh your memory. [5] I can't wait to see the polar bears, the gorillas, the giraffes, and the elephants. [2] And I have made special plans for a behind-the-scenes tour of several of the exhibits by Max Bronson, the zoo's public relations officer. [6] See you Saturday!

QUOTATION MARKS AND UNDERLINING/*ITALICS* (PP. 185–189)

EXERCISE 1

1. "Do you need any help?" my sister asked.

2. In her book Gift from the Sea, Anne Morrow Lindbergh wrote, "The beach is not the place to work; to read, write or think. . . . One should lie empty, open, choiceless as a beach—waiting for a gift from the sea."

3. Sir Laurence Olivier had this to say about Shakespeare's most famous work: "Hamlet is pound for pound . . . the greatest play ever written."

4. In 1999, singer Weird Al Yankovic released a parody of The Phantom Menace; it was sung to the tune of "American Pie."

5. "Civility costs nothing and buys everything," observed Lady Mary Wortley Montagu (1689–1762).

6. Forrest Gump made many sayings famous, but "Life is like a box of choco-lates" is the most memorable.

7. My teacher wrote "Good Work!" at the top of my essay.

8. The first time a contestant won a million dollars on the television quiz show Who Wants To Be a Millionaire? was in November 1999.

9. Karen asked, "Where will you be at noon?"

10. My family subscribes to Newsweek, and we all enjoy reading it.

EXERCISE 2

1. We are reading the book <u>Dibs in Search of Self</u> in my English class.

2. I can't decide whether to call my narration essay "A Day at the Beach" or "The Day I Made Waves."

3. I love to watch <u>Nova</u>, a series of nature programs on public television.

4. My favorite program in the series so far has been "The Life of Birds."

5. "There is nothing either good or bad but thinking makes it so," Hamlet says to Rosencrantz and Guildenstern.

6. "Daddy" is a famous poem by Sylvia Plath.

7. Plath also wrote a children's book called <u>The It-Doesn't-Matter Suit.</u>

8. Martha Stewart publishes her own magazine called <u>Martha Stewart Living.</u>

9. I've heard the expression "Living well is the best revenge."

10. Indira Ghandi said, "You cannot shake hands with a clenched fist."

EXERCISE 3

1. In his play <u>The Cherry Orchard</u>, physician and playwright Anton Chekhov wrote, "When a lot of remedies are suggested for a disease, that means it can't be cured."

2. George Orwell, author of <u>Animal Farm</u> and <u>1984</u>, felt that "At 50, everyone has the face he deserves."

3. On the power of clear writing, Orwell said, "Good prose is like a window pane."

4. The assignment for Tuesday is to read the essay "What Is Poverty?"

5. I have read Kate Chopin's novel <u>The Awakening</u> and her short stories "The Story of an Hour" and "The Storm."

6. Letters to the editor of the <u>New York Times</u> are good sources for research papers; I'm using one titled "Time for Irradiation" and another that shows the opposing view, "Food Irradiation Holds Too Many Risks."

7. The title of my essay will be "Pass the Ketchup: The Two Sides of the Food Irradiation Controversy."

8. "The cruelest lies," said Robert Louis Stevenson, "are often told in silence."

9. "What color," they all asked, "is your new car?"

10. Sir Laurence Olivier felt this way about playing the part of Hamlet: "Once you have played it, it will devour and obsess you for the rest of your life. It has me. I think each day about it."

EXERCISE 4

1. George Sterling described San Francisco as "the cool, grey city of love."

2. One of the most famous actresses of the early twentieth century was Mary Pickford; movie producer Samuel Goldwyn had this to say about working with her: "It took longer to make Mary's contracts than it did her pictures."

3. Goldwyn himself was no easier to get along with: "He would not acknowledge rejection, according to one biographer; He could not be insulted. He could not be deterred. He could not be withstood."

4. When someone suggested that Walt Disney run for mayor of Los Angeles following the success of Disneyland, Disney declined, saying, "I'm already king."

5. Disney knew what it meant to succeed; having dropped out of high school and having moved to Los Angeles with less than fifty dollars in his pocket, he empathized with Mickey Mouse, a character he described as "a little fellow doing the best he could."

6. Mark Twain said of California, "It's a great place to live, but I wouldn't want to visit there."

7. There is a French expression *L'amour est aveugle; l'amitié ferme les yeux*, which translates as follows: "Love is blind; friendship closes its eyes."

8. "Let's keep our voices down," the librarian said as we left the study room.

9. Box-Car Bertha, renowned woman of the rails, suggested that "Nobody can hurt you but yourself. Every experience you have makes you all the more fit for life."

10. "Pain is inevitable," said M. Kathleen Casey; "Suffering is optional."

EXERCISE 5

1. P. L. Travers wrote the book Mary Poppins about a magical English nanny who defies the laws of physics and alters the lives of everyone she meets.

2. Asked about the character of Mary Poppins, Travers said, "I never for one moment believed that I invented her. Perhaps she invented me."

3. Travers believed that "A writer is only half a book—the reader is the other half."

4. Travers never felt comfortable in the spotlight following the success of Mary Poppins. "I never talk about personal matters," she said, "only ideas."

5. And Travers had firm ideas about the audience for her stories: "[T]hey were never in the first place written for children, but for everybody—or maybe to ease my own heart."

6. When <u>Mary Poppins</u> was made into a movie that differed in many ways from the <u>book</u>, Travers felt extremely uneasy.

7. "The characters are entrusted to you," Travers responded; "I don't want it ever to be possible that somebody could take [Mary Poppins] and write a story about her that wasn't mine."

8. Travers also found it difficult to convey to Mary Shepard, the illustrator of the original Mary Poppins books, just exactly how Mary Poppins should look.

9. "Finally," Travers explained, "I went out and found a little Dutch doll and showed it to her. But even then there were disagreements."

10. In an essay titled "Lively Oracles," which Travers wrote for the journal *Parabola,* she shared her thoughts about time: "Where the center holds and the end folds into the beginning there is no such word as farewell."

PROOFREADING EXERCISE

I've been reading the book How Children Fail by John Holt. I checked it out to use in a research paper I'm doing on education in America. Holt's book was published in the early 1960s, but his experiences and advice are still relevant today. In one of his chapters, "Fear and Failure," Holt describes intelligent children this way: "Intelligent children act as if they thought the universe made some sense. They check their answers and their thoughts against common sense, while other children, not expecting answers to make sense, not knowing what is sense, see no point in checking, no way of checking." Holt and others stress the child's self-confidence as one key to success.

CAPITAL LETTERS (PP. 191–195)

EXERCISE 1

1. I have always wanted to learn another language besides English.

2. Right now I am taking English 410 in addition to my writing class.

3. The course title for English 410 is Basic Grammar.

4. English 410 is a one-unit, short-term class designed to help students with their verb forms, parts of speech, phrases, and clauses.

5. I hope that learning more about English grammar will help me understand the grammar of another language more easily.

6. Now I must decide whether I want to take Spanish, French, Italian, or Chinese.

7. I guess I could even take a class in Greek or Russian.

8. When I was in high school, I did take French for two years, but my clearest memory is of the teacher, Mrs. Gautier.

9. She was one of the best teachers that Hillside High School ever had.

10. Unfortunately, I did not study hard enough and can't remember most of the French that she taught me.

EXERCISE 2

1. Sir Laurence Olivier was one of the most famous British actors of the twentieth century.

2. He was well known for playing the leading roles in Shakespeare's plays.

3. He performed in London, on such stages as the Old Vic Theatre and St. James's Theatre, and for several years, he was director of the National Theatre.

4. Of course, Olivier also played to audiences in cities around the world, such as New York, Los Angeles, Moscow, and Berlin.

5. Among Olivier's most celebrated roles were Henry V, Othello, Richard III, and King Lear.

6. Though we can no longer see him on stage, we can still watch the film versions of his classic performances.

7. Olivier also directed many plays and some of his own films.

8. He directed the 1948 black-and-white film version of <u>Hamlet</u> and received the Academy Award for Best Actor for his performance in the title role.

9. One of Olivier's most treasured memories was of a single live performance of <u>Hamlet</u> in Elsinore, Denmark; it was scheduled to have been played outside but had to be moved inside at the last minute, causing all the actors to be especially brilliant under pressure.

10. American audiences might remember Sir Laurence Olivier best for his portrayal of the tempestuous Heathcliff in the movie <u>Wuthering Heights</u>, but he was a Shakespearean actor at heart.

EXERCISE 3

1. My mom and dad love old movie musicals.

2. That makes it easy to shop for them at Christmas and other gift-giving occasions.

3. For Mom's birthday last year, I gave her the video of Gilbert and Sullivan's comic opera <u>The Pirates of Penzance</u>.

4. It isn't even that old; it has Kevin Kline in it as the character called the Pirate King.

5. I watched the movie with her, and I enjoyed the story of a band of pirates who are too nice for their own good.

6. Actually, it is funnier than I thought it would be, and Kevin Kline sings and dances really well!

7. Dad likes musicals, too, and I bought him tickets to see the revival of <u>Chicago</u> on stage a few years ago.

8. He loves all those big production numbers and the Bob Fosse choreography.

9. There aren't many musicals made these days, but my folks did say that they would like a copy of the 1997 movie <u>Evita</u>, starring Madonna.

10. <u>Evita</u> is the Andrew Lloyd Webber musical about the first lady of Argentina, Eva Peron.

EXERCISE 4

1. Jodie Foster was born as Alicia Christian Foster on November 19, 1962.

2. Jodie was raised by her mother, Brandy, who worked for a film producer in Hollywood.

3. At the age of three, Jodie accompanied her older brother Buddy to an audition and got her first job acting in a TV commercial.

4. She was the little girl with a dog nipping at her swimsuit in the Coppertone Tanning Lotion commercials.

5. There were other TV ads before Jodie acted in TV shows such as <u>The Partridge Family</u>, <u>Gunsmoke</u>, and <u>The Courtship of Eddie's Father</u>.

6. As a movie actress, Jodie Foster's credits include the following films: <u>Taxi Driver</u>, <u>Bugsy Malone</u>, <u>The Accused</u>, and—of course—<u>Silence of the Lambs</u>.

7. She has won two Best Actress Academy Awards, which she keeps by her bathtub.

8. Foster attended Yale University in the early 1980s, earning a degree in literature.

9. In the late 1990s, Yale awarded foster an honorary PhD in fine arts, and she was nominated for a Golden Globe Award for her role as an astronomer in the movie <u>Contact</u>.

10. Jodie Foster became a mother in 1998; she had a boy and named him Charles.

EXERCISE 5

1. In 1999, New York's American Museum of Natural History featured an extremely popular exhibit.

2. The title of the exhibit was *"The Endurance:* Shackleton's Legendary Antarctic Expedition."

3. *The Endurance* was a British ship that set sail for Antarctica in 1914.

4. Ernest Shackleton was the ship's captain, and Frank Hurley was the photographer Shackleton took along to document the expedition's success.

5. Shackleton and his crew were attempting to be the first to cross Antarctica on foot and to claim this accomplishment for Britain.

6. Having nearly reached its landing site, *the Endurance* got stuck in the ice, and the crew lived on the ice-bound ship for nearly a year before it was crushed by the ice and sunk.

7. The crew escaped the sinking ship but were forced to live on the ice and eventually to travel to an uninhabited island.

8. Realizing that they could not survive much longer on their supplies, Shackleton took five men with him in a lifeboat named *the James Caird* and covered eight hundred miles before they reached another ship.

9. Shackleton made it back to rescue the crew members he left behind, and all of them returned home safely.

10. The New York exhibit's displays, which included *the James Caird* itself and Frank Hurley's pictures, brought the voyage of *the Endurance* and the heroic efforts of Shackleton and his crew to life for all of the visitors who saw them.

REVIEW OF PUNCTUATION AND CAPITAL LETTERS (PP. 195–196)

1. The Golden Gate Bridge is a famous landmark in the city of San Francisco.

2. Have you ever seen Woody Allen's early films such as Bananas or Take the Money and Run?

3. They've remodeled their house, and now they're ready to sell it.

4. "How much will the final exam affect our grades?" the nervous student asked.

5. We have reviewed your policy, Mr. Martin, and will be sending you a refund soon.

6. The two students who earn the most points for their speeches will face each other in a debate.

7. Ms. Thomas, the new English 4B teacher, recently received a national poetry award.

8. Even though I enjoy my French class, I believe should have taken Spanish first.

9. You always remember Valentine's Day and our anniversary, but you forget my birthday!

10. The most memorable saying from the original Toy Story movie is when Buzz Lightyear exclaims, "To infinity and beyond!"

11. My sister subscribes to Architectural Digest magazine, and my whole family loves to look through it when she's finished reading it.

12. Finding low air fares takes time, patience, and luck.

13. My friend is reading the novel Thousand Pieces of Gold in her English class.

14. I wonder how much my art history textbook will cost.

15. Bill Gates, founder of Microsoft, is one of the richest people in the world.

COMPREHENSIVE TEST (PP. 196–198)

1. (pro ref) She asked her sister, *"May I go to the store?"*

2. (shift in time) Instructors break their classes up into groups when they *want* the students to learn on their own.

3. (p) I wonder if the real estate agent has called yet.

4. (apos) A *man's* overcoat lay on the back of the bus stop near my house until someone finally took it away.

5. (sp) The teacher's lecture had an *effect* on all of us.

6. (sp) We don't know which of the events *occurred* first.

7. (wordy) *Parking is a complex problem on campus.*

8. (cap) My favorite high school teacher moved to *Arizona* when she retired.

9. (pro) The school awarded scholarships to my roommate and *me,* and we're both so happy.

10. (// and wordy) Cranberries can be harvested *dry or wet.*

11. (ro) The dishes need to be done, and the trash needs to be taken out before you leave the cabin.

12. (mm) *By going to museums,* children can learn about dinosaurs.

13. (frag and awk) *The room required a deposit,* but my check had not arrived.

14. (cs) I haven't finished my term paper; the library has been closed for the long weekend.

15. (s/v agr) Each of the branches *is* covered with lights.

16. (dm) *After we took a long vacation,* our house didn't seem as small as it did when we left.

17. (ro) The hills were steeper than we thought; none of us had worn the right shoes.

18. (cliché) *I often eat too much junk food.*

19. (wordy) I *returned the library book;* it had been overdue for a long time.

20. (pro agr) *The townspeople* turned their porch lights on in support of the proposition.

WRITING

ORGANIZING IDEAS (P. 215)

EXERCISE 1 THESIS OR FACT?

1. FACT	**6.** FACT
2. FACT	**7.** THESIS
3. THESIS	**8.** FACT
4. FACT	**9.** THESIS
5. THESIS	**10.** THESIS

TRANSITIONAL EXPRESSIONS (P. 218)

EXERCISE 2 ADDING TRANSITIONAL EXPRESSIONS

I have been planning to take a cruise with my husband and maybe my kids for several years now. *However,* I haven't decided what kind of cruise to go on yet. *First,* there are the romantic couple cruises to the Caribbean. But then I might worry about my children while we're away. *Next,* there are the breathtaking sights of Alaskan cruises. I've seen pictures of cruise ships passing right next to glaciers, although that seems a little dangerous. *Finally,* there are the family cruises that cater to everyone's desire for adventure and fun. While the kids play one of the numerous supervised activities, the adults can relax and enjoy each other's company. *In conclusion,* I think I've talked myself into a cruise for the whole family this summer!

WRITING ABOUT WHAT YOU READ (PP. 236–240)

ASSIGNMENT 17

100-Word Summary of "Men Don't Cry, Women Don't Fume"

We judge the emotions of people differently based on whether they are male or female. Scientists have studied the ways people feel about emotional outbursts. We pay most attention to anything out of the ordinary. So if a man is sad enough to weep in front of others, we worry about him. And if a woman gets mad enough to yell in front of others, we are shocked. This is where some unfairness comes in. We all seem to care more about how men feel than how women feel because we are so used to hearing a woman's feelings discussed.

ASSIGNMENT 18

Sample 100-Word Summary of "Keeping Faith in Kids"

In America, we have given up on our youth. Due to recent news reports, many people believe that the typical teenager is a criminal or a drug addict or both. That's not true, and statistics prove it. Young people today are cleaner than they've been in a long time. But unfortunately, they have more access to guns and can't help being influenced by our society's interest in violence and sex. America has its fair share of weirdoes. That will never change. But the majority of today's teenagers have the ability to make us proud if we trust and nurture them.

Index